Bringing
HOPE to Life

a memoir

CREATING PATHWAYS OUT OF POVERTY FOR YOUNG PEOPLE THROUGH THE BELOVED YOUTHBUILD COMMUNITY

DOROTHY STONEMAN

Bringing Hope to Life (a memoir)

Creating pathways out of poverty for young people through the beloved YouthBuild community

978-1-7368556-1-4

Design by Jason Fairchild, The Truesdale Group

Contents

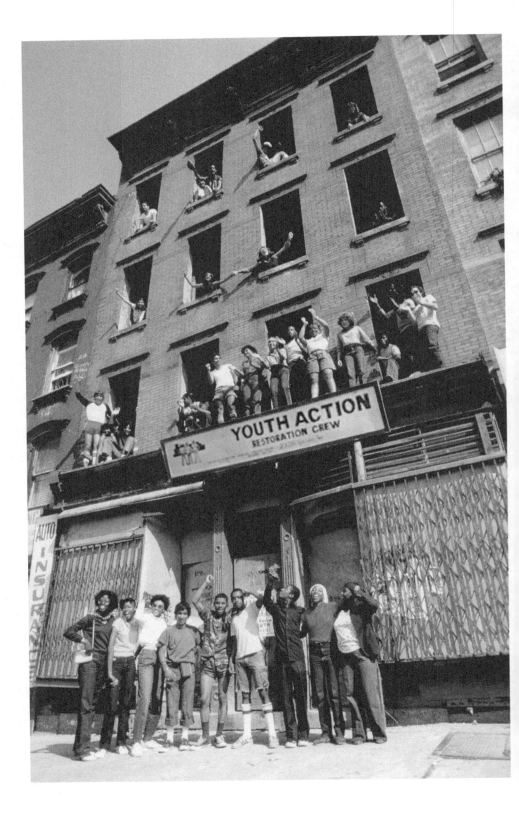

Dedication

I gratefully dedicate this book to:

Helene D. and Vernon C. Stoneman, my parents
John Bell, my partner
Leroy Looper, my guide
David Calvert, Youth Action's organizer
John Kerry, YouthBuild's champion
Roy Priest, YouthBuild's guardian.

Without their personal dedication over decades
this story would not have been possible.

Introduction

I hope many social change activists and entrepreneurs will read this book. The core lesson to be learned is this: "If she could figure out how to do it, so can I!"

I started as a Civil Rights activist in Harlem in the 60's. Then I became a public school teacher, a Headstart teacher, and the director of an independent parent-controlled community school in East Harlem. In 1978 I started the Youth Action Program in East Harlem to address one of America's key problems: the widespread lack of hope and opportunity for low-income youth. We supported teenagers to create community improvement projects of their own design, to address what they defined as the priority needs in East Harlem. One project the teenagers created was rehabilitating abandoned buildings to create housing for homeless people and jobs for unemployed youth. This project was later named YouthBuild.

When that project proved itself successful, for the next 38 years I orchestrated its replication around the United States and in several other countries. In 1990 we named it YouthBuild. Many colleagues kept telling me I had a duty to write a book about it. They said the story would inspire and empower other leaders.

YouthBuild has always been highly regarded by people familiar with it. As one of the most comprehensive and effective programs available in America for low-income young people who have left high school without a diploma, YouthBuild has engaged over 200,000 youth in rebuilding their communities and their lives. YouthBuild students have built more than 35,000 units of affordable housing in over 270 American communities while working toward their own high school equivalency diplomas and then moving on to college, employment, and many of them into significant leadership roles. This was possible because we figured out how to get a federal funding stream for YouthBuild authorized in 1992 and then funded ever since. However, despite this enormous success, most of the general public has never heard of YouthBuild. Many of our members call it "The best kept secret in America." Meanwhile it inspired many other countries to replicate it!

This book will hopefully be exciting for everyone connected with YouthBuild or similar programs. I believe it will also be extremely useful to younger activists and social entrepreneurs aspiring to create something new and wonderful. The YouthBuild story is a pretty good expression of what it takes to stick with a good idea and a positive philosophy through all the ups and downs, all the systems to be navigated, the communities to be organized, the allies to be won over, the policies to be created, the dubious to be persuaded, the organizations to be created, the funds to be raised, and the personal challenges to be weathered.

The book starts with my arrival in Harlem in 1964 to join the Civil Rights Movement through a grassroots storefront organization called the Harlem Action Group. Of course, back then the question suspiciously posed to me by residents of Harlem went something like this: "Why are you here? Are you going to write a book about us? Is that it?" I got the message that it was absolutely not my role as a white person to write any book about black people's reality. In 1964 I assured folks that I was not there for that purpose. But forty years later, black colleagues and board members were telling me I should get off my butt and write the long overdue book about

YouthBuild's history and our essential learnings about the transformational impact of the power of love coupled with opportunity. The combination restored hope and provided a path to a productive future. It decisively improved the lives of young people who had been kicked into the streets by poverty and discrimination.

I had written lots of handbooks about how to implement Youth-Build on the ground; but no public history of how it came to be a highly successful national and later international movement creating essential opportunities for young people to rebuild their communities and their lives, within a caring and loving community.

In the first version of the book, I simply described what I learned through my various professional roles over the years: a summer preschool organizer in the Civil Rights Movement; a public school teacher in Harlem; a teacher and executive director at the East Harlem Block Schools; the founder and director of the Youth Action Program; the founder of YouthBuild; the person who orchestrated its expansion, developed its national support center, guided its internal culture and philosophy, and figured out how to create a permanent federal funding stream to support it; the leader who kept the ideas and vision of young people at the heart of our evolution through youth leadership councils at every level. I shared how we orchestrated the successful replication of YouthBuild around New York City, then nationally and internationally, with private and public dollars, deep community engagement, and great local directors whose passion, skills, and fidelity to the philosophy created inspiring results.

When the first draft of the book was reviewed years ago by a publisher, and by colleagues at YouthBuild USA who had formed a support group to nudge me into writing the book, they all said it was not personal enough. They explained that it seemed too professional, just facts and history. They wanted to get more of a feeling of who I was, what I was feeling, and what challenges I faced. They wanted more joy and pain, heart and soul.

As a result, I went back to the beginning and wrote what I called the "Backstory". I wrote new chapters sharing what was going on in my personal and family life behind the scenes. I inserted these between the professional history chapters. After all, living is never simple. It is never just a matter of fact. We are passionately living out our hearts and souls as best we can under whatever conditions we face, experiencing incredible challenges, getting hurt and healing, overcoming external oppression and internal distresses, falling in love, managing unexpected setbacks, opening our minds and hearts to new perspectives, and always having complicated relationships.

I have set up the book with the **Backstory** chapters clearly labeled. That way readers can skip them if you are only interested in the actual professional history of what it took to create the successful network of YouthBuild programs.

When I was diagnosed with cancer in August of 2020, I decided I should get this book out of my computer and publish it before I died. I decided to skip the time-consuming process of getting a publisher and an agent. The book is self-published. If you like it, please share it with others, because there is no coordinated publicity for it. (I'm also happy to report that my cancer is completely cured, so my eventual death is not imminent. As a result my publishing process slowed down again.)

The first person who read the whole book was Crystal Russell Aryitey, a highly respected young leader in Montgomery, AL, who, after teaching in public schools for several years, and organizing debate teams in juvenile justice facilities, started her own non-profit called Destiny Driven. She asked me to advise her as she produced her PhD thesis and implemented her vision for community organizing. In that context, she read the book and found it extremely valuable as a source of both lessons and inspiration. This strong encouragement from a young black woman scholar and social entrepreneur pushed me on to completion.

I am very happy that whatever is useful in this book is now available to the public. Maybe YouthBuild will be more widely known.

And since social entrepreneurship — along with terms like "servant leadership" and "change-makers" — has become a widely understood concept embraced by more and more people, the detailed stories of successful creation of wonderful initiatives that benefit humanity should indeed be available for anyone traveling on that path. I hope the Backstory, showing the inevitable balance of our complicated lives, is also useful.

I hope you enjoy reading how persistent and caring individuals can make a big difference by putting one foot in front of another, steadily, toward benefiting humanity, finding allies and champions, navigating our existing government, implementing visions that have come to us in response to the obvious needs or the clear recommendations and deep engagement of people we love.

It's always reassuring to hear directly from the people who have experienced what you create. Here is the kind of message I got repeatedly from YouthBuild graduates over the years:

> "I was lost, I was on the streets. Without YouthBuild I would probably have been dead or in jail by age 25. But in YouthBuild I found safety, I found a family, I found adults who cared about me more than anyone had ever cared about me before. I was finally able to care about myself, and then care about other people. Now I want to give back."

Deep and Broad Gratitude, Specific Acknowledgments, and One Detail

There are literally thousands of people who have been deeply engaged in the YouthBuild movement, plus the predecessors of it: the East Harlem Block Schools, the New Action Party, and the Youth Action Program. Dedicated directors, passionate staff, and eager participants; philanthropic and corporate funders; advisors at every level; volunteer board members across the nation; parents, spouses, and children; elected officials from across the country and their staff; advocacy partners and lobbyists; federal, state, and local public officials; researchers and reporters; staff and board of YouthBuild USA, Inc.

There is no way to acknowledge them all adequately or communicate the cumulative power of their dedication. I have infinite gratitude to this broad community. We are all grateful to each other. I have named a tiny sliver of these wonderful people in the book, and I haven't even been able to detail the enormous gifts those named have given. Furthermore, literally thousands go unnamed. I apologize to all of you. I thank you from the bottom of my heart. Together we have spread the love, and the opportunity, the YouthBuild way. You have created unending ripple effects across the country and world.

In 1999 I wrote the "YouthBuild Story of Thanks" to acknowledge as many colleagues as possible at our 20th anniversary. It names many more individuals from the early years than this book does. It repeats and expands on our early history, without the backstory. (You can find it in the Wikipedia references if you google YouthBuild Story of Thanks.) However, even that story is not updated so it still doesn't include hundreds more wonderful people engaged in the last two decades. If you are one of them, please forgive me, and please accept my profound thanks!

There are also innumerable important people in my personal life who don't surface in this book, even in the backstory. I am deeply grateful to all my friends, classmates, colleagues, co-counselors, and family members who have walked through different parts of my life with me.

I have included a tiny cross-section of photos just to give you a visual glimpse of some of the players and feelings. I had to leave out hundreds of wonderful people. That was hard. But I hope the photos enhance your experience of the book.

Specific Acknowledgments Related to this Book

In the final preparation of this book, there were wise and generous readers and advisors. I am profoundly grateful for their time and input. Crystal Russell Aryitey, John Bell, David Abromowitz, Roy Priest, David Calvert, Mason Bishop, Kaleb Lester, Rhea Carter, Chantay Jones, and Malik Looper read parts or all of the book. Collectively they gave me specific edits and broad commentary. Some did line-by-line edits of every single page. Some had participated in key parts of our history and gave me feedback that enhanced my memory. Some shared profound learnings that they took from the book as young social entrepreneurs and activists, or reflections they found fascinating from the point of view of cross-racial experiences and perspectives. Some readers thought I should remove some of the personal stories that they felt over-exposed me; others thought I should include them because they were empowering to themselves and would also be important to other young activists who might go through comparable challenges. (I left them in.) A few readers spent hours with me on the phone debating and laughing about the content of the book, especially the details reflecting race and class. These conversations were so much fun that I considered delaying the publication for a year and expanding the group of readers by a couple dozen with whom I would have deep reflective and joyful dialogue before finalizing it. But in the end, I decided to bite the bullet, and publish it. It would never be perfect, but all the readers said it would be useful and I should get it out there. Nonetheless, if any new readers would like to share with me personally your thoughts and memories, or your disagreements, I would welcome that. Write to me! Enjoy the book! Enjoy our lives that we are blessed to live!

An Explanation of One Detail

You will notice, and some of you may be annoyed when you notice, that I have not capitalized black, nor white, when referencing people's race. In many contexts it is now preferred that Black be capitalized, and white be in small letters. I decided that since the concept of race has been a false construct designed to separate groups from each other and justify and perpetuate oppression, I would not magnify the names of either black or white people. We are equally human. There is in fact neither a white race nor a black race biologically. We are all members of the human race. Therefore, the false distinctions between us should not be magnified with capital letters for either group, and certainly they should both be treated equally. Let's unite to get power to all the people to build a world that is good for all human beings, all other species, and all of nature.

CHAPTER 1

White Girl in the Ghetto

I t was the winter of 1964. It was after the March on Washington in which the great Reverend Martin Luther King Jr. made his most famous "I Have a Dream" speech in front of over 250,000 black and white marchers on the mall. It was after the Birmingham Church bombing, when 4 little black girls were killed, shocking the nation. It was after Rosa Parks was arrested for sitting in the front of the bus, touching off a dramatic confrontation between segregation and dignity. It was after students holding sit-ins to integrate lunch counters in the South were met with relentless, irrational violence rooted in centuries of slave-owning attitudes among whites with property.

It was before Freedom Summer, when northern students descended on the South to register voters and join black organizers in the Student Nonviolent Coordinating Committee (SNCC). It was before the Harlem riots of 1964. It was before Goodman, Schwerner, and Cheney — two northern white students and one southern black student — were murdered in Mississippi for daring to defy the old order with visions of equality.

It was March of 1964. I was on my way to Harlem to join the Civil Rights Movement. I had gone to a rally at Columbia University the week before, just after moving to New York City to attend Bank Street College of Education to learn how to be a nursery-school teacher. Prior to moving to New York, I had gone through a transformation committing me to becoming a frontline activist. However, my plan to go to the Congo to support Angolan refugees had been blocked by complicated factors (to be explained later), landing me in New York for graduate school.

At the Columbia rally, I was moved to tears by a freedom song. I realized in the moment when lovely idealistic voices were rising together that if I couldn't go to the Congo, I could nonetheless be useful in New York City. The Civil Rights Movement was as important in America as the colonial liberation struggles were in Africa.

I picked up the phone the next day to call someone at the Harlem Action Group to ask if I could volunteer for the Harlem rent strike.

Whoever answered the phone said, "Sure you can help. Come on up."

The next day, as I walked up the stairs at the subway station at 135th Street and St. Nicholas Avenue in Harlem, my eyes took in the familiar-looking branches of a maple tree outside the station, not different from the one outside my parents' front door. The tree seemed to welcome me to Harlem. I have never forgotten that moment of climbing those stairs into new territory and seeing the maple tree in the little park above the subway at St. Nicholas Avenue. It was familiar and welcoming.

When I reached the street level, I was struck with a wave of strangeness. I thought, "There aren't many of me here." In fact, every single person was black. I had never been on a street where every person was black, probably hadn't ever imagined such a street in the United States. But here I was, on the first day of the rest of my life.

I turned down 137th Street and walked the block to 8th Avenue to the storefront. It was a tiny little scruffy storefront on the East side of the street, just south of 137th Street, with a hand-made sign in the window that said, "Harlem Action Group." Inside, a large man sat on a tall stool behind the counter, facing the door. He had on a classic businessman's hat, a maroon jersey shirt, and he sported a substantial beer belly plus a beer in his hand. I introduced myself as a volunteer for the rent strike. He said simply, "I'm Leroy. Glad you're here. Bob Knight is in the back."

I followed his direction to the back, and found the tall thin director of HAG, Bob Knight, who I would soon learn was always in the back, talking rapidly and jiggling his knee. I got put to work immediately as a typist. It was a perfect role for an innocent white girl who knew nothing about anything, but who did know how to type. Thank goodness my father had made me study typing in 8th grade telling me, "If there is ever another depression you've got to have a skill. Learn to type." He had no idea it would make me a useful unpaid aide in a ramshackle Harlem Civil Rights storefront in 1964.

I sat at my desk for several days, typing whatever anybody gave me. I was also listening. That's what some typists do. They type, and they listen. Everyone was talking about this rally and that strike and this leader and that meeting. The energy was exciting. Pretty soon I had met everyone in the place, as one by one, people introduced themselves to the young white stranger facing the typewriter against the wall in the middle of the two-room storefront.

Two teenaged boys began to sit next to me every time I came. They talked to me about the movement, about how they wanted to be leaders, how the world was changing, and how much they wanted to be part of it. This was my first lesson in listening to the aspirations of black teenaged boys who wanted to become somebody who could make a difference. They were completely up front with their hope.

They began to tell me about the people in the office. Leroy Branch, who always sat at the front with a beer, was described by them as "the hustler." Nobody knew what he was doing in the Harlem Action Group. The rumor was that he followed the money, so they believed he must have some inside knowledge about money that would soon be coming through HAG. They didn't yet know what I learned later about Leroy — that he was listening also, trying to learn about the Civil Rights Movement, to see if it held any real promise for change.

Leroy had spent too many years as a hustler, too many years as a "dope fiend," too many years in prison. He was 39 years old and ready for a change. His hope had been stirred by Malcolm X, Martin Luther King, and the March on Washington in the summer of 1963 when he saw blacks and whites together calling for change. Now he was just sitting there at the front of the Harlem Action Group office, watching the folks who were coming to Harlem, checking them out. He lived on West 134th Street and he didn't have a job. Ex-convicts couldn't get jobs. His partner, Sarah Kearney, with whom he had lived for 18 years, supported him. As I got to know him, I learned he was widely read, having educated himself in the penitentiary. He had a dream of starting a small business selling watermelons out of the back of a truck because he had decided never to risk selling drugs again. Beyond selling watermelons, he had a bigger dream of helping other drug addicts emerge from the chaos and powerlessness of their addiction. But at that time, he had no inkling of any way to make the second deeper dream a reality. That was to come later, when he would become famous as Leroy Looper, a man who changed the lives of thousands.

The Harlem Action Group (HAG) was sponsored by the Northern Student Movement (NSM), one of the important Civil Rights groups in the North. The Northern Student Movement didn't usually have grassroots operations — it was a college students' organization. But somehow an unlikely affiliation had occurred between HAG and NSM.

NSM had a downtown office that a few leaders from HAG often went to, and NSM had some leaders who occasionally came uptown to HAG. A few of these leaders later became somewhat famous: Danny Schechter and Gordon Davis were in the downtown office. For some reason, I never went to the downtown office, never even felt like going there. I wasn't a leader. I was a foot soldier. I have no idea to this day what the downtown office of NSM was doing or what it even looked like. I was just sitting uptown at my typewriter getting to know people and figuring out my role. This was the beginning of decades of my being completely at home at the grassroots, in the field, with little interest in going to the center of power. When Gordon Davis later became a senior aide to Mayor Lindsay in the downtown office and I was still in East Harlem, he commented on this difference between us, which is why I remember the concept — I seemed to belong in the field, not the downtown office.

The regulars in that storefront were Chickie, Granville, Elsie Chandler, Miss Flack, Bob Knight, Jesse, Luther, Julius, Leroy, Beale, and the two teenagers with hope, both of whom happened to be named Lamont.

Chickie was a charming, poetic, charismatic, energetic, heroin addict who could talk rings around all of us, spouted poetry, was attractive to all the women, including me, and had a vision for change. Granville was an intense, impulsive, father of five who lived upstairs with his wife and children and was always railing at something, frequently threatening to go upstairs and get his gun. Ms. Flack was the grandmother of the group: skinny, warm, friendly, quiet, always available to help everyone. She provided home-cooked food for the rest of us. Jesse was a quiet, slow-speaking, under-educated wine-drinking unemployed man who very much wanted to get educated and make a difference. Luther was an upstanding young man with a job who came to volunteer and whom everyone respected as a straight shooter. Julius was quixotic and outspoken; he surprised me early on by openly propositioning me in the back office because he said wanted to sleep with a white girl. Bob Knight was the director. He came from outside the neighborhood. He seemed ambitious, self-conscious, nervous, self-important, controlling everything. Elsie was another white girl, petite, even elfin, but sturdy in her Jewish commitment to equal rights. She, too, came from outside the neighborhood. Beale was enigmatic, sitting and listening, like Leroy, only much younger.

By the summer, Chuck Turner was also there in that storefront. Chuck was a black Harvard graduate seeking a role for himself. In 1964 there weren't many African American Harvard graduates — black students at Harvard were more likely to be from Africa than Harlem. Chuck would later become a major Civil Rights leader in Roxbury, Boston, for the rest of his life. He served as a City Council member for many years. But this was his first grassroots experience. He was short, round, quiet, smart, also alert for what he could learn by listening.

People were always running in and out, there was lots of energy, and everyone was talking about the movement, the rent strike, the neighborhood, racism, Martin Luther King, Malcolm X, and the politics of it all. But it wasn't entirely clear to me what was actually happening, and I don't remember what I was typing. I just knew that I loved being there. I immediately felt like I had come home in some deep way that I hardly understood.

It seemed to me that I had found reality. I compared the energy and intensity to the sanitized life I had lived under a protective bubble in Belmont Massachusetts, in an entirely white segregated suburb of Boston, where nobody seemed to have any idea about poverty, racism, and struggle. Everybody had what they needed, at least materially. Nobody saw what each other lacked or what each other suffered inside their homes. Everything was superficially fine. The clear and visible reality of the effects of oppression in Harlem seemed to stir in me some unknown memory of genuine human struggle that was somewhere in my own history. I wondered if it was resonating with my Russian Jewish immigrant side, the dark-haired emotional side, the side that escaped the pogroms in the Ukraine just two generations before. That was my father's side of the family.

Soon two things happened to me in Harlem: The first was that I made friends. Elsie moved into my apartment on Broadway and 113th Street. Our apartment soon became a gathering place for Jesse, Granville, and Chickie. Slow-speaking self-effacing Jesse asked me to be his tutor, which I eagerly did. We read books together in the evening at the kitchen table while Chickie charmingly spouted poetry he'd written. We all sat around and talked Movement, along with storefront gossip.

The other thing that happened was that I got an idea. Although I had come to Harlem to support the rent strike, I quickly decided that it did not make any sense at all for a privileged white girl to go door to door suggesting that poor black people take the risk of withholding their rent from their white landlords. I had no idea what the consequences would be for them, and it just didn't seem right for me to be asking them to take that risk.

It's probably worth saying that I didn't grow up viewing myself as a "white girl." Having been raised in a totally insulated suburban white community in the fifties in the North, I never had to think of my race at all. I was simply a human being. My mother was a German Presbyterian, my father was a Russian Jew, and I was raised as a Unitarian. I didn't think of myself as white. None of us did. We never referred to ourselves as white. The distinctions between people in our community were about religion. We had Catholics, Jews, Methodists, Episcopalians, Congregationalists, and Unitarians in our town. And then there was nationality: we had Irish Catholics, Italian Catholics, Armenians (the rest of us had no idea what their religion was), and general European Protestants and Jews. Everyone was white, except the cleaning ladies who arrived in the wealthier part of our town on the public bus on Thursdays, and we never gave that any thought either — it was just the nature of things. Black ladies cleaned houses on Belmont hill on Thursdays. The black lady who cleaned our house on the hill on Thursday throughout my childhood was named Maggie. I never knew her last name.

I did learn about race in college, because my tall blonde roommate from Minnesota, Emmie, spent a year in Kenya in 1961 on the Crossroads Africa program and learned about colonialism, wars of liberation, racism, imperialism, and the Mau Mau's struggle against the British. She came home to teach me we were white, racism was real and bad, and we had to do something about it. So, I began to read: *Black Like Me, Negroes with Guns, Down these Mean Streets*, and other such books. By the time I reached Harlem from Harvard I had a little bit of book learning about race, and I had some African acquaintances from Ghana and Nigeria. By then I did know I was white. And I had developed a passionate drive to work against racism. My generation of innocent white Girl Scouts who had taken a pledge to "help other people at all times," to "be a friend to all and a sister to every other Girl Scout," and had saluted the American flag saying "with liberty and justice for all," were horrified to learn about the existence of racism when it hit the news in the North inside our protected enclaves of white privilege in the early sixties. Our idealism was easily activated. (Of course, activation of previously unaware northern whites went well beyond Girl Scouts, but part of my moral identity was rooted in Girl Scouts.) I hadn't yet learned what it meant to be a "white girl in the ghetto," as we were called in the Movement.

The good idea that came to me in the early weeks at the typewriter was that I should use the skills I was gaining at the Bank Street College of Education to set up a summer pre-school. I had had a similar idea during college when I wrote a paper in my sociology class suggesting a nursery school that would employ and train teenagers as a way of "breaking the cycle of poverty." That vision was what had impelled me to go to graduate school in education. It dawned on me that I might implement that idea for HAG. I asked my two teenaged friends hovering around my desk what they would think of starting a pre-school for the summer, especially for children who had somehow missed kindergarten, to help them prepare for first grade.

They thought it was a great idea. I asked Chickie, Granville, Jesse, Elsie, and Leroy. They all agreed. I asked Bob Knight. He was more skeptical. I was white, after all, and young, and surely wasn't fit to navigate in the community. But he didn't veto it, and Leroy encouraged me to go ahead and do it. He said he would help. So, I began to plan.

Around the same period of late winter, I had applied to join SNCC's Mississippi Freedom Summer to go South to organize voter registration. That would be the front lines, the hot spot of the movement. I had decided in college that everyone committed to justice should go as close to the front lines as their personality allowed. That's why I had been planning to go to the Congo. Emmie, my college roommate, had decided the same thing; she was already in Jackson, working in SNCC's main office.

When I learned that I had been accepted by SNCC, I talked it over with Leroy. Sitting at the front counter at HAG on the tall stool, he shook his head at me and said, "We need you here. You have begun something. Racism isn't only in the south. There are issues here in Harlem. The same issues. We already know you, and we want you to stay. What's the point in going south when you can do just as much good here and we already know you?"

Walking me slowly to the subway, Beale quietly said the same thing.

"Don't go. Stay with us. We already trust you."

I stayed. This was a wonderful decision. I was so lucky. During the next few years, I watched most of my white friends who had gone south be pushed out of the movement because there were too many confident white northerners. They were too dominant. They had deeply internalized the automatic assumption of leadership in all situations, were too inadvertently forceful in pushing their points of view. As a group, they didn't know how to be subordinate, how to listen and learn and defer to the people whose freedom was at stake, whose liberation was at hand, whose leadership was essential. I watched their hearts be broken as they lost their sense of belonging to the greatest movement of our time. They had to leave. Some of them landed as hippies in Vermont for a while. Then some of them married black men from various walks of life and built complicated multi-racial lives with children who successfully navigated our racist society. But they were never quite at the center of the Movement again.

In my invisible little spot embedded in Harlem, where there were only two white girls, and no white men, I was able to learn directly from Leroy, Chuck, and Chickie how to use my skills, that I had received from my privileged white life, to benefit their goals. Tucked into the community, I just put one foot in front of another, quietly, toward creating something they believed would be of value. I will always thank my lucky stars that I never had to be pushed out of this great movement. I am still in it.

The Summer Pre-School in 1964

Once I had the go-ahead from the members of HAG and a promise of support from Leroy and Miss Flack, I began to organize the summer pre-school. It materialized sort of magically. I just walked from place to place in the neighborhood, sometimes with Leroy keeping me company and opening the doors, and we asked for things. Everyone gave us what we asked for.

On Sunday mornings Leroy led me down rickety and sometimes mildew-smelling stairways into basement churches where we gave little speeches to the gathered Congregations about what we hoped to do, and the pastors of the little basement churches always offered us their humble spaces for the summer.

I went to visit the local school principals. The principal at the elementary school on 134th Street and Seventh Avenue gave me contact information for children who had missed kindergarten. The principal at the middle school on the corner of 138th and St. Nicholas Ave. gave us three classrooms for the summer, at no charge!

I called my close friend from high school, Lois Howlett, and asked if she would volunteer for the summer — she was also a Bank Street graduate student — and she said yes. Another young white woman named Donna contacted me, referred through the Northern Student Movement. She had heard we were planning a pre-school and offered to spend the summer volunteering. That was the summer of 1964 when white civil rights volunteers who could afford to work for free were everywhere. Including me, we had teachers for three classrooms committed to volunteer full-time all summer.

At HAG I asked for teenagers who wanted to be assistant teachers or to lead small groups of school-aged children. Before I could blink an eye, we had 17 teen-aged volunteers from the neighborhood. We offered to pay them $5/week and they said Yes. This was before Head Start, before Job Corps, before Summer Youth Corps, before AmeriCorps. There were no pre-schools, no summer jobs, no job training programs. It was the spring of 1964, before the Civil rights movement became national. There was nothing for teenagers to do in the summer in Harlem. Suddenly an exciting project was emerging, and everyone was on board.

Miss Flack and I went door to door around the neighborhood to ask the parents of the children who missed kindergarten if they would like to send their children to a summer preschool to prepare for first grade. Every single one of them said Yes. We asked if they would pay $10/month, and every single one of them said Yes. But they needed one thing: they needed us to pick up their children in the morning because for one reason or another, they could not bring them. That was why they had missed kindergarten. Miss Flack and I enrolled 60 five- and six-year-olds and promised to pick each one of them up every morning at their homes.

At the same time, we found 120 older elementary school children who had nothing to do in the summer. We decided to add a second project: we enrolled them in activity groups that the teenagers would lead in the little spaces in the church basements.

By June we had a robust registration of 180 children, three nearly professional volunteer teachers, 14 teen-aged small group leaders, and three teen-aged assistant teachers. The schools gave us free materials, and the city government provided food for lunches. The whole summer pre-school and activity program cost just $600 for the summer. That was $3.33/student!

All of this was done without supervision, rules, insurance, a board of directors, or oversight of any kind. I was 22 years old, making it up as I went along, optimistic, totally naïve, and surprised at how easily everything fell into place while I was still attending graduate school full time. I had no advice from any professional, no advisory board, no pro bono legal advice: I had never heard of any of those things. I just had the Harlem Action Group behind me, with Leroy as a mentor and Miss Flack as a supporter. This was a risky venture, but we didn't realize it. I was a Unitarian Girl Scout, just putting one foot in front of another without imagining any real risks. I got welcoming support from the community.

I thank my lucky stars — which have been very reliably with me all my life — that nothing significant went wrong. We almost had a disaster when one of the teenagers lost one of the elementary school students in the subway on a trip downtown. The lost child was Granville's son, who was quickly found; but Granville did threaten to go get his gun. Leroy calmed him down, and the crisis blew over.

Another memorable moment also involved Granville. He was angry at his son Junior, who was in my preschool class. He came roaring into the classroom one day, threatening to beat Junior with his belt. I stood up and said he absolutely could not hit any child in my classroom even if it was his own son. I had no idea what I was doing. It was just instinct and principle. Nobody had ever beaten me as a child, and it was nowhere in my psyche to allow the beating of a child. Granville was enraged. What right did this white girl have to get between him and his own son? I hadn't thought about it in racial terms, but in fact everything in Harlem had to be understood in racial terms. Granville left in a huff and ran over to sound off at the HAG office a block away.

Leroy came over to the classroom after school to talk to me, to find out what in the world I was thinking, and what had actually happened. He knew Granville was a hothead. But he thought I must have made a significant misstep to trigger such anger. We had a long talk about hitting children, and I expounded on some theory I had about how black parents hitting their children was the internalized behavior learned under slavery and that it wasn't good for the children and wasn't necessary in 1964. I have no recollection of where that idea came from, but it seemed like it could be true. I don't know whether Leroy believed me, but he decided that my intentions were good, I had something to offer, and he would protect me by watching my back.

This summer project was the beginning of a life-long relationship in which Leroy watched my back. For over forty-five years we worked together bringing opportunities to young people, bridging the racial divide, and bringing resources to low-income communities. I used the access that being white and privileged gave me, acted on my naïve but very committed good intentions, while he backed me up, listened to me, and advised me wisely on all issues related to race and class.

I don't know whether the summer pre-school was a success in preparing children for first grade. We had no capacity to follow up, and simply took it on faith that we were doing the right thing. The morning walk to school, with each teacher plus two teen-aged assistants walking through the neighborhood and picking up the children at their homes was a wonderful daily ritual, much appreciated by the neighborhood.

"Good morning, teacher!" was warmly offered from passers-by, as we strolled down the sidewalk with an ever-expanding group of children holding hands at 8 AM every morning. It was a great way to start the day, one by one, building the sense of belonging and being cared about that comes from having a teacher knock on your door, with your classmates in tow, waiting for you while you finish tying your shoelaces.

We took a lot of trips that summer. Many of the children had never been south of 96th street, so our subway rides to museums and ferry rides to Staten Island were important for them. I will never forget the absolute delight of a tiny little girl named Carolyn who leaped up on the bench on the Staten Island Ferry, ecstatically pointing to the Statue of Liberty, calling out, "There it is! There it is! I see it! I SEE IT! There's the Flatue of Stiberty! The Flatue of Stiberty!"

The HAG summer pre-school occurred simultaneous with the Mississippi summer preschool that was the harbinger of Head Start. The idea was occurring to many people at the same time: preparing young children for first grade was a recognized need.

Growing up in Belmont in the 1940's and 1950's

W e had an amazing sense of safety and freedom when I was growing up in the suburbs of Boston in a middle-class seg-regated white community called Belmont, meaning the "beautiful hill." In fact, I lived on "the hill," which was where the richer people in town lived, where the yards were big, maple and pine trees were ever-present, and open fields were spacious. My family lived in a big brick house, on a street that was called Marsh Street, named after the wetlands, found at the bottom of the street near the pretty place where we would play in the brook that passed through the fancy private golf course toward the real marsh.

We played freely, by ourselves, with no adults supervising, in the streams, in the woods, in the marshlands, in the back yards. We built tree houses and rode our bikes. In the spring we sold flowers and fruit punch to passers-by at little stands we would build on the side of the street. In the winter we would build snow forts and throw snowballs at cars passing by. In the fall we played basketball and baseball in the big backyard basketball court my father had created because he had been a semi-professional basketball player before he became a lawyer.

I look back with amazement at the fact that I had such freedom, and my parents had such a deep sense of comfort regarding the safety of the world. I would come home on the school bus from the Winn Brook Elementary School at 1 PM, have lunch, and then get on my little blue two-wheel bike, at age seven, and ride out the driveway, a mile up the hill to the crest of Marsh Street and then sweep down the steep hill another couple of miles to the neighborhood where the Winn Brook School, my elementary school, was situated. I would arrive at the playground to play with the other kids who lived within walking distance of the school. We would play all afternoon, on the swings and the jungle gym, and in the baseball diamond. I would stop in at my best friend Ellen Furry's house where her wonderful mother, Mrs. Furry, would give us grape juice in the mid-afternoon. Then at 5:30 PM I would get back on my little bike and push it up the hill to get home for dinner at 6:30 PM. As long as I was home for dinner at 6:30 PM I could go anywhere, do anything, play with my friends, without calling home (there were no cell phones), with no adult supervision. Nobody worried about me, and I didn't worry about anything either, except being sure I got home at 6:30 because we always sat down for dinner at that exact same time in our little breakfast nook with my mother and father, who were both always there, and my older brother and sister. A live-in maid, who was typically either Irish Catholic or African American, would serve us dinner, except on Thursday evening when she had the day off and my father went to the golf club, and we stayed home with Mommy.

My father always arrived home from his law office in Boston at exactly 5:30 PM. When we were home, we would hear his gray Cadillac turn into the driveway at exactly the same time every day. We would immediately wonder if we had done anything wrong that day that he could see from his car. Had we left tools in the yard? Had we left our bikes out in the driveway risking getting rained on and rusty? Had we left the porch light on so that we were wasting money on electricity? Had we broken anything that he might find? We did worry about those things, because my father would be quick to criticize if he saw something out of place or broken. There was one period of time when I went to bed early for a few days (or weeks, I really can't remember) in order to avoid his wrath because I had broken the edge off a table in the living room and I wanted to avoid the first round of his anger when he discovered it. I figured if I were asleep then I would be safe, and my mother would not let him wake me up to scold me. She would absorb the first round of his anger.

My mother always created safety for us on every level. Yet she was not in any sense over-protective, because she let us roam freely around the town and never seemed to worry. She trusted us, she trusted the world, she expected the best of everyone, and spent her life volunteering for the League of Women Voters to help make a better world through the democratic involvement of women. She studied every social and political issue and wrote issue briefs on them. She didn't have a paying job. She didn't need to. Her husband made enough money, and women in those days were not really expected to work. She was an educated woman, who had graduated from Vassar College and Radcliffe graduate school. She was interested in everything, especially everything that affected the well-being of American society. She volunteered full-time, contributing social capital to her community and country. She became president of the local and the state League of Women Voters, and later served on the national board. That was her work. She went to meetings, she read books, and she sat in the breakfast nook and wrote papers on social issues on her typewriter.

She always wore a dress and high heels, always had her hair professionally done, was always gracious and almost never angry, a kind and unpretentious woman who was widely respected for her dedication, intelligence, humility, and grace. She was also privileged to have a live-in maid who cleaned the house, cooked the meals, and made the beds, so she had time to study the world and go to meetings to discuss and advocate for the issues of the times. Recently, in 2020, celebrating the 100th anniversary of the passage of the 19th Amendment to the Constitution giving women the right to vote, the Town of Belmont chose to honor my mother, Helene D. Stoneman, who had already been in her grave since 1987.

As a mother to her children, she was unusually unintrusive and undemanding. She did not control and direct us, did not scold or criticize us, did not insult or punish us, did not threaten us with punishments of any kind, did not raise her voice at us, never lost her temper, and did not disapprove of us or our friends in any way that I can remember. She was almost never disappointed in us. She also did not hug and kiss us. She also did not seem to need anything from us. When I needed attention, I would decide to go with her in the car on her neighborhood errands, so I could sit next to her in the front seat, and she would have to listen. I don't know what she did when she needed attention, because she never seemed to ask anyone for anything. She was a German Protestant: self-sufficient, hard-working, self-contained, reserved.

I have often referred to my mother as a perfect mother. The level of trust, respect, and freedom she gave us, asking nothing in return, and imposing none of her own needs on her children, seemed amazing. But her German WASP shyness and self-contained lack of demonstrative affection was also something I had to un-learn. I later had to practice putting my arm around my girlfriend's waist as we walked down the street in order to get comfortable with that simple level of physical affection. I had to watch on TV to see how people hugged after I had found myself puzzled in seventh grade when Bob McBride kissed me, and I didn't know what to do with my hands and arms. I had awkwardly placed my hands on his hips.

But I grew up learning from my father what to do with my arms and hands in sports. He taught us how to play baseball and basketball, how to swim and ski, how to wrestle and box, how to rake leaves and weed gardens. He gave us instructions, and high standards, with criticism being easily available, but he also gave us freedom and respect. I remember well when we first went skiing in Vermont, and the plan was for us to have skiing lessons. I didn't want lessons. I wanted to go to the top of the mountain and ski down it. He actually let me do that, and I will never forget sliding down that mountain largely on my butt, with my father waiting and smiling, giving me instructions, but clearly proud that his little girl had the guts to go to the top of the mountain and make her way down it. I was about eight years old. Nothing made me happier than making my father proud. I also remember that event as representative of a lasting element of my personality: I would figure it out on my own, not wait for direction or teaching, and somehow get safely down the mountain.

It wasn't always easy to make him proud, because he seemed to think that if a person wasn't the best in the world at something, they weren't worth hardly anything at all. Once he saw that I was becoming a good little skier, he decided I should aspire to be an Olympic skier. He would tell my brother and me to lean up against the wall in the hallway outside the kitchen and lower our bodies to bend our knees to strengthen our legs for skiing. When I told him I did not want to be an Olympic skier and did not want to stand against the wall strengthening my legs, he was very disappointed. "How," he asked, "if you have the ability to become an Olympic skier, is it possible that you would not choose to be the best skier in the world?" But fortunately, he did not force me to do the exercise.

This attitude of his that being the best at everything should be core to anyone's aspirations was hard on us. In a way it was the opposite of the freedom and trust that we were given by our mother. There was an underlying expectation that we had to be very good at everything to maintain our father's approval, even to obtain his basic acceptance. The epitome of this message was expressed in the fact that he expected us to graduate from high school as the first in our class. My sister was second in her class: "salutatorian" it was called. I was eight years old when she became the salutatorian. My brother was also second in his class, "salutatorian." I was fifteen when my brother Billy came home and proudly announced that he would be speaking at graduation as the salutatorian.

My father responded with disdain, "Another second best!" This was a horrifying and memorable moment. How could a father be disapproving and ashamed of his son for being "Second best" instead of proud of him for being salutatorian?

When I was a junior in high school, I overheard my father telling one of his best friends that "Dorothy is doing very well in school and is going to be first in her class.... valedictorian." I was very angry to hear him say that. It wasn't fair. I wasn't even in my senior year, and he was setting it up so that I would profoundly disappoint and even humiliate him if I were not the best in my class. He was giving me no choice. Either be the best, or be a failure who shamed my father. Those were the only alternatives. That was not fair.

This pressure did not come only from my father. When I was a sophomore in high school and my brother won a national merit scholarship, my tenth grade teacher remarked, "Oh, yes, your brother got a national merit scholarship... so will you. It runs in the family." The pressure was on. It was the same story in my first term in high school when I asked my English teacher how my grades were coming along. She looked in her book, then looked up at me standing at her desk, and said, "Oh, you're a Stoneman. I'm sure you'll be earning an A. It runs in the family." The pressure was on.

I understood that I was profoundly lucky that I was able to get good grades. But just to belong in my family without bringing shame or disappointment, I had to get all A's. Fortunately, it did run in the family and came naturally to me, so I was able to succeed. I had noticed as early as 1st grade that things were easier for me than for other kids. I knew I was lucky. It had nothing to do with anything I had done. I hadn't earned that good fortune. I was somehow born lucky, in every imaginable way.

I was born lucky that I was healthy and good at sports. I was born lucky that I could do schoolwork easily when other kids were struggling. I was born lucky that people liked me from the minute I entered nursery school. I was born lucky that my parents had enough money and we never had to worry about it. I was born lucky that I had two parents who were healthy and who didn't drink alcohol and didn't get divorced and didn't abuse me. I didn't know it at the time, but I was also lucky that I was born white in America.

I didn't have any idea why I was born so lucky. My only way of dealing with it was to think that I must have been born lucky so that I could help other people. There had to be a reason. It otherwise didn't make sense that anyone could be born as lucky as I was.

Still, lucky or not, the pressure and expectations that I would excel were intense. Maybe that was the only unlucky part. In senior year I anxiously awaited the results from the national merit scholarship test. The week the announcements were due I drove home from school every day during lunch period to see if I had anything in the mail. One day it was there. When I opened it, standing by myself at the bottom of the stairs, I discovered I had indeed been chosen as a National Merit Scholar. Relief and happiness flooded through me. Thank goodness, I had made it! I was safe. I had not disappointed anyone's expectations! I raced back to school as fast as I could drive, leaning on the horn, yelling out the window, crying to myself that I had made it. I was safe. I had gotten the National Merit Scholarship that everyone expected me to get. If I had been religious, I would have thanked the Lord. But I just thanked my lucky stars. I was so relieved, so happy to be able to meet my father's explicit expectation that I had to excel to be worthy of my family's approval.

But once I got that scholarship, and once I got into Harvard on early admissions in the fall of my senior year, I relaxed. I let my grades drop. I didn't have to get all A's anymore. And I certainly did NOT have to be valedictorian. I had a lot of fun that spring of senior year with my friends. When I came home from school and told my father that Mary Austin was valedictorian and Karen Ippen was salutatorian, he was furious. He could not believe that I was not first, nor even second, in my class. Not even second best! I told him I didn't need to be, that I was already in Harvard, that I hadn't tried to be valedictorian. He said, "You are ruining your life." I said, "No, I am ruining your life. You shouldn't care so much that I have to be the best. I don't have to be the best."

That was in 1959. Much later, in 1996, 37 years later, when I unexpectedly got an award I had not worked for nor looked for, had not waited in suspense to see if I would get the letter in the mail, the surprise MacArthur "genius" award that you can't even apply for, one of the greatest honors that American professionals ever get, I was sad that my father was not alive to witness that moment. He would, finally, have been proud of me, on his own distorted terms. He was never proud of my work as a teacher, or community organizer, or even as executive director of a non-profit organization, because it was in Harlem. Even when I was, at age 27, the highly successful executive director of the East Harlem Block Schools, with a staff of 60 people, doing creative work on the cutting edge of school reform, he would ask, "When are you going to get a real job?" That was a horrifying question that revealed his profound class and racial bias. But if he had been alive to see it, he would have understood that a MacArthur "genius" Fellowship would count as success in his terms, and we could have gotten a certain closure on our relationship and the fact that I had not chosen to live up to his particular competitive expectations.

It is sad that as I set out to write this personal autobiographical chapter, it so quickly turned to the feelings generated by the excessively high expectations imposed on me by my father. I sat down to write about the extraordinary freedom and trust we were given, about how the mindset of what I was later to be called — a "social entrepreneur" — was possibly created through the freedom of a seven-year-old on a bicycle who had the confidence to ride wherever I chose, all afternoon, creating my own life and my own path, because my parents didn't force me to be always obedient to someone else's plan. There is something about having the confidence to chart your own course that is central to the role of social innovator. I am grateful for the childhood freedom that kept my confidence to innovate intact.

This life we had in Belmont in the nineteen forties and fifties was a good life. I often think it may not be such a strange coincidence that Michael Brown, one of the founders of City Year, also grew up in Belmont, about twenty years after I did. He also attended Winn Brook Elementary School and we had the same third grade teacher. We got goose bumps many years later when we shared our history with each other and discovered that both our fathers went to Harvard Law School and both our Jewish immigrant grandfathers were auctioneers. In 2019 an award was created called the Stoneman Brown National Service Advocacy Award to honor the similar roles Michael and I played in advocating for national service funding at the federal level. It was an amazing coincidence that we both grew up in Belmont, with Jewish fathers.

Being a Unitarian Girl Scout

What else was going on in Belmont that influenced my perspective on the world? Well, there were Girl Scouts, and the Unitarian Church. I grew up as a Unitarian Girl Scout. I spent twelve years as a Girl Scout. That meant I was saying a pledge, on a weekly basis, that committed me as follows: "On my honor I pledge, to do my duty to God and my country, to help other people at all times...." In those days, the pledge ended with these words: "especially those at home." Later under the influence of the women's liberation movement it was changed to "and obey the Girl Scout laws." The Girl Scout laws were pretty good. They included being "a friend to all and a sister to every other Girl Scout," caring for animals, telling the truth, and other good things that I internalized as a whole but don't precisely remember now.

The Unitarians had a similar positive influence. They taught us to respect the religions of all other people, and to think for ourselves. Leading an ethical life of service was more important than believing any particular theology. This was most helpful for me, because, again, it reinforced my freedom to think for myself. I therefore figured out exactly what I thought about religion when I was fourteen. I saw that my Catholic friends were struggling with the ideas of Heaven and Hell, the fear that if they did not believe the right thing, they would go to Hell.

I decided that any God that I would believe in would not be so egotistical that he would care about whether I believed in him (or, from my current perspective I might have thought if there were a God it was unknown whether God was a he or a she!) S/he would only care about how I lived. So I decided it did not matter what I believed, it mattered how I lived, and I did not have to worry about Heaven or Hell, because I did not believe in life after death; but if it turned out that they existed, if I had lived in a way that was consistent with the teachings of Jesus in terms of helping other people, forgiving my enemies, turning the other cheek, doing unto others as I would have them do unto me, understanding that love was the greatest force for good, I really didn't have to be concerned about any other beliefs or any theology. This was a simple conclusion that carried me a long way. It still seems to be true. Any religion that imposes obedience to a theology out of fear of the consequences of not believing what you are told to believe has always struck me as oppressive and counter to what I believe would actually be the will of God if there were a God.

Somewhere along the way, someone at summer camp when I was about nine years old told me to talk to God as if he were my friend. That was a helpful piece of advice. I did that. Although I didn't believe in God in the theological sense, I did feel that God was my friend, and I would thank him a lot for all of my good fortune. Who else could I thank? It was beyond anyone's responsibility that I had been born so lucky, so my gratitude had to go somewhere more spiritual, more mysterious, to some larger universal consciousness. Having God as a friend was a kind of simple relationship for me, not fraught with any burdens, any expectations, any obligations, any fears, or any beliefs. I never asked God for anything because I already was grateful for everything I already had. I figured if there were a God, he would be very busy with other people's needs and I should not take up his time. I just occasionally said, "Thank you." Now, with a Buddhist husband whom I sometimes accompany to meditation retreats, I still find the most poignant and relevant spiritual attitude is one of infinite gratitude.

Being a Girl

The other themes of my early years were about friendship and romance, and the nature of being a girl. I was a "tomboy", as they called us back then. I was the only girl my age in the neighborhood. All my early childhood freedom was spent with boys. I loved sports, and I liked to wrestle with the boys in the neighborhood. My brother took pride in the fact that I usually beat them. My father included me in sports in a nonsexist way that was a great boon to my development. Even though his extremely high expectations were hard on me, the fact that some of my father's expectations were non-sexist was extremely helpful.

I was, nonetheless, a girl, and I had to be properly deferential. I only got to play basketball with the boys on our backyard court when they needed an extra player. I would sit and watch a lot, until they needed me to even up the teams. I was a pretty good player, but still, I was a girl. The only other girl in my neighborhood was Nancy Baty, who was five years older than I. My very best friend was Vic Taylor, a boy my age who lived two doors up the street. He moved into the neighborhood in 2nd grade. We remained very close friends all through our childhood and adolescence (and we are still friends to this day). Having boys as real personal friends turned out to be very important to my evolution. It was different from what a lot of girls experienced.

I played baseball with the boys in school during recess every day. I brought my baseball glove to school and always looked forward to recess. Unfortunately, one day in fifth grade my teacher, Miss Tracy, said shocking words to me as we stood on the front steps of the school at the beginning of recess. She said, "Dorothy, you must stop bringing your baseball glove to school and stop playing with the boys. You are a girl." I do not remember anything else she said, but I obeyed, and was terribly sad every day afterwards when the boys would call me to play, and I would have to say that I couldn't. This seemed to be the first official imposition of sexism on my life, but I had no word for it back then. It just shocked and hurt me.

That same year, my friend Nancy Baty, who was five years older than I, told me that it was risky to be a tomboy. She told me I should change before I got to junior high school because otherwise I would never have a boyfriend. Fortunately for me, when I reached sixth grade the kids in my neighborhood were switched to a different elementary school because our Winn Brook School was being renovated and was short of space. That meant that I could start over in 6th grade and not act like a tomboy. Then when we got to junior high in 7th grade my old friends from Winn Brook would just think that I had changed in the course of the year and not think anything of it. It wouldn't seem like an abrupt change. This strikes me in retrospect as an extraordinary manipulation on my part of my perceived identity, of deliberately trying to change my image from tomboy to girl. But I remember clearly that I had this consciousness and that I did manage this shift. It was successful. I was not viewed as a tomboy in junior high school. And I did have boyfriends.

The genuine friendships and ease of relationship with boys that I had from my earlier sports and neighborhood connections were useful in the boy-girl social life of junior high school. By eighth grade, age 12, I had started what I think of as a 20-year search for the right boyfriend… or, eventually, the right husband. I "went steady" with Bill Callahan, a tall and smart but quiet basketball player. We barely knew each other, were both very shy with each other, and had no real conversations, but I would feel faint of heart when I saw him enter a room or walk down the corridor. Somehow, we became boyfriend and girlfriend. He gave me his silver bracelet and I wore it proudly. That's what it meant to "go steady" — you had a publicly acknowledged relationship and couldn't date anyone else.

In 9th grade I fell in love with Mark Colby, a football player who had also gone to Winn Brook elementary school, so I had known him a long time. This was an intense relationship. He was not really a happy boy. His father had passed away when he was about nine. His mother was kind. He had an older sister and a baby brother. But he began to confide in me that he was not happy, and that sometimes he thought about suicide. I had no idea what to do with that information. The only possible person to ask was our Unitarian youth group's junior minister at church. I waited for an opportunity to ask for help when the junior minister was driving me home from church one Sunday night. It was a big relief to have a grown-up to tell. Of course, this grown-up was only about 22 years old, and he probably had no idea what to do either. In fact, he did nothing, and I did nothing, and Mark did not commit suicide, and the moment passed. It left me with the understanding of how lonely a young teenager can be with emotionally charged relationships and no place to turn. This happened even in our safe, upper middle class, segregated white town.

Many years later, at our 50th anniversary, my high school classmates began to share how complicated and problematic their adolescence in Belmont had actually been, hidden under the veneer of our middle-class comfort and safety. There were many family problems behind closed doors, many lonely teenagers with nowhere to turn with the problems they faced in their families and among their peers.

All my relationships with boyfriends throughout high school were important to me. They interfaced significantly of course with my relationship with my father. He rarely approved of my boyfriends. I didn't marry until I was 32 years old, so the twenty years between age 12 and 32 were spent in part figuring out what kind of man could I commit to for life, and would that man be like my father? Or like my mother? Or completely different? And would that man come from a background similar to mine, or completely different? And would my relationship with my chosen man be similar to my mother's and father's relationship or entirely different? It did work out very well but not without a lot of exploration, that I share in a couple of the later "Back Story" chapters.

In high school the challenge of being a girl had three other key aspects: relationships with other girls, leadership roles, and appearance. These were actually woven together in interesting ways. There was a kind of internalized oppression among the girls that both kept our aspirations limited and created envy when one of us was outstandingly successful. Receiving that envy was very painful.

One memorable example of the internalized oppression was when we were in ninth grade. It was time for someone to run for class president. I was well-liked and a natural leader, with relationships that transcended the usual cliques, so some classmates began to assume I would become president. Then one of my best girlfriends came to me in the school yard and said, "Dotty, the girls don't want you to run for president because you might win, and we think a boy should be president." I did not have enough consciousness regarding women's liberation in 1956 to say that was ridiculous and for that very reason I should of course run! Instead, I took it to heart and didn't run. Just as I had obediently put down my baseball glove in fifth grade, I deferred to traditional patriarchy — communicated to me by girls — in 10th grade. I encouraged my boyfriend at the time, Peter Dawson, to run, and he won handily. The following year I was elected vice president, an acceptable role for a girl. I began to think that when I grew up maybe I would be Vice-President of the United States, or perhaps a Senator. It took until 2020 for a woman to be elected vice-president in the United States!

Another deeply heartrending example of the envy factor was when one of my two best friends told me that she and Sue (the other one) didn't really like being around me because I was too smart. It made them feel dumb. I was thunderstruck. Deeply hurt, I drove tearfully to Sue's private school dorm in the neighboring town to ask Sue if it was true. She reassured me that nothing like that was true for her, that she was happy when I succeeded, and that she was my true friend, and that our other friend did not speak for her. This was a heartbreaking expression of envy from a female friend whom I loved, a pattern that repeated itself occasionally throughout my life. This pattern made it easier to be friends with women who excelled well beyond me in various ways, because they would be unlikely to have those envious feelings. Both of my best girlfriends at Harvard College graduated phi beta kappa and were much better students than I. Neither of them was ever envious of me, so I was safe from that type of hurt. They would be genuinely happy for me if I succeeded, and I for them.

In the acceptable female role of high school class vice president, I organized my class toward unity by being the person in charge of creating all the activity committees for three years. I would put committees together deliberately that included people from different cliques — Irish, Italian, Catholic, Congregational, Methodist, Jewish, athletes, scholars, richer, more working class. We didn't have any people of color in our class, nor anybody who was really poor, so this exercise was pretty limited; but, in fact, there were moderate lines of separation that tended to produce isolated cliques. The experience of working together in these committees did produce a less divided class. When we graduated, people wondered why we seemed so united. I kept quiet about what I had deliberately done. Forty-five years after graduating, we started holding reunions every year at my house, recreating that same sense of community. The role of social engineer, trying to create unity and community, came naturally to me from an early age.

I have no idea where these ideas came from, except perhaps the absence of negative teachings in my home or church. The fact that my German Protestant mother and my Russian Jewish father were married, against the prejudices and prohibitions of their own families, might have entered my unconscious perspective without my knowing it, to be reinforced by Unitarian teachings about respect and inclusion. Maybe the most fundamental fact was that for some reason I liked everybody, and this in itself had a positive effect. Maybe I liked them because they liked me, and maybe they liked me because my mother had been so nice to me that I had an easy personality. Or perhaps I learned to like everybody from my mother. I don't ever remember hearing her downgrade another human being or group.

I remember deciding in high school that one thing I could do to build unity was to never repeat anything negative that one student said about another. The tendency to pass along negative comments, to whisper behind each other's backs, to share negative secrets as a way of getting close, is always highly destructive to community and trust at all levels. I decided I would always pass along the positive, and never the negative, and in fact I would counteract the negative by sharing positive comments about the person being badrapped. I knew that avoiding negative comments would strengthen trust of me, but also would build greater trust among the group as a whole. This rule has served me well in life.

Perhaps the most difficult part of being a girl was handling the pressures related to appearance. A fundamental part of sexism, the idea that girls must be attractive to boys, and women to men, was a struggle for all of us. I am not sure to this day whether it was an advantage or a disadvantage that I was not beautiful. I was moderately overweight, and I had a big nose and little eyes with short lashes. My father thought I was unattractive due to my weight. It bothered him; so it also bothered me. Most women who grow up thinking they are beautiful do so because their fathers are delighted with them. But my father was not delighted with either my appearance or my older sister's. I was able to take it a little less personally because I had witnessed the same disapproval directed at my older sister, but I still internalized the idea that I was not attractive. It was reinforced along the way by insulting comments of various boyfriends. For example, "If I'm going to marry you, I might as well have my fling with the beauties now." Or "I can't take you to a party in Cambridge, because they don't know what a good person you are, and they will judge you by your looks." My father's comments were even worse. Before I set out to choose what college I would attend he told me clearly, "You have to go to Harvard, so you can date your older brother's friends. You are not pretty enough to attract your own boyfriends." This was a pretty horrible comment. When he made it, at the breakfast table during my senior year in high school, I picked up my coffee cup with the impulse to throw the coffee in his face, and then I quietly put it down, wisely controlling my hurt and angry reaction. Fortunately, he did not perceive my impulse.

The reason I later began to think it might be an advantage not to be beautiful is that no matter whom I was dating, I was reasonably sure that he actually liked me. He was attracted to who I was, not to my appearance. I simply did not attract men who were seeking the beauties, so the ones I dated liked my personality and my mind. I was particularly blessed to have Eddie McDevitt as a boyfriend for several years in high school and college, because he was such a loyal, unpretentious, and good man, who truly loved me for who I was.

I also grew to resent the whole sexist expectation that women would dress to attract men, and I refused to do it. But when some-one liked me for who I was, and we were then dating, I would voluntarily give him the gift of trying to look nice if we went out, because he hadn't required it of me.

Because I was comfortable with men as friends, I never lacked for real boyfriends, in a time when people were allowed to date more than one at a time. I also never worried about their motives. Further, being not-beautiful seemed to protect me somewhat from the envy of other women. Of course, a lot of it is in the mind, and it is possi-ble that I was more attractive than my father and I believed. When I look now at pictures of myself in my twenties, I think it's too bad I thought I was ugly, because actually I looked pretty good.

Becoming Aware of Poverty

Perhaps the most life-determining experience of my teenaged years occurred during our 1956 family trip to Europe. It was a clas-sic white upper-middle-class summer trip to expand the horizons of the children. All five of us went together to England, France, Italy, and Belgium. My father skipped Germany because, as a Jew, he refused to set foot on German soil.

The most stunning impact of this trip was that in both Paris and Naples I saw people who were poor, out on the streets of the cities.

I had never seen poverty in Belmont, because there was none. In Paris I saw hungry children. In Naples I saw a group of orphans in uniform with their group leader. I vividly remember walking through an alley in Paris, catching sight, to my left, over by the wall, of a small child who looked abused and hungry, sort of desperate. I quickly looked away. Afterwards I realized I had been afraid, ... unable to relate to the obvious misery that I saw. I decided on that day, "I will never look away again." I would force myself to look at reality, and I would try to do something about it.

When I saw homelessness in Naples, and talked about it with my older sister, Elinor (aka Nellie), I said that when I grew up, I would like to create housing for homeless people. My sister advised me not to be too idealistic, because homeless people wouldn't know how to care for the homes. I didn't really believe her.

When I returned back to Belmont in the fall, I had a strong motivation to make very good use of the fact that I was blessed with a good education, freedom, parents, a home, and every opportunity to prepare for life. I said to my friend Sue, "We have been given 20 years to go to school with hardly any other obligations. People around the world would give their right arms to have what we have. Don't take it for granted. It is our duty to make good use of it. We should study hard."

My Own Identity

The fact that my father was a Russian Jew and my mother a German Protestant spoke to a powerful courage and integrity on the part of my mother. They married during the rise of Hitler. She had been engaged to a German chosen by her father, Frederick Nieschlag. Her father was himself a first-generation German immigrant who was said to have arrived in the USA with $17 in his pocket. When my mother met and fell in love with Mike Stoneman, my Jewish father, she broke off the engagement with the German. My cousin told me decades later that my mother did that after wedding invitations had already gone out, and that my grandfather was furious. I recently learned from that same cousin that the man my mother had been engaged to marry was the German Nazi who later led the invasion of Norway. That gave me the chills.

When my mother eloped with my father, she was disowned by her parents for marrying a Jew. Her father deeply believed that his grandchildren, mixed Gentile and Jew, would belong nowhere. They would be rejected by the world as "misfits." In his view my mother was destroying the lives of her children. My mother believed that she could raise children whose identities transcended the prejudices of the day. In 2010 I found a wonderful essay she had written after a painful fight with her father in 1935 when he insisted she would find out he was 100% right about the terrible impact on her children of being mixed. The essay asserted her confidence that she could effectively defy and rise above those prejudices.

My mother was right, of course. I have a clear memory of myself as a child, standing next to the washing machine in the basement, thinking to myself, "There's no point in being a Jew like my father. They get killed by the Germans. There's no point in being a German like my mother. They are killing the Jews. I am neither a Jew nor a German; I am simply a human being." This did seem to become my identity.

In an all-white community, religion was often the divider. I think I applied the same universal identity in that arena. As a child I used to answer the question "What is your religion?" — which was always asked in white communities — like this: "My father's a Jew, my mother's a Presbyterian, my sister's an atheist, my brother's an agnostic, and I'm a Unitarian." It was my way of saying that my family includes everybody, and I belong everywhere.

Overall, I had a blessed childhood, for which I am forever grateful.

Daddy and Mommy

With brother Billy and sister Nellie

Skiing with Daddy and Billy

With my close friend Nancy Baty

Dancing with my best friend Vic Taylor

At the prom with Eddie McDevitt

Making it Through Harvard

When I graduated from High School in 1959, I went on a summer-long Experiment in International Living to France. I had studied just one year of French, so I was not very well prepared. Yet it was a life-changing experience because I met Emmie, one of the other students in the Experiment.

Emmie was a tall, blonde, athletic success story from St. Paul, Minnesota. She had been a superb student at an elite private school and was already truly fluent in French. She had also been the State tennis champion. She fell in love with our group leader, who also fell in love with her. I followed them all summer on bike rides all over the hills around our little town, acutely aware of their forbidden romance.

Emmie and I had immediately bonded on the first day of the Experiment, and when we learned that we were both heading to Harvard, we asked to be roommates. As a graduate of Harvard Law School, my father was able to arrange it. He chose to do that because Emmie had already been selected as the "Most Promising Freshman." He thought I would be in the right company. He didn't know about the relationship she was having with the group leader and didn't anticipate for a moment the radical effect she would have on my life by the end of four years.

Harvard was a kind of strange place. Virtually everyone there had been outstandingly successful in high school. When we arrived, the new ranking of us in competition with each other was a weird and unpleasant experience. For example, I was a National Merit Scholar, and had received the New England High School Teachers' Award for outstanding writing, yet I was placed in a General Education writing class rather than advanced writing. It was as if I needed a remedial class. That was my first blow upon arrival. Then they gathered us all together and asked how many of us had been at the top of our high school graduating class, how many of us had received various merit awards, and the like, and warned us that this would not be like high school, that the competition here would be stiff. The general effect on most of us would be to lower our self-esteem.

Harvard was at that time a very sexist and somewhat stodgy place. The women attended Radcliffe College, lived in separate dorms, and were not allowed to go to the Harvard houses for dinner because it was said that we would ruin the intellectual caliber of the dinner conversations. We were only allowed to join the men for dinner on Saturday nights. We had a midnight curfew every night, and were only allowed to let men visit our rooms on Sunday afternoons between 1 pm and 3 pm, and then only if we left the door of our room open and both the man and the woman kept at least one foot on the floor at all times.

In 1959 nobody smoked weed, meditated, or practiced yoga, although by 1962 weed and LSD were creeping in. Absolutely nobody was on medication for depression. The relatively recent growth of that tragic phenomenon throughout the Ivy League and other colleges needs some serious attention and I imagine it may be primarily the result of a profit-making campaign of the drug companies.

People were somewhat isolated and lonely in their intellectual competitive boxes, trying to succeed academically in a context where a lot of smart people had been admitted on a competitive basis to compete with each other anew for ever higher status. The dominant values were about academic success in preparation for individualistic careers, without a strong ethic of service, social responsibility, or any visible drive toward social justice. At graduation I remember being quite disappointed at how few people planned to take any direction driven by social responsibility. Most people were heading into their ambitious personal careers, usually in the corporate sector if they were not going to graduate school to become doctors or lawyers.

There was one important counter-cultural entity at Harvard called Phillips Brooks House (PBH) that offered an explicit path toward community responsibility through volunteering in various community service activities. Through PBH I led a small after-school activity group with seven-year-olds at a settlement house in East Cambridge, throughout my time at Harvard. This was my first experience getting to know people in a low-income racially diverse community.

Perhaps the competitive Harvard environment had something to do with my brother's emotional breakdown in his senior (my sophomore) year. It was a devastating and mystifying experience. Billy had always been a completely handsome, smart, successful, popular, athletic, humorous, sociable leader. Everybody loved and admired Billy in high school and again in college. He was president of his high school class, a successful forward on the basketball team that won the state championship, and the winner of all sorts of awards including his National Merit Scholarship. He seemed to be my parents' favorite, and I adored him. He included me in his social circle, which was great for me because he had a lot of interesting and attractive male friends. (My father had been right about how helpful it would be to have an older brother at Harvard.) But all of a sudden, in the midst of an intense love affair, he became so depressed that he had to leave Harvard.

He couldn't manage school. His friends couldn't help him. I couldn't help him although I tried hard, and neither could my parents. He dropped out of Harvard for a year, his love affair dissipated, he lived off campus, a few of his best friends also dropped out and they all lived together. He tried therapy but it didn't work. This crisis is one reason why all my grades dropped in sophomore year. I couldn't justify being happy and successful when my beloved brother was suffering. I spent a lot of time with him that year, trying to be supportive, but really not understanding why this was happening. We theorized that it had something to do with the pressures from my father, but we really had no way of understanding this depression. More recently, my brother shared his own interpretation that it had to do with the fact that he was not ready for the love affair he was in, and it troubled him not to be able to match the love of his girlfriend.

Prior to that year I had been planning to be a doctor, inspired by Albert Schweitzer, to help the people of the world. But when I did poorly in chemistry (I had made the mistake of taking Chem Two without having taken Chem One. I had thought I could just read the textbook in the summer and jump into a second-year course. The result was a D.) I decided that helping people did not require becoming a doctor, so I quit pre-med. I majored in History and Science — American history and biology, and also studied Russian language and history. The three courses that grabbed my strongest interest were the history of the Russian revolution, physiology of the brain, and sociology related to poverty and youth development.

Professor Leon Bramson taught the sociology course that I took in my junior year. In 1961 I wrote a paper for his course putting forth an idea about how to break the cycle of poverty and juvenile delinquency. I would create pre-schools for poor children, taught by professional teachers with local teenagers as assistant teachers. This would help the young children, but equally importantly it would help the teenagers prepare to be parents. As described in Chapter 1, it turned out I unexpectedly got to implement this idea in the Harlem Action Group in the summer of 1964.

Throughout my time at Harvard, Professor Bramson was the only professor I ever got to know at all. I was not one of those students who automatically gravitated toward the professor. They typically did not notice me, and I did not talk to them. This pattern of not being entirely comfortable with the people who had power and authority has remained with me all my life. It has undermined my effectiveness to some degree. It is probably rooted in my father's somewhat intimidating style.

I vividly remember my introductory meeting with Professor Bramson when I stepped outside of my timidity for one brief moment. He had written kind words on my paper about interrupting the cycle of poverty, so I went to his office hours. I stood tentatively in the doorway and told him I had come to see him because he was the only professor in all my time at Harvard who had ever taken any interest in my work. He looked at me quizzically, then realized this might be an important moment for me. He invited me to come in and sit down. We had a nice talk, got acquainted, and somehow it evolved into my babysitting for his family. I did a lot of babysitting throughout college. It allowed me to contribute some of my earnings to my boyfriend, Eddie McDevitt, who was attending Tufts University on scholarship and working his way through. When I met Professor Bramson's wife, I discovered with great excitement that we had gone to summer camp together as children. Being sentimental, I always love earlier connections.

Overall, other than the ideas I developed in that one sociology course, Harvard's intellectual environment did not influence me very much. I was busier learning from my friends, working through relationships with men, trying to understand my brother's emotional breakdown, serving in the neighborhood through Phillips Brooks House, serving one summer as a social work intern in the mental hospital in New York City on Ward's Island, participating on the edge of the anti-war movement, beginning to learn about racism through the tutelage of Emmie when she returned from a year in Kenya through Crossroads Africa, and learning about Soviet communism through getting to know Russian exchange students.

Through these activities I was exposed to powerful influences that shaped my life toward social activism. After freshman year, Emmie went on Crossroads Africa to spend a year in Kenya. She returned transformed into a revolutionary anti-colonialist who radically influenced my understanding of the world.

In my senior year I fell in love with an incredibly handsome and charming 39-year-old Russian exchange student, Ilya Berezin. He was a professor of chemistry who was also chairman of the Communist Party at Moscow University. Getting to know him, across the Cold War barriers between Russians and Americans was my first profound cross-cultural experience. Fortunately, Harvard was flexible enough to give me credit for independent studies learning Russian in my regular evening meetings with him. I got at least 3 credits for learning the basics of the Russian language from Ilya!

I watched President John F. Kennedy's speech addressing the Cuban missile crisis in Ilya's dorm room with three other Russian professors who were together on the international exchange program at Harvard. None of them believed a word President Kennedy said. They were shocked when Premier Khrushchev acknowledged the truth that Russia did have missiles in Cuba. It was fascinating to watch that historical moment through their eyes. It was a lesson in not believing what any of us had been taught in our own national contexts.

By that time in the early sixties, Harvard students were beginning to participate in peace marches against the Vietnam war, and I was with them. A few people, like Todd Gitlin, were making their names as activists. A few others were using LSD and claiming breakthroughs of consciousness. Still, there was no real social justice movement to join at Harvard. Nor was there even a national service movement to attract the idealists among us. There was no Peace Corps, no VISTA program, no Teach for America to recruit us. City Year, created by two Harvard graduates, wouldn't exist until 20 years later.

But outside Harvard, the incipient Civil Rights Movement was simmering under the surface, in the South, about to break forth into visibility for northern whites to see.

When the Birmingham 16th Street Baptist church was bombed in September of 1963, and four young black girls in Sunday School were killed by hateful whites, some of the nation woke up.

Before that most of us northern suburban segregated whites didn't really know much about racism. We grew up in protected bubbles of privilege. We were profoundly ignorant. We had benefited, sometimes for generations, from the exploitation and oppression of both black and white poor and of all working-class people, without ever realizing it. These injustices were the hidden sources of some of our good fortune as upper middle-class white Americans... they were also the hidden sources of our ignorance.

But Emmie had seen the world from a different perspective when she spent a year in Kenya in 1961, the year the Mau Mau's, who had been led by Jomo Kenyatta to oppose British colonial domination, came out of prison. They became her friends and she fell in love with one of Kenyatta's chief aides. Falling in love across cultural barriers turned out to be a good learning experience for lots of us in the sixties. When she returned, she educated me about colonialism and racism.

She later fell in love with a Ghanaian Harvard student. Because he has become a famous author and hasn't reviewed a draft of this book, I will give him a pseudonym: Ampah, a Ghanaian name that means "faith." At Harvard he was a determined revolutionary.

Emmie and he steadily tried to persuade me to try marijuana, which I finally did inside Ampah's dorm room at Harvard with Emmie, Ampah, and a young African American Harvard student. This experience was a seminal one, because the combination of an unusually sensitive and receptive consciousness influenced by drugs, and a deep conversation with my fellow student about his experience of growing up black in America, seemed to create the beginning of a more personal conversion in my awareness of racism. After that I read all the current books on racism and liberation.

I did not choose to keep getting high on any drug, because it struck me as a disorienting and excessively powerful experience. I liked life the way it was. I liked my mind and my heart and didn't feel a need to be in some other state of consciousness. I thought the one experience was so powerful it would be best not to keep repeating it because it could become addictive. As a result, it was more than a year before I ever smoked weed again, and then I only did it a few more times.

After that first time, I went home and shared the experience with my mother. I am not sure why I dared to do that, or why she didn't seem upset. It was memorable to me that I sat at our breakfast table and told her what it was like. I told her I didn't want to do it more because I liked life the way it was. I imagine now that she was probably quite relieved to hear that.

During the spring of senior year, I continued a profound conversion to activism. I decided that it was my responsibility to go as far out on the front lines to fight racism, colonialism, and injustice as my personality would allow. Emmie was planning to drop out of Harvard to become a guerilla fighter and go to Angola with Ampah to fight the Portuguese colonialists. One night, lying in bed deliberating on my future role, I realized in a deep epiphany that I could never be a guerilla fighter because my psyche is resolutely constructive. There was no way I could commit violence for any cause. I therefore decided to go to the Congo and set up schools for the Angolan refugees who were fleeing from the war with Portugal over Angola. That would be my way of supporting the anti-colonialist revolution. I had decided I was willing to risk my life... which I thought I might be doing because I had agreed to join the CVAAR (Cuerpo Voluntario de Assistencia a Angolanos Refugiados), a leading organization giving aid to the refugees.

But before I could go to Angola, I had already arranged through Phillips Brooks House to go to Utah for the summer of 1963, to teach preschool on the Ute Indian Reservation. In addition, before I had even thought of going to Angola, I had followed up on my idea of creating pre-schools by applying to Bank Street College of Education, where I had been accepted as a graduate student for the fall of 1963. But when I decided to go to Angola, I postponed Bank Street for an indefinite time.

Oddly, I don't actually remember my graduation from Harvard. I don't know whether I attended, whether my parents were there, where it took place, whether there was a celebration, and whether I got a diploma. But probably all of those things did occur. I do remember a moment's conversation with my sister outside of my dormitory after graduation, when we were packing up my stuff to leave campus and I was bemoaning the fact that I would never see all my friends again because everyone was taking off for parts unknown.

She said, wisely, "Don't worry, you will all meet again in New York City in a few years." She was mostly right.

From Harvard to Harlem

I graduated from Harvard in June of 1963. I went immediately off to Utah for the summer, in a project organized by Phillips Brooks House, working on the Ute Indian Reservation. I taught nursery school to Ute children during the day, and I lived in a summer camp with Ute teenagers. At the summer camp I came to be friends with an older working-class Native American man named Laffie, who was very important to me as a friend with an entirely different class and racial perspective.

Each day I traveled by school bus down from the summer camp in the hills to the town, where I taught in a preschool class and tutored older children after school. In the evenings I studied Portuguese in my cabin in preparation for meeting Angolan refugees in the Congo. At the same time, I prepared a language primer in Portuguese for the children who would be in my school, whose language of origin would be Kikongo. I maintained my correspondence with representatives from CVAAR (Cuerpo Voluntario Angolano de Assistencia a Refugiados). They were welcoming me to the Congo. I was on a mission.

At the end of the summer, several Harvard Phillips Brooks students who had been serving in various sites for the summer took a road trip to visit a series of Native American reservations in Utah and three adjacent states. When we stopped at the Hopi and Navajo reservations, I was totally blown away by the sophisticated cross-cultural wisdom of the tribal leaders we met. They had figured out how to manage both white society and the tribal world. I never forgot the awe and respect they inspired in me.

Once back in Boston after the summer, I set out to earn enough money to go to the Congo as planned. My parents had made clear that they were not subsidizing this trip and thought I was somewhat out of my mind. My mother kept encouraging me to join some kind of structured international program, not to set out on my own to join a revolutionary group, imagining that I could set up schools in an unknown country where I didn't even speak the language.

While looking for a job to earn the money for my own trip, I also started trying to raise money for the CVAAR, because they needed a truck to deliver food to the refugees. It was extraordinary that Deolinda Rodriguez, who seemed to be in charge of CVAAR, had taken me seriously enough to write to me, to send me updates, to trust that I would raise the $500 she needed. I did.

I took a position as a counselor in the Metropolitan State Hospital, working on a ward with autistic boys aged 8 to 12. It turned out I was very talented in communicating with these boys. I was able to tune in, listen, connect with them, and create safety for them. They began, one by one, to talk to me. I was on the ward for eight hours a day with them, so there was endless opportunity to get through their barriers, their terrors, their isolation and to build real relationships, even though they were in various stages and intensity of autism... enough to be put in a mental hospital. I'll never forget the day when one of the boys, who had never talked to anyone, looked up at me and said, with a poetic rhythm In his voice, "I feel sa-a-a-fe with you! Carry me!" I picked up his tall lanky body and carried him out to play on the swings in the small playground outside the ward. It was a beautiful moment. A similar feeling was expressed by another boy who would run over to me every day when I arrived in the morning and say energetically, "Talk to me, 'Dorofie!' Talk to me, 'Dorofie'! Never mind about the other boys! Talk to me!" Then he would tell me his life story, starting from the beginning. Each day he would add one more significant memory.

I loved these boys. Their hearts were aching for caring attention. When they got it, they began to share. I realized that I could probably cure several of them, at least enough for them to lead real lives, but only if I spent my whole life doing it. It seemed inefficient. I decided I should not use my whole life to save five boys, that there must be many children for whom a lighter touch could qualitatively change their lives. If I were to help children, I should find a way to help thousands, not just five.

I was working on this ward when John F. Kennedy was assassinated. None of the young boys had any comprehension of what had happened, so I experienced my own shock largely alone, in this strange world of a hospital ward with autistic children.

During the time I was working at the hospital, Emmie and Ampah had successfully made their way to Algeria, on a mission to get trained as guerrillas to join the Angolan revolution. I was planning to meet them later, in the Congo, after I had earned the money to come. However, they got de-railed. The Algerians refused to train them as guerillas. They said, "First of all, Kwame Nkrumah does not want us training the Ghanaian intelligentsia as guerillas. There are enough Angolan peasants to fill that role. Ampah, you should go home and be an intellectual. And second, Emmie, we are not going to train Americans as guerillas. You are probably a CIA agent anyway, so you are not welcome in our guerilla training."

Emmie and Ampah were stunned. This was an unexpected setback to their revolutionary fervor. Their newfound identities that they had built up over about a year of preparation and travel through the South, through Cuba, and to Algeria, as a radical bi-racial couple, were shaken deeply. They had both dropped out of Harvard without their degrees, partly as a statement of commitment that they were breaking their ties with the upper class. They chose not to graduate, even though both of them had been working for many years to become Harvard graduates. Emmie had already received the Phi Beta Kappa award for her all A's through Junior year. Ampah had left Accra as a high school student and attended a privileged white private school in Groton before going to Harvard. And then, despite all that success, they dropped out to fight colonialism. If the revolution wouldn't accept them, who were they and what would they do? Ampah had a nervous breakdown. Emmie found herself traveling in the Algerian desert with a disoriented and emotionally disturbed lover who had lost his identity.

The money I had saved to go to the Congo was spent bringing Emmie and Ampah back to the United States. Ampah became a patient at McLean Hospital, a mental hospital in Belmont. Emmie joined SNCC and went South. Then, having spent all my money saved to go to the Congo, I went to New York City to Bank Street College as I had originally planned to do before the anti-colonialist fervor had changed my direction.

You can imagine how crazy this all felt. Forces beyond our control seemed to take over our lives. We each landed unpredictably, separately, on track for a wholly unexpected next stage of our life. For me, once I was in NYC attending Bank Street College, my path led directly to Harlem, to the Civil Rights Movement, as explained in Chapter 1.

It was 1964. I joined the Harlem Action Group in March. That was a very direct path to the rest of my life.

Falling in Love with Leroy

In Chapter One, I shared about the key role Leroy played in encouraging me to stay in Harlem rather than to join SNCC in the summer of 1964, and how supportive he was of the pre-school program we created.

Somewhere between March and August, Leroy and I fell in love. This was a complex process. I hardly remember when it began, and when it became love. But it did, and once in motion, it lasted a lifetime.

I remember a moment at a HAG party that winter, when Leroy was talking to someone about how he would like to improve his life, and how he would never get involved with a woman who didn't have the potential for helping him do that. The moment stuck in my mind as an honest expression of his aspirations. It was a precursor to an afternoon in the late spring of 1964 when we sat together at the top of Morningside Park, overlooking Harlem, talking at length about his past life and his current desire to start a business, selling watermelons from the back of a truck, so he could support himself; and his dream of creating a bookstore; and his more deeply held dream of helping addicts recover from their addictions, somehow, somewhere.

As I got to know him, I felt the intensity of the tragic gap between his enormous intelligence on the one hand, and the opportunities that should have been available to him as a child but never were. I don't remember when and where he first told me about his childhood, his alcoholic father, his years in the reform school to which he was sent at age eight for snatching a pocketbook. He was there for years. He tried to run away but would be caught. They punished him by making him stand up for hours in a doorway with his wrists pressed up against the door frame, whenever he did something wrong. He wet his bed in fear and would be punished for it. He would wait hours on Sunday afternoons for his mother to visit him, but she was always late. In his later professional life, Leroy would never be late and never could tolerate anyone else being late.

There was one very positive element of the reform school story. Leroy had a teacher named Mr. Orange who cared enough to teach him how to read and to bring him books from home. Leroy felt that Mr. Orange saw something good in him, saw that he was smart, and cared enough to pay attention to him. This story was a lasting lesson for me about the unpredictable ripple effects of kindness from a teacher to a student. Later when Leroy went to the penitentiary for adult crimes, he was prepared to read widely. He educated himself in a way that prepared him for his later role as an effective social entrepreneur. Mr. Orange will never know the amazing impact of his kindness.

Leroy told me how he later fell prey to a heroin addiction, became a drug dealer and spent years in the penitentiary. He educated himself through reading broadly while in prison, and he played a role as a counselor to other prisoners. He told me of his near-death experience after he emerged from prison when he found himself unconscious from an overdose in a closet next to a friend who was dead. Evidently people had thought they were both dead and left them in the closet together. At that moment he determined to give up drugs. He succeeded. He wanted to live.

He was like no man I had ever met. Our experiences were totally different. Many of the values governing our lives were in conflict. The class and racial differences between us were enormous. Yet we shared something more profound than the differences between us. We shared a fervent desire to make a better world for everyone. We came from opposite corners of America, opposite experiences of privilege and oppression, opportunity and exclusion, white and black, rich and poor. But in our hearts, we were human beings aching for a world of love, justice, and opportunity for all.

As we began to merge our talents and our energy toward creating the summer pre-school, our hearts merged, and we became a deeply connected team. I don't remember when it became a sexual, romantic relationship, but the moment it did I knew we had to be careful about how we were perceived. If the community thought I was "his woman," it seemed dangerous to my ability to do the work of the pre-school. Since he had a reputation as a hustler, and a man who lived off women, it seemed risky.

When I promised on the Morningside Park hillside to give him the money to buy a truck to create a watermelon business, he immediately told other people. I felt the perception of me giving Leroy money would undermine my role as the organizer of the preschool and undermine the perceived integrity of our cooperative relationship in the school, so I pulled back and said I wouldn't give him any money until the fall, after the summer preschool was over. I don't know if I was imagining this danger or not, but I was definitely in new territory on every front. I was trying to walk carefully through minefields. I also felt betrayed and used when he immediately went public with my offer to give him money. It was as if he had to prove that he knew how to manipulate women financially, and that his only reason for being close to a white woman was to obtain resources. I was unwilling to be used or perceived in that way. I had experienced that earlier in our relationship when we entered a bar one evening and he made it clear to me that I had to pay, and clear to the bartender that I would be paying.

Leroy and I were struggling with our different values. Every stage of our relationship was accompanied by deeply dissonant expectations and mistakes in what we expected of each other. I wrote him long letters trying to communicate my values and expectations. He would read them over and over, trying to take in what I was saying. He would adjust his behavior or his attitude, partly out of respect for what I was trying to communicate. But for a long time, I wasn't sure if he truly cared about me, or was simply determined to manipulate me into being a financial resource for him like so many other women had been. For a long time, he didn't know either. He was resisting being vulnerable, "getting his nose open" as he would say. His life had been lived in a totally different world where he had maintained control of his feelings and had managed his intimate relationships in a mercenary way. That was anathema to me. Yet I had to try to understand his reality and he had to try to understand mine.

Overall, our attention to each other was supremely healthy. First of all, reaching across the class, race, gender, and age barriers to understand each other was a prodigious and admirable undertaking in itself. Many people in our generation of the sixties went through cross-cultural love affairs, and the result was healthy for society. For a while I believed that no white person who had not had the experience of loving a person of color across the barriers of bias and ignorance could actually be a whole person in our society or actually know how to join forces with people of color to oppose oppression. I still believe that cross-class and cross-racial relationships are extremely important for our individual and collective consciousness.

Later, when I was in a position to hire folks to work in East Harlem, and at YouthBuild USA, I would routinely ask every white applicant if they had ever had a personal cross-racial or cross-class friendship. Those who had, seemed to work out better as employees in a multi-racial context. One white middle class woman answered that question after a long pause with, "Yes, in college I had a friend who lived in an apartment instead of a house." I didn't hire her.

The process of getting to know each other was also very good for Leroy and me personally. The fact that I took his deeper aspirations so seriously was crucial for his personal transformation. I listened, and I heard, and I validated, and I supported who he really wanted to be. He was a brilliant man, with incredible charisma, emotional power, vision, and compassion. He had simply never had the opportunity to fulfill his potential or even define his aspirations. His life had been seized and twisted through poverty, crime, drugs, and prison. But underneath, his heart remained whole. Being seen clearly and taken seriously by a person of the dominant white culture was useful to his evolution.

For me, the fact that Leroy found me attractive in a way that contradicted the negative view my father had held of my appearance, was useful to my evolution. Leroy wasn't turned off by my being over-weight. He didn't need me to be a "glamour girl" in my father's terms. He was also bigger than me in various ways — taller (6'4"), stronger, older, more experienced in many ways. His passion and energy were enormous. He was fascinating and the struggle between our perspectives was also fascinating, and it engaged both of us very thoroughly as we tried to learn each other's perspective, tried to understand the world through each other's eyes and heart and mind.

We were working together, creating something of value to the community, using our respective talents and connections to create something bigger than either one of us could have created alone. This was a lesson in the value of our different life experiences. We each brought different strengths, knowledge, and skills to the venture. I would see this dynamic play out later among other couples whose combined power far transcended their separate potential, because it transcended society's barriers.

By the time the summer came, we were emotionally involved. By that time, the living arrangements in our little HAG community had changed. I was no longer living with Elsie, who had moved on. I was living with my friend Lois Howlett and with Chuck Turner in a big apartment on West Side Drive that we had been given for the summer by a family who had left town. One day that summer Chuck gave me a lecture. It went something like this:

"Dorothy, your relationship with Leroy is going to jeopardize his way of life. He has survived financially in a racist world through his relationships with women. He is opening up to you emotionally, and you would never submit to being his source of financial support. What happens if he falls in love with you, and you won't support him? He has no way of supporting himself, and you will have destabilized his life."

This speech made an impression on me. I didn't want to jeopardize Leroy's life. Chuck's perspective as a black Harvard graduate on the damage I might inadvertently be doing was a whole different voice. I wasn't sure what to do about it until later.

The story of Leroy's and my relationship, its power, joy, conflict, pain, and long-term positive impact weaves through the rest of both of our lives and work. For me he was the first example of a person who had been profoundly oppressed by the racism and classism in our society, whose liberation occurred through the combination of feeling the love and respect of another person, finding opportunity and resources to set different goals for himself, belonging to a social change movement he could believe in, providing service to his community, and taking on leadership roles for a better world. Leroy's transformation, I later saw, was similar to how YouthBuild students changed when they found their way into the combination of a loving community coupled with the opportunities that Youth-Build provided.

When my father heard that I had become close with Leroy, he went into action. His deeply held belief was "Once a criminal, always a criminal." He hired a private detective to research Leroy's background and to watch us. He went to visit the Dean at Bank Street College to find out how I was doing in school. He took a moral position that Leroy's relationship with Sarah Kearney, his long-term partner with whom he lived and who supported him, was the important relationship and that Leroy should have married her.

While my father adamantly opposed Leroy's and my relationship, he took no steps to actually interfere. Perhaps the fact that he had himself met disapproval for marrying someone who was not Jewish, and that his wife had been disowned temporarily for marrying a Jewish man, gave him some degree of constraint or perspective about judging relationships. Or perhaps the fact that one of my previous boyfriends at Harvard, Bob Johnson, said to my father in one heated conversation about Leroy when I was not present, "Mr. Stoneman, the truth is that Dorothy has chosen a man just like you, except that he happens to be black. He is just like you in that he is smart, feisty, entrepreneurial, and charismatic and defies conventional wisdom in various ways. You should take their relationship as a compliment." Or perhaps it was just a form of the respect that my parents always seemed to give to their children's right to make their own decisions. At the time, his disapproval felt powerful; but actually, it was relatively benign compared to the types of interventions that parents of some of my other friends made to disrupt their cross-racial relationships.

Later, in 1968, after Leroy and I had reached a point in our relationship where it was clear we were not going to marry, I began to date a man who was much like my mother. His name was John Bell. He and I married each other In 1974. John understood Leroy's importance to me, and through lots of delicate negotiations, agreed that Leroy would be my friend and movement partner for life, as John would also be. Once again, I was lucky, well beyond normal expectations.

CHAPTER 6

Teaching Second Grade
in PS 92

In the fall of 1964, I accepted a job teaching second grade in PS 92, on 134th Street between 7th and 8th Avenues, also known as Frederic Douglas and Adam Clayton Powell Boulevards. This was one of the two elementary schools in HAG's neighborhood that had given me the names of the children who had missed kindergarten. Being in the neighborhood, hearing how people thought the schools were very bad for their children, made me intensely curious about what it would be like to serve as an actual teacher in the public elementary school.

The principal of PS 92 at that time was Dr. Elliot Shapiro. He had become famous through the compelling book, *Our Children Are Dying,* written by Nat Hentoff. This book explained the real challenges facing the children and described the principal's efforts to address them. Dr. Shapiro was a marvelous, kind, older Jewish activist who had been the principal for many years. He welcomed me in a very kind way. Since I was a beginning teacher, he put me in a classroom next to his office in case I needed help. He gave me the class that was number two among eight second grade classes. Children were tracked according to perceived ability and achievement, so the number two class was filled with bright, eager children. It was a gift to a beginning teacher.

Thirty-two beautiful children piled into my classroom on the first day. I was certainly not prepared for them despite my experience as a student teacher in two private and public schools elsewhere in Manhattan. How in the world could I get them to sit still and be quiet and work hard all day?! Despite their beauty and intelligence, they clearly carried the weight of society on their shoulders and had enormous emotional needs and energy flowing out at every moment. As soon as they realized that I was a harmless, nice, inexperienced teacher, half of them were out of their seats all day. The kind of activity program that would have worked was not the teaching style of this school. Instead, there was a common curriculum for all the children and an expectation that they should sit still in their rows of seats. Thirty-two seven-year-old children and me behind closed doors together: that was not a workable system.

I decided almost immediately that teachers were drastically misunderstood, frightfully underpaid, and that the conditions in which we worked, trying to address all the issues that children brought into the classroom after being born into poverty and racism, were impossibly difficult. That was in 1964. I don't think it has gotten any easier.

Within five days, noticing the noise emanating from my classroom and sympathetic to my plight, Dr. Shapiro offered to move nine of my most unruly students to the classroom of a seasoned, much older, hard-nosed teacher who ruled like a tyrant. I welcomed the offer, and I said good-bye to those nine children. I saw them occasionally during the year, lined up silent, walking single file in the hallways under the watchful eye of their famously and unambiguously tough, older, black, woman teacher.

Still, with the remaining 23, it was no picnic! Soon the children began to tell me that I should hit the "bad" children. "Hit us, Miss Stoneman, hit us!" said Walter Garcia, pleading for order from his seat in the middle of the outside row. I said, "No, I don't believe in hitting children. I will not hit you. I'll have to find some other way to persuade you to be quiet." "Oh, come on, Miss Stoneman, hit us!" he said. "It's the best way! Everyone does it."

But I refused. I tried every other form of persuasion. One day I said, "Please, children, please be quiet and sit down to do this lesson. Please. I am trying to teach you because I care about you. I don't need to be here. I do not need the money. I could be in lots of other places. I am in this school because I asked to be in this school, because I care about you and your neighborhood. Please listen to me." I said this passionately with tears flowing down my face.

I had been embarrassed to "break down" emotionally in front of them. I was absolutely not taught in graduate school that it was a good idea to cry in front of my students while pleading helplessly for cooperation. But two days later in the local snack shop I overheard a conversation in which Joan, one of my students, who was sitting with her back to me, having no idea I was hearing her, said to her friends, "My teacher cares about us. She was crying in class. She told us she doesn't have to be here. She's here because she wants to be. She cares about us. She's not here for the money."

This was a memorable lesson. It turned out that showing my feelings was a good thing. They didn't assume I or any teacher cared about them. It had to be shown, and even stated, and then it had enormous meaning. To my student Joan, it was worth telling her seven-year-old friends after school.

This would happen to me a few more times during my life in Harlem... when I spontaneously choked up about something important to me, someone would say to me afterwards, "Now I know you care." It was always a mystery to people why a middle class white woman would be in Harlem. Silently, people were observing, weighing the possible answers that came to mind: she was assigned here against her will; or, she failed at everything in the white world and thinks she can hang with us; or, she thinks she can "save" us; or, she's here to study us and to write a book about us; or, she actually, for reasons we don't understand, cares about something important to us and can be trusted to some degree. Of course, the degree of trust deserved would be continuously tested.

Throughout the first year with my second graders at PS 92, I struggled with every way of caring, entertaining, persuading, cajoling, yelling, teaching, bribing, creating exciting projects, and organizing the classroom so that they could learn. I worked long hours, stayed until 5 PM every day with children after school, made home visits, corrected their papers all evening, and generally poured my whole self into teaching them. I definitely cared, and they began to feel it.

There were moments, however, when I lost control. One day a boy named Terry provoked me with such persistence that I lost my temper and slapped him across the face. I was instantly ashamed, filled with remorse, and completely apologetic to him. Surprisingly, he was so grateful that I cared about his feelings, we became very close from that day on. After that, he always tried to please me. He had realized through my remorse and apology that I cared. He told me that he had been hit many times in his life by people who never apologized.

Caring was something I couldn't help but do. When I was 18, working as a summer social work intern at Manhattan State Hospital on Ward's Island, the advice given to me by experienced social workers was, "You care too much. You will not survive in this job if you care so much. You have to learn to protect yourself." I was deeply distraught at the plight of the old people who had been put in the mental hospital not because they were crazy but instead because they were poor and had no other place to be.

In graduate school a few instructors and head teachers told me similar things: "Learn to keep a professional distance. Set up professional boundaries. You can't get so close to the children. You'll burn yourself out if you care so much." I did not agree with them and did not try to learn to distance myself. In hindsight, I think this is a terrible way to teach social workers and teachers and is the opposite of what would be effective training. This distorted concept of the importance of setting "boundaries" is something that deserves

deeper discussion. I think one reason YouthBuild has been so effective is that we deliberately taught staff to surprise students by how
much they cared, to go outside of the normal expectations, to show
up when they were needed and least expected... at the hospital, in
the court, after school. The students needed to know that someone
really cared. When someone did, they began to open up their own
ability to care about their own lives.

Since I was so open, so young, and so opposed to punishment
and authoritarian approaches, I had no way of scaring the children
into obedience. Caring and reason, building relationships one by
one with each child, were my methods. Voluntary cooperation was
my goal.

I did observe and collect the methods of other teachers, because
my approach was apparently failing. One of my white male teacher
friends in the third grade had a system of putting the names of the
children on the blackboard when they spoke out of turn. Then he
would put check marks next to their names every time they did
something else that was out of line. When they got a certain number of check marks he spanked their hands with a ruler. He said it
worked for him. His children sat in their seats. Several black wom-
en teachers had a way of talking to the students that inspired their
respect and their fear.

For the first few months, none of my own approaches seemed
to work. All I had was caring, and reason, although occasionally I
invented a clever gimmick. For example, one day when Abilene and
Janet were facing off in the middle of the room yelling at each other, I
went to my desk, sat down silently with a piece of paper, and began
writing every word they said to each other. Soon the rest of the children had surrounded my desk to see what I was doing. When they
saw that I was writing every word, they ran to Abilene and Janet and
told them. This mysterious action silenced their fight. They sat down.

Despite my hard work, I was not gaining the respect of the
assistant principals, Miss Jones and Mrs. Chapman. One day Miss
Jones came into my classroom to tell me that I simply must achieve
a much greater level of discipline. "No deviations, Miss Stoneman.

No deviations!" was her message. She stood over me in her powerful clarity, actually backing me into the coat closet, while I timidly asked, "What do you mean?" There was no way that I could, or even wanted, to achieve a context characterized by "no deviations." No deviations from what? Did they have the perfect structure or curriculum that worked for everyone?

I kept a pet white rat named Louie in the classroom because some of the children loved to play with him. It had a calming influence to have a pet to put in their desk and stroke softly in their lap. As often as possible one of my students, Calvin, had the rat under his shirt while he worked. If "no deviations" meant that Calvin was not allowed to get up and go get Louie the rat in the middle of math class and hold him under his shirt, it wasn't my approach.

Little by little, my reason and my caring, plus my hard work, paid off. The children began to feel loved, and they began to love me. They began to want to please me. They began to cooperate. They began to put peer pressure on each other to cooperate with Miss Stoneman so they could learn. They began to learn. I was able to tolerate a certain amount of disorder and they were able to cooperate increasingly with me and each other. I had rearranged the seats from the straight rows to working groups of desks, and individualized the work as much as possible, with individual assignments for each student. I gave them prizes for successful work. The prizes were little things, like puzzles, but they knew I bought them with my own money and that made a huge difference. Any demonstration that I was not there for the money and was chipping in my own, always made an impact.

We put on plays together, even doing one very successful and creative rendition of Hansel and Gretel for all the other second grade classes. Miss Jones left me alone, even smiled at me occasionally. Dr. Shapiro remained kind.

In the spring during a large school assembly, I realized we had reached a turning point. Mrs. Chapman was demanding that the huge gathering of several hundred children be quiet. She was insulting them in the process. Walter, the same boy who had insisted I should hit the children in the first months, turned to me and said, "Miss Stoneman, you should run the assembly. You wouldn't yell at us!" I said, "Walter, there is no way that I could handle the assembly. Nobody would listen to me. Don't you remember how it used to be in our classroom?" Walter responded, "Oh, that ain't nothin', Miss Stoneman. You could do it. I know you could!"

I felt my refusal to hit or insult them had won the day. Walter's praise meant the world to me. It still rings in my ears as one of my great successes and lessons in life. They... at least Walter... had internalized the idea that people should not be yelled at or hit. That was a very big achievement. Furthermore, when the test scores came in, it turned out my class had gained an average of more than two years in reading scores during that one year. I breathed a huge sigh of relief and joy. I felt vindicated. My wonderful students were succeeding. Therefore, so was I.

My first year of teaching was successfully completed, I thought. Everyone had warned that the first year of teaching would be difficult beyond belief. It was certainly among the hardest things I have ever done, to this day.

I had grown very close to some of my students, especially those who tended to stay every afternoon in my classroom to be with Louie the rat and me. So, in the summer, with their parents' permission, I took Calvin Thomas, Kevin Washington, and Wesley Terry to Cape Cod for a week. On our way to the Cape, I pulled into the parking lot at Howard Johnson's Restaurant for lunch. Surprisingly, the boys would not leave the car. They refused. They wanted me to get the lunch and bring it back to them. I got impatient. They revealed that they did not want to leave the car because all the people in the restaurant were white. They were scared. I vowed to remember that moment. I thought I had learned that being black in America was a constant struggle, but I had already forgotten that these three little boys from Harlem, who had never been south of 96th Street, might be deathly afraid of stepping into a white Howard Johnson's restaurant in 1965. I went in and got their lunches for them.

Once we got to our little house on Cape Cod, they had a wonderful time. They loved the little stand-alone house, with a little yard, with nobody living above or below who could be disturbed by our noise. Neither Calvin, Kevin, nor Wesley had been to any place like this before. It caused them to begin to fantasize how they would change Harlem if they could. With my encouragement, they wrote a thoughtful letter to Mayor Lindsay telling him how he should change the neighborhood.

This was my first experience helping children communicate their vivid ideas about public policy. It turned out they had very important ideas, from a fresh perspective. I did not send it to the Mayor, because I had no confidence and no experience yet that indicated it would make any difference at all. The downtown powers felt almost as far away and untouchable to me as they did to Calvin, Wesley, and Kevin. But the first step of what was to become part of my life's work was begun: I knew how to draw out the young people's ideas and take them seriously enough to write them down. But the second and third steps — getting them communicated and later implemented — I hadn't even begun. It was also the case that their Ideas at that moment were overly Influenced by being on Cape Cod: they were advising Mayor Lindsay to change all the housing in NYC from apartments to little free-standing houses.

Carmen Maristany Ward and Tony Ward, Founders of EHBS

CHAPTER 7

Finding the East Harlem Block Schools

In the fall of 1966, I returned to PS 92 for what I expected to be a much easier year of teaching. After all, the first year was over. Everyone knew the first year was the worst.

I would have been a good candidate for Teach for America, the national service program now attracting young teachers to difficult schools. Back then there was a similar initiative called Teachers, Inc., started by Roger Landrum and others. Roger later became the founder of Youth Service America, which played a key role in the creation of the national service movement, from which AmeriCorps and Teach for America grew, and which still plays an important role.

But I was not a member of Teachers, Inc. and I didn't have any professional support system or on-going source of training, except my small group of white friends who had graduated from Bank Street College of Education and who started a little group called Teachers for Educational Change. We were all young and inexperienced, and none of us had the answers for the inner-city schools we were in. All of us — Tim Parsons, Tom Roderick, John Bell, Karen Weiskopf, and others — remained educators for the rest of our lives, and got more knowledgeable as we grew, but we were really struggling at the outset.

Unfortunately, as I entered year two, Dr. Elliot Shapiro retired. Miss Jones was elevated to acting principal, Mrs. Chapman became my direct supervisor, and I was given second grade class level 5. That means they were a group considered less talented and prepared than levels 4, 3, 2, and 1.

I started from scratch. This was a whole new group of students who didn't know me, didn't know I cared, didn't want to sit still all day, had not progressed well in school, and didn't feel good about themselves as learners. If the weight of the world was on my level 2 second graders, it was even heavier on my level 5 group. I could not believe that I was back at square one, no more effective than I had been on day one of my first year.

In the first month, Mrs. Chapman took me aside in the cafeteria and said, "Miss Stoneman, your class last year was a failure. You must do better this year." I was stunned. My eyes opened wide, and I responded, "How can you say it was a failure? My students gained an average of more than two years in their reading level!" She answered, "Oh, yes, that. But they never learned how to walk through the halls quietly or sit in their seats."

I was horrified that meaningless order and obedience were actually valued more than learning. My inability to achieve instant order, under supervision that valued only order, made me a failure, destined to fail, over and over again.

Meanwhile, my close friend from high school, Lois Howlett, who had joined me in running the summer pre-school for HAG and also went on to Bank Street College of Education, had found a position teaching five-year-olds at the East Harlem Block Schools. We talked every day. She was completely happy, well supported by a supervisor who understood early childhood education — Alice Graves — and an executive director — Tony Ward — who understood community organizing.

Tony was a young white Quaker man who had come to East Harlem to join the East Harlem Tutorial Project. Tony fell in love with Carmen Maristany, a young Puerto Rican mother with four children who lived on East 111th Street between Park Ave. and Madison Avenue. Carmen and Tony married, and then together they set up the East Harlem Block Schools as a parent-controlled pre-school. They were among many inter-racial couples whose deep connection to each other enabled them to create wonderful community-based initiatives that married their respective cultures and roots and their unique skills and connections, bringing the resources of the white world to ensure fulfillment of community members' vision. Carmen brought the parents to the table, who supplied the wisdom and knowledge about what they wanted for their children. Tony brought the funders and the money to the project through his confidence, white and male privileged connections, and writing skills. Together they produced a marvelous little parent-controlled school, perfect for the children and parents in the neighborhood. A good part of the story of school is well told by Tom Roderick in his book, *A School of Our Own: Parents, Power, and Community at the East Harlem Block Schools.* (2001, Teachers College Press).

In the fall of 1966, due to the painful challenges of my new 2nd grade class, I was persuaded by Lois to apply for a position teaching the class of three-year-old children at the Block Schools. Very professional in my light brown suit with skirt and low heels, I was interviewed by Carmen Ward and a group of black and Puerto Rican East Harlem parents. Luckily for me and its impact on the rest of my life, they chose to offer me the position. Being hired by parents was my first lesson in community-based parent-controlled education. They were in charge. They had the power to choose the teachers for their children. I learned that I was accountable to them. They called the ultimate shots, and I needed to be alert to what mattered to them, even if it differed from what I had learned downtown from my white professors. In fact, it would turn out to differ in some important respects. By and large, I came to believe that the parents were more on target than the professors.

Separating from my public school classroom at PS 92 in December of the school year was incredibly painful. It is one of very few responsibilities in my whole life that I abandoned in failure. I felt that if I could not achieve order among seven-year-olds in a context that was hostile to my emerging philosophy, maybe I could achieve it among three-year-olds within a supportive school whose philosophy welcomed children moving about and exploring their environment. The nursery school arrangement, with its blocks, paints, toys, hands-on activities of all kinds that the children were free to choose and free to move around, with only 18 children plus two assistant teachers from the neighborhood to help me, seemed much more conducive to success.

Unfortunately, the students in my second-grade class at PS 92, who by December had gotten to like me, felt that I must be leaving because of how bad they were. Mrs. Chapman did not miss the opportunity to tell them that it was their misbehavior that had caused me to leave, so if they wanted to keep their next teacher they must not misbehave. This pattern of threatening children with terrible results if they do not improve their behavior and blaming them for things that occur that are not their fault, is one that adults frequently demonstrate. It never has a good effect. Of course, I tried to tell them it was not their fault, but they never believed me. Our parting was very sad.

Once I had separated myself from PS 92, I was amazed at the nightmares I began to have about going back, about failing, about making terrible mistakes. I had not even realized the level of stress and shame I was carrying. At the same time, the relief and delight at working in a school that had a clear positive philosophy, cohesive staff, teacher training built in, and parent involvement, told me I had made the right decision.

The Block Schools are a great story, one that I was blessed to be part of. The children who went to the Block Schools were part of a joyful, committed, experimental community that they still remember as a source of love and the origin of their intellectual creativity and analytical skills. I have gotten calls all my life from graduates tracking me down to tell me they have never forgotten the joy of going to school at the East Harlem Block Schools. One such call came from Victor Soler, who called to say, "As I was walking in my back fields here in Georgia with my stallion, I thought how happy you would be that my life turned out so well, so I tracked you down to tell you." One of my first grade students, Chantay Henderson Jones, is still active in my life and was a reader for this book!

The East Harlem Block Schools (EHBS) was really one of the first of what would later be called "charter schools," established outside the existing system by idealistic and creative people with a vision, but still publicly funded. It steadily expanded, adding one grade each year, until it went up through eighth grade. Meanwhile, it had negotiated its way into the Public School District and was therefore fully funded publicly but was still parent-controlled and managed by the parents' Board of Directors. Seeing the value of this structure, back in the early seventies I organized something called the Committee for Independent Public Schools to try to get state funds for schools like the East Harlem Block Schools throughout the State. However, we were before our time. I didn't actively pursue it, and so it went nowhere. Charter schools hadn't yet been invented or named. (I won't go into it deeply here, but I will mention that non-profit community-based charter schools as an innovative force in the public school system are entirely different from for-profit private charter schools that should not receive public funds. The debates over charter schools rarely explicitly distinguish between the non-profit and the for-profit schools. That is the most significant factor. No public schools should be for profit.)

My shift from PS 92 to the East Harlem Block Schools was a life-changing and life-guiding decision. Everything I learned at the EHBS, at the hands of the wise parents and under Tony Ward's leadership, would guide me for the rest of my life.

Some Key Lessons Learned at EHBS

The most important thing I learned was to respect the intelligence and the wisdom of low-income community people who do not have a formal education but who have clear ideas and deep caring and if given adequate information and a chance to deliberate are likely to make very good decisions about important issues. I had already learned some of that at the grassroots storefront of the Harlem Action Group, but this was a formalized administration inside a funded public education system, and it worked perfectly. The structure in which professionals were accountable to community people meant that the decisions made had the best of both perspectives. This relationship was similar to the marriage between Tony and Carmen. The professional teachers brought their good training and resources; the parents brought their knowledge of their reality and their heartfelt desire to make things better. We all brought a very deep level of caring and mutual respect. Together we made good decisions.

It would be this same marriage of perspectives that I would later implement in YouthBuild. Realizing that the perspective of the young people was as valuable as the perspective of the adult staff was fundamental to the way YouthBuild was set up. Perhaps it was similar to my own partnership with Leroy in Harlem earlier. Cross-class, cross-race, cross-age, cross-gender partnerships bring a greater wisdom to difficult challenges than does a more limited perspective.

I learned that reversing the power relationships between traditionally privileged and traditionally oppressed groups had the effect of equalizing their relationship and allowing for real partnership. At the Block Schools, there was no doubt in anyone's mind that the parents had the ultimate power. They were the board of directors.

They could fire Tony Ward. They could fire every teacher. Tony was completely accountable to them according to our legal by-laws.

Tony was fundamentally a community organizer. A big part of Tony's job was to bring information to the parents, to talk through every significant issue with them, to prepare them to take complex positions and understand the implications. It was also his job to listen to their ideas, to make sure their ideas were sorted out, and their best ideas dominant. Then it was his job to write up their best ideas to raise funds for them, and then to guide the implementation of their best ideas. This is the role of any executive working with his or her board; but in most cases the boards are not made up of people living in poverty with a substantially different life experience than the executive.

To me, this accountability of the outside professional to the local community became a core principle of community organizing, community development, and community service. I wrote my Master's thesis at Bank Street College about the profound positive impact of reversing this power relationship.

Accountability to the community is a factor that is important in every aspect of social justice and social service. It is also important in the national service movement when the service-receivers are struggling with poverty. They have been marginalized, silenced, their knowledge and wisdom made irrelevant to solving their own problems. In reality, their engagement is crucial to changing the conditions in their communities. "Maximum feasible participation" was the correct watchword of the War on Poverty, which was unfortunately called off within two years of its launching in the 1960's. Unfortunately, many institutions of the War on Poverty did not genuinely or solely empower the people living in poverty; they empowered many politically ambitious, upwardly mobile opportunists who happened to live in the community but were driven by personal ambitions, so things got a little mixed up.

One of the safeguards at the East Harlem Block Schools was that only parents of children in the schools were eligible to serve on the board, and only people who lived in the tenement buildings were eligible to send their children to the schools. Thus, people who might have joined the board to achieve their personal ambitions were not involved. Only low-income parents with an interest in their own children were eligible.

A core group of totally dedicated and deeply wise parents emerged. Rosie Gueits, Rosie Tirado, Carmen Rios, Ethel Velez, Anna Rivera, Sonia Medina, Josie Comas, and many others who came and went with their children, ran those schools with love and dedication, for decades. Based on her learning at the Block Schools, Ethel Velez became a major community leader, chairman of the Johnson Housing Project Tenant Association. She created a fabulous community center. She later became the chair of the city-wide tenants' association, and is still actively leading in the 2020's. Most of the other parents I named have passed away, as has Carmen Maristany Ward. But the wonderful East Harlem Block Schools lives on. In 2022, Carmen's daughter, Margie LaFosse, succeeded in getting the 111th Street block between Park Ave. and Madison Ave. renamed in honor of her mother.

Some of the core group of EHBS parents

Leroy and I Go Through Hell and Back

In January of 1965, while I was teaching at PS 92, I found I was pregnant. It should not have been too surprising, since Leroy had refused to use birth control because he was 40 years old and claimed never to have gotten anyone pregnant and desperately wanted a baby. To insist on actively preventing pregnancy would have offended him deeply.

I was just 22 years old. Still extremely young. I felt obliged to have his baby, since he wanted one so much, but I was not ready to be a parent. Nor was I ready to commit to marrying Leroy. Our relationship was still new and tumultuous. I thought I should have the baby and give it to him and Sarah to raise. That would make him happy, I thought. I also knew it would be extremely difficult for me to give away my baby once it was born.

I went home to Belmont for a visit with my family. I had a long talk with an older close friend who was a psychologist. He persuaded me that I had to tell my parents, that I had to face the reality of how they would react if I planned to have Leroy's baby out of wedlock. If I could stand up to them, then good, I could go forward.

If I couldn't, I should find out in advance. So, I followed that advice and confided in my mother, who told my father, who confronted me with the reality that he would make me leave the country if I had a baby. He said I could not do that in "his territory." It would ruin his reputation. He also told me I would be completely disowned and not welcome in the family.

I called Leroy. With me sitting in the corner on the floor behind the bed in my parents' bedroom, he and I spoke quietly and at length. On that call Leroy gave me permission to have an abortion. He said he did not want to ruin my family relationships, and he did not want me to feel obliged to him to go through with it. This permission was the most extraordinary expression of love I had ever experienced. I knew that with all his heart and soul he wanted me to have that baby. Yet he gave me permission not to have it, and he promised not to let it ruin our relationship if I honored my parents' feelings or felt too conflicted or upset to happily have a baby at this point in my life. Nobody had ever put my well-being so far ahead of his own. It was an unforgettable experience that made me realize that Leroy truly loved me. Any lingering question about whether he was still managing our relationship for his personal gain was answered.

In retrospect, I think I really did not want to have a baby, and I was in no way ready to do so. It was a fantasy that I could have it and give it to Sarah. Maybe I unconsciously went home so that my parents would force me not to do it, and so Leroy would forgive me because it was their decision and not my own. That is what happened. My parents arranged an illegal abortion for me that took place in their home, on March 11, 1965. My mother was home, vacuuming the rooms downstairs while the abortion doctor took me through the traumatic experience in my bedroom. He said unkind words during the procedure. Then he flushed my baby down the toilet.

Although Leroy forgave me as best he could, and absolutely kept his word, neither of us ever really got over it. We always regretted that our offspring, who we believed would have been amazing, had been denied life. I felt profoundly guilty for years, until I had worked it out in co-counseling through many hours of sobbing guilty regret. Then I no longer felt guilty, just sad, even though I realized objectively that if I had given birth to Leroy's baby my entire life would have been different, in totally unpredictable ways, and all the wonderful things that happened later — like marrying John, and having Sierra and Taro as our beloved children, and welcoming Freddy as our extended family, and launching YouthBuild — might not have happened. There was no way to tell what path life would have taken, but it certainly would have been different. So, as people like to say, "Everything happens for a reason."

Clearly Leroy and I were not meant to have that baby together in 1965. But both of us always felt that there was supposed to have been a person produced by our union who would have been wonderful and deeply loved. Fortunately, I was able to know and love the four children that he later had, two with each of his wives, all of whom came under his custody with his second wife, Kathy. I became the godmother of all four. He became the "god-grandfather" of my children who both admired and loved him. Most recently, in 2021, his oldest son, Malik, chose to become an active part of John's and my family. He comes to visit us for a week each year. He also supported me with weekly co-counseling phone calls during the chemotherapy I underwent in 2020. Our relationship is another sacred gift.

After the abortion, I returned to NYC, my womb empty. We continued seeing how our relationship would evolve. We had been together less than a year. I was living on the upper West Side, on 75th Street just off Central Park West in a little one room apartment. Leroy came on alternate nights. He spent the other nights with Sarah. I was still woman #2 in his life, technically; although I was pretty sure I had become, emotionally, number one.

Traveling to Africa

In the summer of 1965, we traveled together to Africa. This was a dream come true for Leroy. I had inherited something like $20,000 from my German grandfather, who had made his money importing coffee from Ghana and Brazil. (Somewhere along the way, Grandpa had reversed his original disowning of my mother for marrying my Jewish father. However, my father never did set foot in his German anti-Semitic home.) Happily, as a result of that inheritance, I could afford to take Leroy and me to Africa. For me this trip was also important, given my previous unfulfilled plans to go to Africa in 1963 and set up schools for Angolan refugees fleeing the colonial liberation war against the Portuguese. I had a deep lingering desire to go to Africa.

In June, Leroy and I hopped on an ocean liner, leaving from the dock on the west side of Manhattan. It took about 14 days on that boat to get to Morocco. Our time on the ocean liner was amazing. At first Leroy refused to leave his room and come upstairs to the deck. He was not accustomed to being around so many white people and had an irrational expectation that someone would throw him overboard because he was black. And, of course, if that happened, he knew he would drown because he couldn't swim.

It took him a few days to overcome this fear. When he finally came upstairs, he began to make white friends on the upper deck. This was the beginning of a new skill. He turned out to be very good at it. Over the next 40 years he made many white friends who lived on the upper decks of society. Many of them helped him fulfill his vision for ways to assist addicts, mentally ill, and homeless people.

We enjoyed Morocco where we were scheduled to stay only briefly before going on to Ghana through Mali. We went biking around Casa Blanca, and we walked everywhere. I spoke enough French to help us navigate. However, a mysterious repetitive event began to occur. Policemen would stop and question us. We could see it coming... a policeman would see us and get on his phone. Re-enforcements would arrive. They would surround us and ask for our identification. After checking it, they would doff their hat and leave peacefully. Finally, one of them explained that they were seeking an inter-racial couple accused of counterfeiting. The man they were seeking was bald, so we learned that if Leroy would take off his hat when they arrived to show them that he wasn't bald, they would let us go. But after it happened 5 or 6 times, we went with them to the national police station to get some papers stating clearly that we were not the criminals they were seeking.

On our way to Ghana, we stayed in Mali for a night or two in a little hotel that cost $1 per night. This was 1965, but even back then $1 was very cheap. There were many bugs in the bed, so we got up and walked around the city almost all night. We enjoyed an unforgettably beautiful sunrise by the river.

Ghana turned out to be unforgettable in another way. We did, again, enjoy sight-seeing, visited our Ghanaian friend Ampah who was now back home. We visited a number of schools, and traveled through Accra and Kumasi, with Leroy having many reflective conversations with Ghanaians about what it was like to be black in America.

The critical turning point that entirely changed the trip occurred one afternoon when we were taking a walk up the beach on the Coast. We came to a point where the rocks jutted out over the water and prevented us from proceeding. We took a detour up toward what looked like a hotel, planning to go around the rocks, through the hotel, and then continue on up the beach. There was a wall around the hotel. We noticed a guard asleep outside the wall, leaning up against it, but we didn't think anything of it. We didn't wonder why there was a guard. We noticed a spot where it would be easy to jump over the wall because someone had thrown cut grass and leaves over the wall and created a nice little hill we could walk up and then basically just step over this wall that was about six feet high. There were no signs, no barbed wire on top of the wall, nothing unusual except a sleeping guard.

We easily leaped over the wall and continued walking toward the hotel, holding hands, aiming to find our way back to the beach. Suddenly a jeep pulled up, a military officer jumped out, and asked how we got inside the wall. We pointed out the spot. He and another officer went to look over the wall. They shook their heads and whispered to each other, apparently both amazed and embarrassed to see that the grasscutters had unwittingly created a walkway into the guarded area.

They led us to an office where we were made to sit and wait for an hour or two. We had time to look around, to read what was on the wall, to see what was going on. One sign on the wall referred to the location as The Castle. We gasped. We had evidently climbed over the wall around Kwame Nkrumah's Castle. We had stumbled innocently, blindly, and stupidly, into the President of Ghana's palace.

Leroy went into high gear to use his charm to make friends with the guard, who had been on the phone trying to get instructions about what to do with us. Leroy made it clear we had no idea where we were, intended no harm, were innocent Americans on a sight-seeing tour. Fortunately, Leroy had lost his baggage in Mali so that he was not carrying the self-protective cudgel that he usually carried as a reflection of his left-over street mentality. Soon he began the conversation about being black in America. These conversations were always extremely interesting to Ghanaians and always created a real emotional and cross-cultural connection.

Soon the befriended guard gave us a tour of the grounds, and then let us go. He waved a warm good-bye. Relieved, we went walking happily down the street, laughing about our foolishness and the close call that we had created. As we were enjoying this moment, another military vehicle sped around the corner, came to a screeching halt next to us, and a colonel jumped out. "Get in!" he said harshly. We did. No questions asked. They put us in the back of the truck and drove us through many winding back roads to a distant building that turned out to be a prison run by the Ghanaian equivalent of the CIA. We sat there in the waiting room along with hordes of mosquitoes for the better part of the evening.

We were a mystery to them. We did not ask to call the American Embassy, because my parents did not know I was traveling in Ghana with Leroy, and as a result I preferred to stay below the radar. The Ghanaians sort of believed we were innocent Americans, but they couldn't afford not to investigate the situation more deeply. They thoroughly searched us, and they interrogated us for several days, each in separate rooms, asking questions of us both for hours on end. The interrogator spent eight hours with Leroy. They chose not to put us in the actual cells where a fairly large group of prisoners were locked up. They let us stay in an office, on a mattress, and they brought us fairly decent food, while they carried out their investigation. We couldn't actually see the other prisoners, but we could see their hands reaching out above the cells because they had somehow learned that Leroy had cigarettes and they wanted some.

For me these events were an adventure. It was fascinating and not scary to be going through this interrogation. They were treating us with some respect and some care, as unknown Americans. But for Leroy, who had spent most of his life locked up, this was no adventure. He had come to Africa to return to his roots, connect with his ancestors, and learn about life in Africa. He had not come to be locked up ignominiously for jumping over the Castle wall.

Through his interrogations Leroy told the investigator his entire life story. He decided that if they were going to ask him questions, he was going to give a totally full answer and teach them about being black in America. He won the interrogator's heart. For Ghanaians who were curious about life in America, Leroy's story was totally fascinating. They became his champions. The head of the investigation called me into his office to chastise me for not having given Leroy more money to start his business and to scold me even further for having sent a postcard to my parents (Ghanaian officials had intercepted it) saying that there was a lot of malaria in Ghana. He said, "Knowing that your father is a racist, why would you say such a thing? You embarrass us."

Ironically, the next day I came down with a high fever, which resulted in my being sent to the military hospital where they diagnosed me with malaria. The mosquitoes in the waiting room the first night had evidently gotten to me. The investigator apologized for his comments. We were getting to know each other.

The most memorable and important comment by this official before letting us go was this: "We can believe that you had no evil intent when you jumped over that wall because you are Americans. Americans have a colonialist mentality. They think they have the right to go everywhere and anywhere, whether it belongs to them or not. If a Ghanaian had jumped over that wall, we would know he had evil intent." He was absolutely right. We had a colonialist mentality and thought we could go anywhere, jump over anybody's fences, and find our own way through their property. As a white privileged American I had that attitude more deeply than Leroy did, but as an American he must have had some of it, because we jumped over the wall together. I was extremely grateful that this Ghanaian official had such an enlightened perspective that he could understand our privileged mentality and forgive us.

Before we could leave, a final check-off was required by the head of the national intelligence agency. He came to the prison for an exit conversation with me. He was quite casual, dressed in a colorful sports shirt. He was primarily interested in what it was like in America to have a cross-racial relationship and asked why a Harvard educated white woman would choose to do that. In 1965, the assumption in Africa was that such relationships were not allowed in America. With no explanation of why not, he did not talk with Leroy.

Finally, after five days of being sequestered in the office at the secret prison, they took us to the airport, stamped our passports as not welcome to return, and sent us on to England.

Arriving in England

When we got off the plane in London and tried to go through customs, the officials blocked our entrance and took us to a detention area. They were highly suspicious because Leroy had no suitcase (it had been lost in Mali) and we had no plane tickets to America. They had rules against people of color immigrating into England. They suspected that Leroy planned to stay there illegally. I explained that my sister planned to buy our tickets. The official said, "I understand why your sister would buy your ticket, but why would she buy his?" This remark landed on us as a very offensive racial comment.

They called my sister, who was at the theatre. She was married to the brother of a prominent playwright. She came to the detention center, signed for us, and assured them that she would indeed pay for Leroy as well as me.

We went on to her home where she and Leroy became friends. She was the one member of my family who was able to transcend the racism of our time and appreciate Leroy for who he was. This might have been possible because she herself had been close friends with a black woman at Oxford, who became her roommate and life-long friend. In general, the prejudices and distance created by racism in our society are best overcome through real and close personal relationships with people of different backgrounds.

The Painful Crises, the Growth, and the Change

Eventually we were back in America, and I was back at PS 92, on W. 134th Street, teaching 2nd graders. It was the fall of 1965. I had moved to the Lower East Side, on East 4th Street between Avenues C and D. Leroy still lived with Sarah Kearney on West 134th Street.

My life at PS 92 was all-consuming. As described in the earlier chapter about being a teacher, I was basically starting over with an unruly class of students who had even greater problems than those I taught in year one. Before I left PS 92, Leroy and I weathered another unthinkable storm. While he had shed his addiction to drugs, he had not overcome his alcoholism. One night he drove his car while drunk, down 8th Avenue, and ran into a man near 132nd Street. The man was killed. He was a father of four children. Leroy was taken to the police precinct, where I went to wait for him for many hours throughout the night.

The next morning my 2nd graders filled the room with emotional talk about the terrible accident the night before on 8th Avenue where a drunk man killed one of their neighbors by driving into him. You can imagine how I felt as their teacher, knowing the driver of that car was Leroy.

He did not go to prison, and for that I am infinitely grateful. Leroy chose never to drive a car again. His guilt at killing that father, that neighbor, was everlasting, as was his decision to express his remorse by never driving again.

In the winter of 1966, we had another traumatic experience. With what I thought was Leroy's permission, I slept with another man. When I told Leroy it had actually happened, he flipped out. I don't think he was under the influence of alcohol, but he was clearly under the influence of a jealous violent rage.

We were at Leroy and Sarah's home. Leroy pushed me onto the bed, picked up his dog's leash which was nearby at hand, and started to whip me. I jumped up to reason with him and he struck me across the face. The leash was in his hand, and when he hit me, the clip went clean through my nose. It was an inch from my temple, a half inch from my eye. I fell to the floor, with blood spurting out of my nose.

Leroy panicked. He ran to the phone and called his doctor (or on second thought, maybe it was his lawyer). I overheard him say, "I need help. I just beat up a white woman."

Even more powerful in my memory than the beating itself was that statement. Forget about who I was. I was not Dorothy at that moment. I was a white woman. And beating up a white woman could cost him his life. He was absolutely terrified. Much more terrified than I was.

To me, I realized I had profoundly misjudged something. I had thought he was ok with my getting close to another man. After all, he was still living with Sarah, and he had given me permission. I did not expect him to go into a jealous rage. At this point Sarah came forward from the other room and offered to take me to the hospital. As she and I got ready to leave, and were walking down the narrow hallway past Leroy, I turned to Leroy and apologized. "I'm sorry," I said. "I'm sorry I drove you to do this to me." He answered, "And I'm sorry. I never wanted to hurt you."

Sarah took me to the hospital on the Upper West Side. When the admitting nurse saw the leash clip jutting out of my nose, she gasped. I lied and said I had fallen while walking my dog. That was obviously a ridiculous lie. The clip would have been on the dog's collar. There's no way on earth a person could fall and get the leash clip forced through their nose. But she didn't push it. She pulled me out of the room onto a cot in a safe room where nobody could see me. I thanked Sarah for bringing me and then I lay on the cot alone, reading a book about the Vietnam war. I can't imagine in retrospect how I was so calm, and how I even had a book with me, but I evidently was not in extreme pain.

The doctor came in, examined my nose and said, "We can remove it. But I cannot guarantee that you will have a nose. You might need reconstructive surgery."

Fortunately, they removed the clip, and I kept my nose. I had only a faint scar for the rest of my life. I also kept to my unbelievable lie. No matter who asked me what happened, I said I had fallen while walking my dog. It was surely clear to them that I had been the victim of domestic violence but that I had no desire to make that claim. When Leroy visited me in the hospital, they probably made up their own story about what had happened.

I never told anyone at the time what had happened. It was humiliating to be in this position. I also wanted to protect Leroy from any consequences. He had not intended to be so angry, had not intended to hurt me, and certainly not to put a dog's leash through my nose. He realized through this event, that he had, in his terms, "gotten his nose open." He was more emotionally vulnerable than he had ever been.

Although I forgave him immediately because I understood him, this near-death experience did scare me. On a deep level, I realized that with Leroy my life might be in danger. Anything could happen. The passions were dangerous. He came very close to killing me without intending to.

The Turning Point

The next trauma turned out to result in an irreversible turning point in a positive direction that changed Leroy's future.

Leroy was still in the grip of alcoholism. Every few weeks he would go on a binge. In between those times, he didn't drink. But the moment he had even as much as a beer, his whole body would go crazy. I could smell it on his hands, the beginning of a chemical change that would end in a serious drunken state. One of these binges brought him to such a state of delirium tremens that I took him to the hospital and checked him in. Luckily, during his stay there, his doctor noticed that he had an extraordinary vocabulary for a drunken black man. The doctor took an interest in him. As Leroy recovered from the immediate impact of his stupor, he found himself having long philosophical and political conversations with this doctor. Soon the doctor engaged Leroy in leading the recovery groups they were holding in the hospital for people who had arrived in a drunken state.

His obvious leadership skills resulted in the doctor referring him to a job at Exodus House as an ex-addict counselor. A wonderful man who became Leroy's professional support and friend for life, Rev. Stephen Chinlund, was the director of Exodus House. Soon thereafter, Leroy became the first official ex-addict counselor hired by New York City. Suddenly he was on track to do what he had always wanted to do. From the bottom of his very deep heart, he wanted to help other addicts recover more than he wanted to do anything else.

During his own recovery from that episode in the hospital, he made an amazing decision. He decided he no longer wanted to depend on women for his livelihood. He needed to become self-sufficient. He needed to grow up into a professional role as a therapeutic counselor who had mastered his own weaknesses and fears. He left Sarah and went to live in his own apartment on East 104th Street in East Harlem, across the street from Exodus House, where he was employed. Before too long, I moved in with him. He was paying the rent. This was a totally new experience for him.

He and I began to attend therapy groups informed by "reality therapy" and sponsored by drug rehab programs like Synanon and Encounter. We studied the writings of William Glasser and learned to lead encounter groups in which people were challenged to take responsibility for their actions and free themselves of their addictions. We made friends in this new community. Meanwhile Leroy thrived as a staff member at Exodus House. We were enjoying living together, had bought a German Shepherd whom we named Kofi, and I was by now working around the corner at the East Harlem Block Schools on E. 106th Street. Still, he was occasionally still drinking, and risking his extraordinary progress.

In the process of exploring reality therapy, we attended a "marathon" therapy session. This was a 36-hour marathon of a small group sharing deeply, confronting each other, challenging each other to take responsibility. The theory was that by being together for so long, without sleep, people's defenses would lose their strength and they would therefore slide into very deep emotional sharing and catharsis that otherwise could not be reached. It did work, although I later learned through training in Re-evaluation Counseling (aka Co-counseling) that there were much more efficient and effective ways of getting to the same level of deep emotional release without taking 36 hours.

When Leroy and I talked in this group about our relationship, and about his drinking and the violence that it inevitably led to, the group leader closed in on me. He said, "You should not tolerate Leroy's drinking. You need to make it very clear that if he ever takes another drink, you will leave him. You are not doing him any favor by tolerating this self-destructive behavior. Your compassion is doing him no good. You must make an absolute commitment that if he ever drinks again you are gone." This was a transformative moment. It had never occurred to me that I had either the power or the responsibility to take this position, to make the difference in Leroy's recovery. But they persuaded me, and I did make that commitment. After that marathon, for as long as Leroy and I were together, he did not take another drink, he never hit me again, and he was thriving in his new professional role because his natural charismatic intelligence and emotional power were both having a catalytic positive effect on other addicts.

It was during this period that Leroy made friends with Sam and Judy Peabody, wealthy and influential individuals who became guardians of his first entrepreneurial creation: Reality House, a drug rehab center he created in Harlem. It was also the period when I introduced him to Cathy Merrill, a Radcliffe graduate who had access to significant wealth, some of which she donated to Reality House as well as to his later ventures. His new comfort with white people allowed him to build genuine relationships with rich people who backed his creative humanitarian ventures. This may be another lesson to learn: a lot of rich white people are wondering what to do with the surplus that they may have inherited, or even if they earned it, they know it is more than they need and that there is suffering in the world that needs redress. Figuring out what to do with it is a major challenge for many of them.

The Resolution

Now it was the winter of 1966. A lot had happened in a short time. I had grown up a lot since arriving in NYC in the winter of 1964. No other two-year period in my life would turn out to be so full of drama and learning. The white girl in the ghetto was becoming a white woman in the world deeply connected to a talented black man who had internalized all the ills and oppressive impact of a racist and classist society, and who was determined to rise above it all and help other people. Sharing and witnessing this transformation had a profound influence on my entire life. Because I understood this process so deeply from experiencing it with Leroy, I gained the insights that informed the creation of YouthBuild, which became the catalyst for thousands of other men, younger than Leroy, and also many women, to find their own best selves that were yearning for expression.

But there was still a problem to be faced. Leroy wanted to marry me. He was by now 41 years old, and I was 24. I was not ready to be married. He at least wanted me to make a life-long commitment. I was not ready to do that either. So, he set a deadline. If I was not ready to make that commitment by June 30, 1966, we would separate. I would move out of his apartment and go back to East 4th Street, where I had retained my earlier apartment that I was subletting.

As June 30 approached, the tension grew. I was getting splitting headaches as I tried to make up my mind. I never figured out how much the underlying feeling that my life could be in danger at some level in the future due to the violence I had experienced with Leroy affected my reservations, or how much classism and racism played into it, or how much the desire not to permanently separate from my parents, or how much it was just my age. I was only 24, after all, and I was definitely living in a different world from my family of origin.

As June 30th came, we faced the terrible reality. We were going to separate. I didn't want to separate. I wanted more time. But Leroy was clear... he didn't have time or patience to wait. He wanted a family, and if I would not be his wife then he needed to find some-one else who would bear his children and be his partner with no reservations. On June 29th, he took me to a wonderful performance at the theatre, both of us all dressed up. And on June 30th I moved out, with his help.

But Leroy and I were not through. Without dragging out the details of this account, the short version is that we went through a few more rounds of love and separation, a few more tries. I even decided to marry him, wrote to my father and mother bravely announcing my plans, explained it to my brother, went to Montreal with Leroy for a sort of preliminary honeymoon, and got blood tests for an appearance before the magistrate to marry us.

But 24 hours before the planned union, I found myself up against an absolute internal barrier that I could not cross. In the evening that I was talking to my brother about my decision to marry Leroy, I was sitting in the bed next to Leroy, and he, sad to say, was sleeping off a drunk. It was deeply humiliating to explain my marriage plans next to a drunken Leroy. I had evidently not kept my commitment to leave if he ever took another drink. I do not remember exactly how the drinking resumed, but I believe it happened after I had moved out of his apartment the first time. The fact that he had lost me even though he hadn't had a drink after I made that commitment, lowered his own commitment to be permanently sober. After all, what could he lose? I was already gone.

I was having intense conflicted headaches. I simply couldn't marry Leroy. My body was protesting, even though my heart was still glued to him. We sat in the car on Morningside Drive and 135th Street while I told him tearfully that I was backing out. I took him home and then drove to my friend Judy Gueron's home where I cried all the night through, in total upset. Just writing this page has brought me to heavy crying as I recall the incredible pain of that irreversible decision, that separation, that moment of convulsive separation, forced by some fear or some wisdom deep inside me that was out of my rational control. I loved Leroy. But I could not commit my whole life to him.

That stage of our relationship was over. We would never reconsider marriage. Leroy went on a drunken binge, and I went into a state of deep grief. Within a year Leroy married his first wife, a very young woman who had served as a teenaged assistant teacher in my summer preschool in 1964. He married Pat and fled to California where he succeeded in starting the family that he had longed for. He had two beautiful baby boys, Malik and Esan. I stayed at the Block Schools and carried on as best I could, still just growing up and figuring out the course of my life. Leroy and I remained in touch from a distance, by telephone, because we were destined to be friends for life.

Staff and students of the EHBS outside the main office at 94 E. 111th Street

CHAPTER 9

Growing with the Block Schools

After Leroy and I separated, I remained depressed for at least a year. At the same time, I was working hard because in the fall of 1966 I had been promoted to a new position at the Block Schools: director of the nursery school on East 106th Street. At the end of that year, Anna Rivera, one of the parents on staff, said, "Dorothy, you haven't been yourself this year. You have been depressed." I felt totally grateful to her because instead of deciding that I was simply a depressed person, she could realize that I wasn't myself, that I was in a state of confused unhappiness that did not reflect my true self. That seemed incredibly generous. It was a reflection of the supportive community that existed for everyone at the Block Schools. I had landed in exactly the right place.

That year I lived by myself in the 6th floor walk-up apartment on the Lower East Side, on 4th Street between Avenues C and D. I vividly remember dragging myself up the six flights of stairs one midnight after a long day's work, when a thought burst into my mind: "Most people who work this hard have wives." But I didn't mind the work. It was meaningful and satisfying. I had recovered my idealistic optimism that had made the summer preschool for HAG successful, and I had found a context in which to express it.

In 1967 the parents again asked me to take on a new role. They asked me to teach the first-grade class of the new Block Schools independent elementary school that was expanding upwards grade by grade. Meanwhile, Tom Roderick, who was a student at Bank Street with me and a teacher at PS 92, had come to the Block Schools to teach in the elementary school. In a storefront on Madison Avenue, Tom and I taught the first and second graders in shared space. This was a marvelous teaching experience. Unlike the public schools, even though we were now responsible for teaching reading and math to elementary school students, we were encouraged to do it with fun, with activities, in small groups, with two assistant teachers from the neighborhood to help create a loving community for shared learning. It couldn't have been more different from PS 92.

One of my first-grade students that year was Chantay Henderson Jones. I mention her here because she played a key role a few years later in starting the New Action Party and the Youth Action Program. We remained friends for life. In fact, she is one of the readers of the draft of this book who strongly encouraged me to publish it.

In 1969, when Tony Ward left his role as executive director, the parent board asked me to step up into that role. I did. As executive director I was suddenly, at age 27, in charge of an organization with a staff of 30, two nursery schools, an expanding elementary school, a tutoring program, and a substantial debt.

Meanwhile, my father continued to ask me, "When are you going to get a real job?" The fact that I worked in East Harlem meant to him that I had not grown up, didn't have a real job, and was still on the margins of society.

I was, indeed, still at the grassroots, in the field, not part of the downtown power. But as executive director I gained valuable experience in both confronting and negotiating with the downtown bureaucracy. There were challenges that had to be solved.

There were endemic weaknesses in The Anti-Poverty Program. One of them was that there were neither adequate financial controls nor training in financial management for the community-based organizations that emerged rapidly in low-income communities. Another problem was that there were rules that prevented success. For example, although Tony and Carmen had gotten the Block Nursery funded under the Community Anti-Poverty Program as a nursery school, and they had received a $50,000 revolving fund in advance to pay its expenses, there was a rule against spending on any capital improvements. This meant they were not permitted to prepare a space that met the code requirements for a nursery school.

Tony made the daring and radical decision to take the risk of using the $50,000 advance to build a space that the Board of Health would approve. In the end, this turned out to be a wise decision, because it positioned the Block Nursery to be accepted for permanent funding as a part of the Day Care Department of the Division of Social Services in New York City. But it caused the near demise of the East Harlem Block Schools when the CAP agency discovered that Tony didn't have the $50,000 revolving fund because he had spent some of it on essential capital improvements despite the regulations forbidding such expenditures. Furthermore, the Block Schools' bookkeeping systems were so poor that we could not account completely for all of the funds.

I therefore inherited not only two fully funded Day Care Centers, but also a debt to the Community Anti-Poverty Program and a bookkeeping mess. My administrative assistant, Peggy Fahnestock, spent two years rebuilding the entire financial history of the Block Schools' first four years. She found the bills, in the drawers and file cabinets, wrote to vendors to find missing bills, and re-did all the monthly voucher submissions to the CAP. I will never forget the day when we arrived with a full set of four years of quarterly financial submissions to the CAP agency. The man in charge looked with amazement, and said, "We thought your organization was dead and gone! We never expected to see you again."

After they reviewed our submissions, they acknowledged that they owed us $38,000 for legitimate expenditures that had never been submitted for reimbursement. This was true because Tony had raised significant funds from private sources over his four years to support the nurseries. I loved getting that check, but even more I loved the congratulatory letter from the heads of the New York City Day Care Council, Nancy Stewart and Marjorie Grossett, saying, "Congratulations. This is unheard of. You have succeeded in squeezing money out of a stone."

Many people suspected that the lack of training for community-based organizations in financial management, which set them up for failure and for being shut down when the powers that be wanted to end the anti-poverty program, was not entirely accidental. Or, they thought, perhaps the harshness with which these organizations were treated when their errors were discovered was not accidental. Certainly, there was a double standard, whether intentional or unconscious. When a low-income community-based organization had lousy financial records or spent money against the guidelines to create a safe space for their children that would pass codes, it was shut down. When NASA blew up the spaceship called the Challenger, it was given many extra millions of dollars to prevent future mistakes. It was always more important to some people to go to the moon than to end poverty and despair on earth.

Reaching the Downtown Decision-Making Table

Soon, at the recommendation of the leaders of the New York City Day Care Council, and perhaps with the recommendation of Mayor Lindsay's aide, Gordon Davis, who used to be at the downtown office of the Northern Student Movement (NSM), I was appointed by the Mayor to his Day Care Task Force. The Task Force was set up to create the new Agency for Child Development, taking day care out from under the welfare department. This Task Force was a very big deal. It was chaired by Trude Lash, the most distinguished leader in childcare in the city. It had emerged after much conflict led by Bob Gangi and Dorothy Pitman who ran the community-based day care coalition. They had staged various demonstrations, even blocking the bridge to the Bronx, to get more day care and more parent-controlled day care. Those were the days when blocking bridges got you to the official decision-making table instead of exiled for life, as it would in the eighties.

Sitting on this Task Force was exciting. It was my first time at the downtown center of power. We really hashed through the issues. Dorothy Pitman and I both fought for parent control, and to a large extent we won the day. Dorothy was African American; she and I worked together in such a way that some people put the similarities in our names together and called us the "Dorothy Seedmen." I felt that as a great honor. The final report had all our recommendations built into it, including the idea that all publicly funded day care centers should have substantial numbers of parents on the boards of directors.

Trude Lash was very kind to me. The fact that I tended to shed tears and get choked up in my youthful fervor whenever I got passionate about an issue was not held against me here any more than the children in Harlem had held it against me. It was, however, more embarrassing to me among these high-level professionals than with my 2nd grade class. I never really got over the tendency to choke up with feeling, but it never seemed to do any perceptible damage. The first time I testified before a Senate committee, fifteen years later, the same thing happened: the sudden change in tone from professional preparation to emotional fervor caused Senator Barbara Mikulski to look up from her papers and listen more closely. Much later, when I choked up in 2016 about how hard I had been pushing uphill for decades in the battle to end poverty, in a meeting including Howard Schultz of Starbucks and former Secretary of State Madeleine Albright, they both offered heartfelt empathetic support.

Mayor Lindsay's Day Care Task Force was quite a wonderful expression of how government could function when the grassroots organizers and the city officials spent days working through to real conclusions about what policies would work best on the ground. Of course, it helped to have the meetings well facilitated by respected leaders and well-staffed by people doing careful research and capturing the agreements in documents. Georgia MacMurray staffed the Task Force. She did an extraordinary job. She became a model for me of the kind of staffing any decision-making body should have. She was later made Commissioner of The Agency for Child Development which Mayor Lindsay set up in response to our recommendations.

The full story of this struggle for parent engagement in Day Care in New York, and the East Harlem Block School's role in it, is well researched and captured in the book written by Tom Roderick mentioned earlier: *A School of Our Own*. I strongly recommend it!

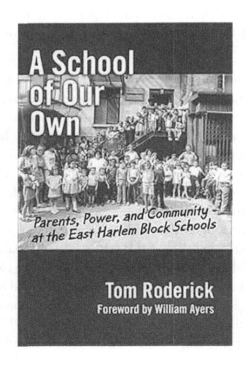

Finding the Right Man to Marry

I n March of 1968 I met the man I would marry in 1974. I was 32 years old when John Bell and I committed to being married for the rest of our lives. By that time, John was also a teacher at the East Harlem Block Schools. We had a marvelous outdoor wedding at the Hudson Guild retreat center with about 100 of our Block School students along with dear friends and family members.

Finding the right man to marry took 20 years, through many relationships. I think the whole process was unconsciously figuring out whether I would marry a man like my father, or not. I didn't. I married a man a lot like my mother.

As mentioned in an earlier chapter, I always liked boys and men and had no problem being close friends with them. I loved sports, was the only girl in the neighborhood, and my best friend for many years was my next-door neighbor, Vic Taylor. I had many close male friends. I also had many important lovers over those 20 years and naturally a certain amount of drama and heartbreak in the process. Leroy was the most important and most dramatic relationship prior to John, but he was not the only wonderful man I was close to and with whom I also remained friends for life.

I met John the Sunday after Martin Luther King Jr. was murdered in 1968. I went to church with my fellow teacher, Tom Roderick, at the liberal mostly white Judson Memorial Church in lower Manhattan, not too far from my apartment on the Lower East Side. Normally I didn't go to church, but this moment in time drew me to where like-minded people would be grieving together. Outside the church Tom introduced me to his friend John Bell, also a young white teacher working in Harlem. In 1968 he was teaching at the middle school, IS 201, on E. 127th Street between Madison and Park Avenues. That school was at the center of an enormous city-wide controversy about community control of the schools. John was on the side of the parents. We knew him because a letter from him had been published in the New York Times supporting community control of schools, and we had reached out to get to know him. After the church service, Tom and I agreed to meet with a few friends at John's tiny apartment on East 11th Street, not far from the Church.

Leaning up against the brick wall in front of his building, waiting for the others to join us, John and I struck up a conversation. I don't remember the words we spoke, but I remember the warmth and kindness of his wide blue eyes, his casual and youthful comfort leaning against the wall, and the sincerity that emanated from him. I had an immediate attraction to his heart.

Our group climbed the many stairs to his tiny 6th floor studio apartment. We sat on the floor around a small, low table in the center of his front room. We talked for hours about the meaning and impact of King's work and his assassination. When I went home to East 4th Street, I called my brother and said, "Billy, I met the man I want to marry. His name is John Bell. We just had a great conversation at his apartment about Martin Luther King, Jr., and I want to marry him." John still loves to tell that story.

This day was the start of a courtship in which I pursued John until he agreed to marry me six years later. He was two years younger than I was, only 24 when we met in 1968. He was innocent, and good, had probably never committed any significant sins nor done any harm in his life. He had been raised Catholic in Bremerton, Washington, in a tiny house on Puget Sound. He had been an altar boy, and the president of his high school. He was the newspaper delivery boy who took the papers to all his neighbors on his bike, with his big Labrador retriever running behind the bike. He also worked in the grocery store bagging goods at the check-out stand.

His father owned a tiny, unsuccessful photography business, and his mother was a nurse, who left nursing to help start his father's business. Sadly, his father was an alcoholic who regularly got drunk, became maudlin or super-critical, filling the household with his irrational rantings and repetitive songs hollered out while pounding on the old electric Hammond organ. John grew up partly afraid, avoiding the verbal attacks by hiding in his bedroom, or taking his little boat out on the Sound to find peace. Sometimes he escaped to the home of his wealthy neighbors down the beach, who had a warmly welcoming lifestyle and served as a "second chosen family" for John.

After high school he escaped not only his family but the limited horizons of his working-class town by going to Stanford University where he worked his way through by waiting on tables and taking out big student loans. None of his high school guidance counselors had encouraged him to go to Stanford... Washington State University was about the farthest anybody from Bremerton ever went... but John had a random meeting on the street with an older friend who encouraged him to apply to Stanford directly, skipping the guidance counselor. John followed his advice and was accepted.

By the time I met him he had become a teacher, partly because he opposed the Vietnam War and wanted to avoid the draft. He had also joined the Civil Rights Movement and moved even further away from his roots...all the way to New York City. Meanwhile his younger brother had been drafted and was serving in Vietnam.

John could not have been more unlike my father. In fact, he was a lot like my mother. Kind, generous, smart, under-stated, lean, blue-eyed, blonde, idealistic, optimistic, peaceful, reliable, and shy. He had no apparent temper and no expressed needs. He was entirely trustworthy. But unlike my mother, who seemed to naturally know who she was, he was searching for his real self, his true identity, his spiritual purpose.

John did not have a father whose identity he had naturally internalized as part of growing up. He had not wanted to be anything like his alcoholic father. Instead, he had to invent his own idea of who he wanted to become. He was always studying philosophy and various disciplines of thought and personal practice. He was the most disciplined person I ever met. I was amazed to witness his search for truth, for purpose, for connection, which has continued throughout his life. He has been successful in this search, visibly becoming more and more of his real self, more and more sure of who he is. He served from 1988 to 2016 on the staff of YouthBuild USA, Inc., leading the departments of training and leadership development. As he got older his confidence, his energy level, and his willingness to take responsibility in a visible way all steadily increased. In 2010 he was ordained by Thich Nhat Hanh as a Dharma teacher in Thich Nhat Hanh's Buddhist Order of Inter-being. Now, as a Buddhist priest, he confidently leads others in their search.

Going back to the day of our meeting: the moment when Martin Luther King Jr. was assassinated was highly emotional for everyone in my generation who had any contact with the Movement. The day after his murder I went to the demonstration in Central Park and hovered around the stage, frantic with feeling, wanting to somehow take the microphone and communicate the depth of my grief, rage, and desire for a better world. Of course, I did not seize the mike, I just paced back and forth near it. I walked in the large march out of the park toward downtown with my friends, until several police officers galloped through our group on their horses, forcing us to disperse. I threw my large cup of iced coffee at the rapidly passing officer, hitting his leg. I surprised myself with that random act of reactive aggression. I realized that I could have gotten myself in trouble. Fortunately, he did not stop. Clearly, I had a well of violent rage stirred up by the assassination of Reverend King.

A few years later I went with John to a non-violent demonstration against the Vietnam War in DC outside the White House. As a longtime follower of Gandhi's work, John was committed to nonviolence. He had decided in advance that he was willing to be arrested, to make his stand against the war. A small group had positioned themselves on the ground, sitting in front of the White House, prepared for the tear gas and the intimidation of the police. I had not made the decision to be arrested when I went with John to the demonstration. I stood with the crowd, looking at John seated with the disciplined group of demonstrators facing the police who were sitting on their motorcycles, staring down the demonstrators, revving up their motors as if about to attack. The demonstrators were gently waving their hands toward the police with uplifted peace signs, quietly singing, "All we are saying, is, 'Give peace a chance!'"

Suddenly my heart rose up. I felt I belonged at John's side, in solidarity, taking the same risk he was willing to take for the cause of peace. I crossed the rope line and sat down beside him, facing the police. This was as much an expression of love for John as it was a political statement. It was a spontaneous expression of what was to become a lifelong commitment to each other, in the context, always, of being committed to something larger than ourselves.

I remember very well the day my older sister said to me regarding Leroy, "Dorothy, if you marry Leroy, your relationship will become your life's work. He will be at the center of everything you decide. He will consume your energy. He is a very complicated and demanding man. You may choose to do that, but you must understand

in advance what you are doing." I believe that she was right. Had
Leroy and I married, he and his own work would have absorbed
enormous amounts of my attention. The wonderful second wife he
married and stayed with until his death, Kathy Sofos Looper, devoted much of her life to supporting and enhancing his projects and his
life, once he put alcohol completely behind him and stepped into his
shoes as an effective social entrepreneur. Together they produced a
treatment center for addicts called Reality House West, also a residential home for the mentally ill called Hotel Agape, plus a hotel for
the homeless called the Cadillac Hotel in the Tenderloin district of
San Francisco, all while raising four children together. I think Leroy
and I would have faced each other and his priorities in a similar way.
We might have had ongoing struggles of various sorts with each
other, and, like Kathy, I might have become the support system for
his big ideas to save people in dire straits. I would probably not have
had the extra energy to create the Youth Action Program or the
YouthBuild movement.

Marrying John was different. He and I stood, or sometimes sat,
side-by-side, sometimes even back-to-back, facing outward to the
world. He supported my big projects. We had minimum struggle,
minimum conflict, minimum differences, minimum worry between
us. Both of us had been trained into a generous but nonetheless
privileged white identity of social justice activists. We easily loved
and trusted each other. Our energy was always available, in tandem,
to face outward to the world, supporting each other.

Not too long after John and I met on that Sunday after Martin
Luther King Jr. was killed, I called John in his apartment on East 11th
Street, from my apartment on East 4th Street, and said something like,
"John, you are the first man I have been attracted to since I broke up
with someone I was deeply in love with. It is a wonderful relief to
know that I can be attracted to someone else. It is very good for me
to spend time with you. Would you be willing to spend some time
together to help me recover from my sense of despair and loneliness?"

He answered immediately, "Yes! I'll be right over." This was a
response that flowed from his generosity. It had nothing to do with

being attracted to me, because he wasn't. It was just kindness. But it resulted in our building a deep friendship. We talked endlessly together and traveled to Vermont and Puerto Rico with friends. Pretty soon John moved into my apartment, as a friend. Shortly after, John's best friend from High School, Marty Hotvet, moved to NYC and joined us.

At the time, John was in a long-distance romance with a woman named Louise on the West Coast. In 1970, Louise moved to NYC to be with John. At that point John, Marty, and Louise planned to move to the Harlem house on W. 137th Street owned by our other teacher friend, Tim Parsons. John asked me if I would come too because he didn't want to lose his close friendship with me. I didn't want to lose him either, so all four of us moved to 212 W. 137th Street between 7th and 8th Avenue, in Central Harlem. We joined several other white Harlem Public School teachers, including Tom Roderick, who all lived there together because they believed that if they were to teach in Harlem they should also live in Harlem. John roomed with Louise. I stayed in a tiny room on the third floor by myself.

I invited John to apply to work at the East Harlem Block Schools as a second-grade teacher. He did. The parents interviewed him and hired him. Our work lives began to merge. We were teaching together with Tom in the same open storefront space with the first and second graders together. At that time, for a brief period, I was both the first-grade teacher and the executive director.

In early 1970, John's relationship with Louise foundered, she left NYC, and I stepped forward. In the spring of 1970, our relationship blossomed into shared love. By this time Leroy had married Pat and successfully created his first drug re-hab center called Reality House on West 125th Street with the active support of his prior parole officer, Sydney Moshette; and his prior boss at Exodus House, Steve Chinlund; and the wealthy couple, Sam and Judy Peabody. He soon moved to California, partly to get away from the pain associated with me. I had also largely emerged from my conflicted grief about not having married him. Healing takes time, but it does happen.

John and I took a kind of honeymoon trip that summer ... four years before we actually got married ... to Nova Scotia. We hitch-hiked all over the area, made love in the blueberry patches by the side of the road and in the fields above the oceans, slept by the side of the road in empty lots and in pretty cemeteries, and sang songs to each other. Someone who gave us a ride in her car taught us a song that became our wedding song. The first verse went like this:

> I haven't got a mansion,
> I haven't any land,
> Not even a paper dollar
> To crinkle in my hand.
> But I can give you morning,
> On a thousand hills,
> And kiss you,
> and give you,
> Seven daffodils.

That was our spirit. We were completely free, without material possessions or aspirations, still working in East Harlem and living in Central Harlem, paying $60/month rent, owning no proper-ty, and having no children. We still sing that song, although now we have a near-mansion, and some land, and some paper dollars. Whenever possible we still love to share "morning on a thousand hills."

In June of 1971, I left my position as Executive Director of the East Harlem Block Schools, and John left his position as teacher. I had decided earlier that it was not appropriate for me as a white woman to remain for a long period of time as the executive director of an or-ganization serving 100% black and Latino children in East Harlem. I had kept my promise to myself to turn the leadership of the school over to a person of color. Judy MacAulay, former board chair of the Block Schools, stepped up. I served as her assistant for three months as she settled in. Then John and I took off in my little blue Volk-swagen bug across the country, with our pet white German Shep-herd, Christy. We planned to explore the world, hike in the Cascade mountains, and go to Latin America on a yearlong expedition.

We started by visiting his parents. That was no fun. I didn't like his father at all, and his parents were both horrified that John and I slept in a combined sleeping bag on their lawn by Puget Sound. His father was upset that John was "shacking up" with "an older woman." Sometimes he referred to me disapprovingly as "an older Jewish woman."

We soon took off on the most wonderful backpacking trip in the Cascade Mountains down the Pacific Crest Trail. It lasted for a full 30 days, covering 200 miles. As we prepared for this hike John revealed his extraordinary attention to detail and his ability to plan for every eventuality. Packing for 30 days in the mountains is no easy trick. But he did it, and we took off with everything we needed on our backs.

The first day out we walked only 4 miles and were exhausted. The last day we walked 22 miles, from dawn to dusk, down and up over mountain after mountain. In between we weathered storms, had gorgeous hikes, and read books including *Fanshen* (an amazing book about the Chinese revolution) and the *Pentagon Papers* (revealing the inside story of the politics behind the Vietnam war). There is nothing like removing oneself from the daily grind, being totally in nature, eating simply, and being together with your beloved partner on a thirty-day hike. We would never be the same. We talked a lot about what we wanted to do in life, where we would want to be in 5 years, 10 years, 20 years. But we actually didn't know the answers to those questions. On that trip I was 29 and John was 27. We fell even more deeply in love.

When we hiked out of the mountains, we were jubilant. We hitch-hiked back to Bremerton to pick up our VW and our dog Christy, and we headed on down to Santa Cruz where we planned to spend a week with my high school friend, Lois— the same one who had joined me to teach the preschool in Harlem in the summer of 1964 and later persuaded me to come to the East Harlem Block Schools. By then she had married my college friend Wally Goldfrank. They lived together on the Santa Cruz campus where Wally was a professor. We planned a short visit, after which we would take off to Latin

America for an unplanned adventure. On our way to Santa Cruz, we stopped to visit Leroy and Kathy in San Francisco. Kathy had the same amazingly welcoming and confident quality that John did: she was comfortable with Leroy and me being friends and was happy to have our families close. Kathy later welcomed Leroy's former partner, Sarah, to San Francisco. She and Leroy provided Sarah with housing in one of their nearby projects as Sarah aged.

Surprisingly, John and I stayed in Santa Cruz for 10 months, encouraged by Lois and Wally, sleeping on their couches in the living room on the campus of the University. We all built a profoundly deep lifelong friendship. Wally brought us food from the dining hall. Our two big dogs took turns, one being in the house and the other locked on the porch because they would otherwise fight. While there, I wrote my Master's thesis for Bank Street College of Education, we participated in campus demonstrations against the war, and John hung out at the bookstore reading widely in his lifelong search for various forms of truth. We had a kind of on-campus sabbatical year, from September 1971 to June of 1972, while the young people across the country were organizing ever more actively against the Vietnam war.

We joined the demonstrations on campus. We actually influenced them, because the students were being more oppositional than we thought was wise. In our opinion they didn't need to attack or disrespect faculty or other students nor shut down the school. They just needed to express their own strong views in the most dramatic and simultaneously respectful ways possible.

While in Santa Cruz we also read all about the primal scream therapeutic approach, and we tried it for a weekend with friends. It was interesting, but we didn't embrace it. Previously I had tried psychotherapy for myself, and I had been trained with Leroy in the "reality therapy" approach to drug counseling. Little by little I was learning the methods of the day, searching for what would work best for me.

As the year went on, John and I gave up the idea of our adventure in Latin America. We felt pulled back to what felt like our roots in East Harlem. After all, the struggle against poverty was critical, we had friends in Harlem and East Harlem where we could belong to a wonderful multi-racial community, and we loved the Block Schools. It seemed like our sabbatical had been long enough. It was time to go home to Harlem. And so we did.

I'll never forget the end of our drive across country as we passed through New Jersey, into New York, back to our big, big City, up the East River Drive to 125th Street, back to the brownstone, our home on 137th Street. This was clearly where we belonged at that moment in our lives. We had left. I had given up my leadership role as a white person in Harlem and turned the reins at the Block Schools over to Judy MacAulay, a highly competent black woman who was also a parent in the school and a resident in the neighborhood. But the magnet of the struggle for justice and equality, for the beloved multi-racial community of action, pulled us back. Fortunately, we were welcome. We were home.

But we were not completely at home with each other. That awful thing that happens when couples have been together for a couple of years had happened to us. Our own deepest distresses had surfaced, had hooked themselves onto our relationship, had discovered each other, and begun to scream. John's core distress pattern that he internalized from his father's criticisms was that he didn't know how to love. His father steadily communicated disappointment that John didn't show his love to him enough and was too busy with his own activities and was therefore selfish. John began to confess to me that he didn't love me, that he couldn't love anyone.

My core distress that I had internalized from my father's criticism was that I was unattractive and therefore unlovable. Not surprisingly, these two distress patterns began to hook each other. John would guiltily confess that he didn't love me. I would feel depressed and unlovable. We both began to suffer, and our relationship was spiraling downward.

Finding a Method of Healing that Worked for Us

One night when we were ensconced in one of these struggles, stuck in guilt, hurt, and hopelessness, we talked about needing some sort of therapy. At that precise moment, my friend Janet Pfunder called on the phone. Janet had attended Harvard/Radcliffe College a year behind me and was part of my friendship group. She had called a few times recently to tell us about the amazing counseling process she had learned and was now certified to teach called Re-evaluation Counseling, aka Co-Counseling. She had previously invited us to her class, but we had repeatedly declined. This time, when she called, we were sitting on the couch in our living room, locked in painful tension, anxiously wondering what to do. We listened to Janet, looked at each other, and said, "OK, we'll try your therapy."

This was one of the best decisions we ever made. Co-counseling solved our problems. We learned the theory and practice, then tackled our underlying distresses, separating them from each other's distress, helping each other overcome the effects. Co-counseling helped us over the hump at that moment, and then kept us on track for the rest of our lives. It also provided a theory and practice that we could gradually integrate into our work in a way that would benefit others. Our life within the Co-Counseling Community is a story in itself … because we both took on major local and national leadership roles for a period of years, in addition to using it personally. (There is more information about co-counseling in the final chapter about Lessons Learned.)

We solved our problems. But we weren't married … not yet. John was still not ready. He couldn't commit. He was still searching for his true self and his meaning in life. He also was not ready to have children. I was 30 years old, ready and waiting… in fact, I was a little impatient.

We Made It!

Without sharing all the ups and downs, I will simply say that we made it! On June 13, 1974, we had a marvelous hippy-style wedding. I sewed both my fancy orange, yellow, and white full-length wedding dress and John's cool daishiki out of the same brightly colored fabric. We drove our blue VW bug to New Jersey to the East Harlem Block Schools spring camp for the big party. We sent rexographed invitations to our friends that asked them to either give us no gifts, or limit gifts to pretty fabrics I could use for sewing. We had no professional photographer, spent hardly any money on the event, took no honeymoon, and exchanged no rings.

Children from the Block Schools sang to us, baked the cake, and decorated our VW Bug. Young Chantay Henderson Jones witnessed the official marriage certificate and Victor Soler was the official bearer of the flower necklace that John presented to me instead of a ring. Our friends Tim Parsons and Tom Roderick played the trombone and the clarinet while we walked happily to the minister who stood in front of the crowd that was sitting on the grass.

Some of our friends asked why we had to get married, why we had to do something so traditional as getting married. Why not just live together? Our answer was twofold: we wanted our parents to have an unembarrassed relationship with their grandchildren; and we wanted to be together for the rest of our lives. When our minister, Rev. Steve Chinlund — the same person who ran Exodus House where Leroy had first worked as a counselor — asked me in a ministerial query the day we got married "WHY" we were getting married, the immediate and only thought that came to my mind was, "Because I want to live with John for the rest of my life."

It was a blessed union, that would indeed last all our lives, and support all our work and dreams. Our worldview was completely in sync. John would stand with me and behind me for the rest of our lives, helping me succeed at every successive venture, making decisive contributions in his own way, and I would do the same for him.

Sadly, there was some painful drama on the wonderful sunny day of our wedding. Three of the third-grade boys in the Block Schools came to us prior to the service and said that a teacher had touched one of them sexually, inappropriately, on his private parts the night before when he was sitting on his lap. They were upset. Already dressed in our wedding garb, in our bedroom, we called the teacher to us and asked if this accusation was true. He confessed that it was. We made him promise to go to therapy, and to take responsibility for never doing anything like that again.

This was in 1974 before there was widespread awareness of the issues related to sexual misconduct. I did not know that I needed to fire the teacher. I thought I just needed to get him to correct himself and apologize. I had no legal advisor. Later I felt guilty that I hadn't understood how serious the action was and had not taken stronger action. Later in my life as the head of various non-profits, more than once I had to fire men accused of similar actions. But the one that occurred on our wedding day just resulted in therapy for the offender. I don't know whether he ever did it again. He said he didn't. He died of AIDS about eight years later.

Most of the time, John and I don't mention this as part of our wedding day. It would cloud the story of that joyous day. But it was definitely part of the Backstory. And it is important for younger readers heading into leadership to know that you will probably face unpredictable imperfections in your life, even on the best of days.

The most important thing was this: I had definitely found the right man to marry, and with a lot of help from our friends and from co-counseling, we got across the bridge. Neither one of us has ever regretted it for even one minute or ever wondered if it was the right decision. I could not be more grateful to John for our lifelong partnership. Behind the scenes, whenever I was scared, or hurt, or uncertain, or sleepless, John has been there to hear my feelings and support my strongest most confident self. We did extraordinary professional work together for decades, each doing what we did best and complementing each other's talents. We have been exceedingly lucky.

CHAPTER 11

From the Block Schools to the New Action Party for a Human Society

As mentioned earlier, in 1969 the Block Schools' board of directors appointed me Executive Director of the East Harlem Block Schools when Tony Ward decided to step away.

One day in 1970 I walked down the stairs at the E. 106th Street Block Nursery School into the basement playground where the four-year-olds and their teachers were playing on the complex wooden jungle gym that staff had constructed. As I appeared on the stairs, two young teachers jumped nervously up from where they were lounging on the equipment. Clearly anxious that I, the Executive Director, would see them as derelict in their duties, they sprang to their feet and joined the children.

That moment bothered me. Staff evidently viewed me as an authority to be feared. They jumped up when I walked in. I was 29 years old. Too young to scare anybody. I didn't want to be separated from my age peers by my role. I made a mental note to get out of that role soon. I could tell it was not only affecting others' view of me, but also my own view of myself in relation to them. I was internalizing the viewpoint of a managing authority and it made me uncomfortable to be always thinking how to get others to do their jobs better.

Around the same time, I attended a gathering at a local settlement house at which a new executive director, a young Latino man, was being ushered in. They were saying good-bye to the middle-aged white woman who had presided for many years over the settlement house. I made another mental note: not to become that woman; not to be the white woman who stayed forever in a leadership role in East Harlem in an organization that should have been led by a person of color.

By then, I was living in the brownstone at 212 West 137th Street in Central Harlem. with a group of friends including several Block Schools teachers. It was a marvelous community household for a group of nine single men and women in our twenties. We shared the kitchen, dining room, and living room space, and we each had our own bedroom. All of us were teachers. All of us became life-long friends. All of us were white. Only two of us were women.

We were treated warmly by the people who lived on the 137th street block between 7th Avenue and 8th Avenue. It was a beautiful block. It had a block association, virtually no crime, and was largely populated by people who looked out for each other and would knock on our door to warn us if the police were ticketing cars. There were a couple of deteriorated buildings, and some apartments filled with depressed and debilitated people, and some absentee landlords. But mostly it was a great place to live.

We never experienced any hostility from the black residents to our presence as white teachers on this block. The general attitude toward us seemed to be that young white teachers who came to live in Harlem must be good folks. During the 18 years we lived there the block also changed. Absentee white landlords were replaced by middle class black homeowners, led by Barbara Ann Teer, who ran the National Black Theatre in Harlem. She and her friends planted and watered lovely baby oak trees up and down the block. Those oaks are today very large and beautiful. One very pleasant memory for me is of the Halloween party that we hosted one year for the children on the block. The block association welcomed our offer, helped to organize it, and all the children on the block came to our home and ducked for apples.

One Saturday night John and I went out to get a snack on 7th Avenue and a gentleman stopped us to ask, "What are you doing here?" We answered, "We live here." He shook his head, stepped back, looked quietly at us and said, "How is it that you are safe here in Harlem but that I can't go to Queens without getting attacked?"

Later, when John and I were married and had a daughter, Sierra, who lived on West 137th Street until she was nine, the story was similar. Starting at age six, Sierra took the school bus every morning to the public elementary school in East Harlem. She was the only white child on the bus. Never, not once, did any child insult her for being white. We remained alert for problems, but never did Sierra complain that she had been mistreated as a white girl by any child on that bus, nor does she now remember any such experience related to her race, although there were two older girls who bullied all the younger children including our daughter.

We had known that racism, defined as mistreatment coming from the race with institutionalized power, was by definition a white problem; but our experience began to suggest that even interpersonal racial hostility was a white, not a black, problem. We never experienced any mistreatment or hostility directed at us as white people living in Harlem.

To the outside world, still totally steeped in racist expectations, it was surprising that we lived in Harlem. There was an article in Newsweek that announced an "influx" of white people into Harlem. It had an arrow pointing to our block. We kept our heads low, believing it should not be a big deal, but still someone had noticed our presence and pointed an arrow to our house in the national news media.

I loved living on 137th Street. Whenever I walked home from the bus stop, I would feel the profound significance of being embedded in the black community. From this vantage point the world looked entirely different from what I saw when looking from the perspective of the privileged white world on the top of Belmont hill where I was raised. I felt I was where I belonged. Every day I got to perceive society from a viewpoint that would keep me rooted on the right side of the struggle for justice and equality.

When we returned from California to NYC and to the Block Schools in 1972, I created a college program in partnership with Bank Street College. As project director, I reported to the Executive Director, Judy MacAulay. Through this program, the parents who served as assistant teachers at the East Harlem Block Schools got certified as head teachers. They got credit for their practical work as teachers, and they took courses in educational theory and practice. They then served their community for decades as certified teachers, eliminating the inequality and the slightly awkward professional relationship that had existed in the Block Schools between the privileged white teachers who passed through on their career path or on their idealistic movement path, and the low-income paraprofessional parent teachers who resided permanently in the neighborhood and had the deepest stake in the schools' excellence.

Conceiving of The New Action Party

I left the Block Schools again in the spring of 1974. I was beginning to feel ready to step into leadership in the national arena. I was convinced that we needed a new political party, one that would unite all people for a more just society that would address the issues of poverty in a more global way. I wanted to do something that went beyond the neighborhood, that would face the need to change our nation.

With the freedom that came from being unemployed, with John's support, in January of 1975 I went off to spend a month with Leroy and Kathy to help tape-record Leroy's life story. We were taping in the evenings and weekends.

During the days I read a lot. I read the history of Students for a Democratic Society, the radical student organization of the sixties, led by Tom Hayden. I was struck with amazement that it had spread so rapidly on such a weak base of knowledge about low-income communities and with such a polarizing political approach. Tom Hayden had spent only one year working in a low-income community in Newark before taking off to become a national leader. Through SDS he attracted large numbers of angry young people who wanted change. Most of them were white and privileged. But it seemed to me that they were doomed not to get change by simply acting on their anger through an oppositional approach.

I conceived of a new political party: The New American Party for Truth, Justice, and Joy.

Given how few people were voting in American elections, I felt that idealistic activists had the obligation to learn how to use the electoral process to take power to create a more just and caring society. It seemed there was an enormous hunger in the country for more real and humane politics, but SDS-style politics seemed to be the wrong approach. I felt that many radicals were hostile to authority and had a certain kind of revulsion against power. But radical idealists would need to come to terms with power and win it to make change.

I sat at the kitchen table at Leroy and Kathy's home and wrote the "Party Papers" of the New American Party for Truth, Justice, and Joy. It was my plan for how to build a totally new kind of people's party. The challenge was to face our responsibility to gain power, but to build toward the responsibility of power with total integrity, slowly, in a way that was clearly designed to engage and serve the interests of the largest number of people in a way that would inspire justifiable trust.

After a month, I returned home. Back in Harlem, I began to build the Party. One by one, I persuaded 70 friends to join me. Five of us — John Bell, Tom Roderick, Susan Kosoff, Tim Parsons, and I — became the core planning group. We went camping in the

Rocky Mountains during the summer of 1975 to think through issues regarding the Party. They were uncomfortable with the name — they thought it was a little too pretentious or idealistic or "corny." They persuaded me to change it to the "New Action Party for a Human Society."

This was, it turns out, the same year that Newt Gingrich and his friends were in the mountains in Utah preparing to take over the country. They had less fear of being pretentious than we did. That summer also turned out to be the moment in which I became pregnant with John's and my daughter, Sierra.

Sierra was born on April 27, 1976, a perfect little girl, destined to bless our lives with her goodness, intelligence, compassion, drive, and conscientiousness. For the first two years of her life, while I was unemployed and primarily caring for her, I worked to build the New Action Party for a Human Society.

I proceeded in a totally unrealistic way. I believed we didn't need money. We used rexograph machines (remember them?) for copying our written materials and we all volunteered our time. We worked only with invisible, ordinary, grassroots folks who had no influence or connections to people with power, with the exception of one college professor and author, Mark Kesselman, who gave us a kind of legitimacy in our own minds.

We thought a Party needed to be built by ordinary people including low-income people of color who had been disconnected from politics and who would work in their own communities to improve the world. None of us had ever participated in any way in any electoral campaign. We were not in a hurry and figured we had 30 years before we would be in a position to gain real power. We were a racially diverse group of powerless idealists with a powerful vision and lots of grassroots experience, but no connections or experience in the world of politics. I suppose it was a continuation of the foot-soldier, out-in-the-field pattern of my life until then, only now I was thinking about how to lead the world forward from that unlikely position.

I wrote a 50-year plan that was pretty good. The plan and the Party Papers were quite easily embraced, with some modifications and additions, by my 70 friends. But I had no strategy or ability to reach more people than the ones I knew personally. If I had had a few million dollars to implement the plan, it might have worked. But I didn't, nor did I try to get any money because I never had a strategy or a vision that involved money or people with money. In fact, our plan involved avoiding all forms of monetary rewards in order to be completely pure and trustworthy.

Part of the plan was to create a Central Action Program focused on one of five key areas of life that we identified as having enormous impact on all Americans, and to demonstrate over twenty years that we could do something so wonderfully and uniquely effective in one key area of life that we deserved to be elected to office. After demonstrating the power of the compassionate, smart, and revolutionary policies and programs we would create, then we would flood the electoral arena with candidates who had already earned the people's trust through the Central Action Program. At that stage we would make a profound political impact and implement more far-reaching policies that would eliminate poverty and injustice and create a world in which every human being could fulfill his or her potential.

The five areas we outlined as potential Central Action Programs that affected all Americans were: 1) meaningful and well-paid work for all; 2) a dignified and secure old age; 3) a positive role for young people in society; 4) protection of the environment; and 5) health care. We would probably choose the same issues today, although I would be inclined now to embed them in understanding that we need to restructure our over-arching economic system to be a fair and sharing economy. The rules governing our economy have changed a lot since 1975, resulting in greater concentration of wealth and power at the top.

I was infected with a driving impulse to improve the world to the best of my ability — perhaps early influenced by Robert Frost's poems or the Girl Scout pledge in which we raised our hands to commit to "do my duty to help other people at all times." However, I also was eager to see if someone else had already thought of what I had in mind and could carry it out better than I could. I went to meetings of existing progressive Third Parties. Unfortunately, none of them appealed to me. They all reeked of the same Harvard-style domination by fast-talking white men who created a culture that was intellectually competitive, unemotional, and slightly alien to me as a woman. Furthermore, none of them were rooted in low-income communities.

So, it appeared that there was no escape. I would have to grapple with my own insecurities as a woman and move steadily toward national leadership to gain power to serve the people and eliminate injustice.

I knew I had a certain terror of visible leadership, despite the fact that I had already been given surprising leadership responsibility in one organization in East Harlem. I first noticed this fear in 1971, after I had been executive director of the East Harlem Block Schools for two years. One day a community relations official at the Bowery Savings Bank, Pazel Jackson, said to me, "If you keep going at this rate, you will be appointed Commissioner of Human Resources in New York City." That struck me as a shocking idea. I absolutely had no ambition to become a commissioner. In fact, it was terrifying. I had such a revulsion to his comment that I took my reaction into a therapy session to try to understand what was at the root of it. In the session I got a bloody nose and wept at various early experiences that made me afraid of leadership. It wasn't that anything bad had happened to me as a leader. The fear seemed to flow partly from first grade when I discovered that everything seemed easier for me than for the other kids, and I didn't understand why. It was somehow profoundly scary.

The next four years, during which I was "Chairman" of the New Action Party, I grappled with my underlying resistance to imagining myself as a leader who would acquire power or visibility. Every time any of us said the word "Party," it forced us all to realize that we were talking about power, not protest. Building a "Party" meant building access to power. It was a very good antidote to self-depre-cation, avoidance of responsibility, or timidity of any kind. It was one of the reasons for calling ourselves a Party. I felt that the mem-bers of the various oppositional movements were too content to pro-test, to be morally correct, to be angry. What they really needed to do was take responsibility and gain the power to make a difference.

Bringing Hope to Life

CHAPTER 12

Launching the Central Action Program of the New Action Party

To build the New Action Party (NAP), we established a core group of participants in Boston, New York City, and San Francisco. My friend Sue Kosoff, who had been a teacher at the East Harlem Block Schools in the 1960's, led it in Boston. Leroy led it in San Francisco. We designed and practiced what we called Action Support Groups, in which a small group of members would listen to each other's ideas for how they would like to change the world, and back each other in launching their projects. We thought these should be set up across the country as a core part of our fifty-year plan to activate ordinary people.

We held retreats, wrote a lot of wonderful documents, and tried to integrate the ideas of Re-evaluation Counseling (aka Co-counseling) into our practices to insure a culture of safety, mutual support, and rational thinking.

However, I got restless and decided it was time for me to start the Central Action Program that we had conceived of as part of our fifty-year plan. The idea was that we would demonstrate the ability to solve a key problem facing society, using our principles and practices, over time. This would win us the right and the reputation to run successfully for office, so maybe in 20 or 30 years we would begin to run for office.

For me, of the five core issues we had laid out, the most appealing one for a Central Action Program was creating a positive role for young people in society, and especially the young people who had been kicked to the curb by the various injustices of poverty and racism. Soon after I began to propose doing that, one of our members, Micaela Hickey, who worked at Bank Street College of Education, saw a request for proposals (RFP) for funding from a federal agency that seemed a reasonable resource to support this idea. Micaela brought me the RFP.

I leaped on it. The Community Anti-Crime Program of the Law Enforcement Assistance Administration was offering substantial grants for community-based initiatives designed to prevent crime by engaging the community in activities designed by the community. This initiative emerged from legislation created by Congressman John Conyers, an African American from Detroit, who deeply understood how low-income communities could help themselves to diminish crime.

Writing this proposal was my very first effort to obtain federal funds. I knew how to write. But I had no experience writing federal proposals. I had a colleague who had won a federal grant. I asked to read his winning proposal so I could learn the ropes. It was a wonderful model that provided great guidance. The discipline with which the written proposal had to respond precisely to the detailed questions in the Request for Proposals was clear. I set out to do it.

Starting this project was scary. Just before starting to write the proposal, I attended a weekend co-counseling workshop in which I explored my fears of leadership and visibility. I found myself standing up in front of 200 people making a commitment that went like this: "On my honor, I pledge, from this moment forward, to succeed at everything, let all my abilities flourish, or die trying." It was a momentous commitment, "to succeed at everything." When I returned home and shared it with Tom Roderick in our kitchen on W. 137th Street, he said, "That doesn't sound wise. You might choose to die trying. Why don't you change it to, "On my honor, from this moment forward, I promise to succeed at everything, let all my abilities flourish, and enjoy myself in the process." That struck me as extremely wise advice, so I changed it. To this day I repeat that commitment on a regular basis. In Co-counseling, there is a regular practice of making commitments that counteract feelings that we carry from past distress experiences. Powerless feelings are widespread. This commitment against powerlessness was useful. Over the years I have developed a multitude of commitments helpful in counteracting both personal and societal hurts I have experienced.

With that particular commitment in mind, I wrote the proposal. Day and night, in the office at 94 East 111th Street, with Peggy Ray, another NAP member, volunteering to help me with the typing, the re-writing, and all the details. It was the first of a lifetime of repeat performances of all-night proposal-writing experiences working to get federal funds.... for Youth Action Program, for YouthBuild, re-entry programs, and all sorts of anti-poverty initiatives over the subsequent years.

We submitted that first ambitious proposal on time. It described a process by which we would engage seven different groups of teenagers in East Harlem, on different blocks, to implement community improvement projects of their own design. I did not say what the projects would be, because that would be up to the young people. I just described the process of engaging the teenagers in designing and implementing them.

One of the requirements for submitting this proposal was getting a fiscal sponsor. I asked the board of directors of the East Harlem Block Schools if we could submit it under their legal 501c3 corporation. Of course, they said yes. I don't remember if I clearly understood the implications of this move. Getting a federal grant for what would be the central action program of the New Action Party for a Human Society meant that we would have to abandon the Party, because a federal grant can't fund the development of a political Party! I don't remember when I realized that, but it did cause the eventual abandonment of the Party. Not only would it be illegal to use federal funds to build a Party, but the Youth Action Program took all of my attention. The concept of a Party was of course nowhere referenced in the proposal itself.

A few weeks later I got a call from a man named Jeff Nugent, who worked for the Community Anti-Crime Program. He said our proposal had promise. He wanted to come from DC and meet me in East Harlem to talk about it and to suggest a few modifications.

I will never forget sitting with Jeff in our office in the basement at 94 E. 111th Street. He told me that the proposal was overall excellent, but it suffered from a kind of self-effacing quality. He walked me through it and asked me to take out all the language that he identified as understating our proposed projects and impact. He also said that the budget would not be acceptable because we were proposing equal pay for everyone including the director and that would be viewed by the government as inappropriate. He said I had to pay the director more than the rest of the staff. The proposal was to pay each of us $11,000/year plus benefits. Back in 1974 that was not a stunningly low salary, but it was a modest level of pay. We had set the salaries at a modest level to make sure we were attracting people for their level of commitment, not for their financial self-interest.

I did what he suggested. I took out all the language he said was self-effacing, I raised my salary to $14,000/year, and I re-submitted the proposal to launch the Youth Action Program. Then we waited, the way people always wait to see if their proposal has won the competition, or not.

Victor Ortiz and Chantay Henderson Jones, founding teenagers of YAP

CHAPTER 13

Early Youth Action Program
including Another Go-Round as White Girl in the Ghetto

The money came! It was about $220,000. My first task was to hire eight staff members — one administrative assistant, and seven community organizers who would each create a youth-run community improvement project designed by the young people in the neighborhood.

Hiring the Staff

True to the Block Schools' basic philosophy of reversing power relationships in order to create equal partnerships between traditionally more powerful and less powerful groups, and thus to get the best possible decisions and to generate enormous energy by counteracting the powerlessness of poor people and the unaware arrogance of professionals, I set up a hiring committee of youth plus a couple of our adult volunteers from the New Action Party for a Human Society.

By this time, we had attracted a group of teenagers who obviously were eager to be involved and had shown themselves to be reliable: Chantay Henderson Jones, Victor Ortiz, Kenny Cox, Billy Cox, Tony Minor, Cynthia Orchart, Taino Cruz, Jenny Macias, John Sainz, Freddy Acosta, and others. We divided into two groups, then arranged for each group to hold interviews two afternoons a week. We had 60 candidates from which to choose seven.

We put together a set of questions and designed several role-plays. They planned to ask how people would change the world if they had the power. They also wanted to see how a person would react to a real situation likely to occur with teenagers, so the role-plays were important to them. In the first interview they actually did a role-play without telling the candidate. They became deliberately unruly and rude during the interview, even throwing spitballs at each other. The candidate had no clue as to what was going on. He was speech-less. Afterwards the group reflected on the fact that this had not been fair or respectful, and decided to invite this candidate back for a second interview if he would come. They determined henceforth never to do a role-play without getting the permission of the candidate. He did return for a second interview, but did not happen to be selected.

At the close of each interview, in the decision-making stage, we always followed this process: we would do a quick go-round, in which each interviewer would say "yes," "no," or "maybe." That way we could get a sense of how close we were to consensus, and also make sure that each young person's initial judgment was equally re-spected before the most talkative persuaded the others of their point of view. Then we would go around again to listen to the reasons behind all of their opinions, and discuss until consensus to hire or not to hire was reached.

We interviewed, and interviewed, and interviewed, every afternoon for at least two months. It was a useful project in itself. Throughout the interviews the teenagers learned a lot from the complicated philosophical and political answers they received to their questions. It was not only educational but very empowering, as the typical roles between youth and adults were reversed. They got to exercise their power and judgment on the most critical question that would determine the success of our venture: that is, which of these adults would become the full-time paid staff employed to guide the youth?

About ten of us would sit around a long table each afternoon for a couple of hours in our crowded little room in the basement of the East Harlem Block Schools at 94 East 111th Street, still at that time the most crowded block in New York City.

One afternoon we interviewed Orlando Rivera, a young man who had grown up in East Harlem, graduated from Yale University, and was returning to his community to contribute. On our rapid go-round every single person in the room said, "Yes!" This was the first time we experienced unanimous approval on the first go-round. A cheer went up, Victor started stamping his feet, all of us pounded on the table in unison, with total glee that we had found a guy who impressed everyone so much, on the first go-round. "Yes! Yes! Yes!" We hired Orlando. Of course, we had also checked his references. I made a point of always checking these in depth before each interview, so the young people would internalize the importance of building a positive track record, and so we would have sufficient information in hand to inform our final decision.

One by one, we put together our staff. It was an intense, highly committed staff: Orlando Rivera, Raphael Flores, Maria Anglada, David Calvert, Kwame Gandy, Julie Cherry, Vicky Eye, Kent Edwards, Ros Greenstein, John Bell, and me. We discovered later that all but one of this group had birthdays in the first two weeks of March, making us Pisces. We didn't know what to make of that coincidence, but we liked it!

After hiring them, I learned slowly more about the underlying ideologies that informed their commitment. Among them we had one born-again Christian, one Marxist, one Maoist, one Democratic Socialist, one Black Nationalist, and one Civil Rights activist. We also had a couple of regular neighborhood organizers with no ideology beyond the commitment to make a difference. Three of them had grown up in East Harlem or still lived there. We had a marvelous week-long orientation and training in which we bonded with each other and got our minds around our basic principles, and then....

Launching the Projects

We were off and running! What a thrilling time it was. The beginning of 1979. Each organizer was responsible for finding a group of young people on a block somewhere in East Harlem; getting office, church, or basement space donated on that block for gatherings; helping the youth come up with a tangible and substantial community improvement project; finding a supportive group of neighborhood adults to help; and raising the money to make the young people's vision a reality. We planned to tie the seven local projects together with a Youth Congress, on the theory that once the young people were engaged in building something of their own design on their own block, they would become interested in taking another step toward political and policy issues affecting the whole neighborhood. This was the basis of leadership development: demonstrating that you could make a difference. The larger youth movement could then emerge organically from very tangible youth-designed projects.

This worked. The energy we unleashed was quite wonderful. The poem below was written by a 12-year-old boy in March of 1979. It expresses the clear and simple vision of loving kindness expressed consistently by all the young people as they developed their projects.

THE WAY PEOPLE SHOULD BE TREATED

by Hilton Marrera, East Harlem

> Bums should be treated nice
> Give them Food.
> Give them Clothes.
> Give them love.
> Respect them.
>
> Children should be treated nice.
> Give them love.
> Give them things.
> Kiss them.
>
> There should be no fighting.
> Be friends every time.
> No smoking, no drinking wine.
>
> The old people: help them when you see them.
> Give them love.
> Respect them.
> Don't bug the old people, kiss them.
>
> Little kids that don't know how to do nothing —
> Teach them how to play.
> Don't hit them.
> If they're in trouble, help them.
>
> If you see somebody sick
> Call the ambulance.
> Take them to the hospital.
>
> The way people should be treated,
> Forever, with love.

Not only did poetry emerge, but the organizing process worked as planned. Great ideas emerged on every block where our staff organized a group. We created the following:

- a playground, park, and huge mural on 103rd Street;

- a Home Away from Home for young single mothers and their children on 118th Street and 2nd Avenue;

- a Leadership High School on 110th Street and 5th Ave.;

- the Youth Action Restoration Crew, rebuilding housing on Second Avenue and 119th Street;

- the Johnson Housing Projects Youth Patrol to prevent crime in the projects on 112th Street between Park and 3rd Avenues;

- Hotline Cares — an emergency telephone staffed by young adults in an office on Lexington Ave. and 112th St., giving emergency service to teenagers people anywhere in East Harlem;

- the East Harlem Youth Congress based at our headquarters on 111th Street and Park Avenue.

The spirit of YAP! Some of our young leaders enjoying being together.

Each block's project was, in its own way, original, state of the art, emerging directly from the ideas and needs and vision of the young people in their own neighborhood. It turns out that teenagers are always a few years ahead of the adults working with them, in terms of the accuracy of their ideas about what they need and want. Each project was implemented with ingenuity and dedication by the organizer, supported by me in various ways. And then, with all the projects united in organizing neighborhood-wide conferences, The East Harlem Youth Congress produced a Youth Agenda for the Eighties that was a smart platform for political change in the community and that laid the groundwork for creation of the Coalition for Ten Million Dollars that we would launch in 1984. (See Appendix B for the East Harlem Youth Agenda for the Eighties. It reflects conditions remarkably similar to the ones we still face today, sadly.)

The Conflict and Resolution

In addition to our successes, we naturally had some struggle, conflict, and drama. The hard-edged ideologies of some of our organizers created factions and friction. Some of them, the black nationalist and the Maoist in particular, began to quietly oppose my being in leadership, as a white woman from a privileged background. Somewhere around 1980, I got a call from Jose Cintron, the District Manager of East Harlem's Community Planning Board, who said, "Dorothy, are you aware that some of your staff are undermining you and planning to try to get rid of you because you are white, and they believe an organization in Harlem shouldn't be led by a white woman? I just thought I would put you on the alert. Are you aware that somehow some of the young people have been turned against you and are getting a petition signed for the board of directors asking for your removal?"

There is nothing worse than learning that people are plotting against you. It's a terrible feeling to learn that people who work for you are actually against you, talking about you behind your back, undermining you, while pretending to respect you. Not being inclined to paranoia, being told by a respected source that in fact people were out to get me, was deeply unsettling. Those were some very sleepless nights.

I decided to confront it head on. I scheduled a meeting with Kwame, the black nationalist. We had a candid and full conversation. He confirmed that while he had nothing against me personally, he was ideologically against having a white director in East Harlem. The end of our conversation went something like this:

I said, "I understand that you oppose a white person being in charge in East Harlem, and I understand why. But I have lived and worked in this community for 16 years. I decided a while ago not to withhold my abilities just because I am white. I started this youth movement in East Harlem instead of somewhere else because it is the closest thing to my own community that I have; and it is where I personally know a lot of teenagers. I think the idea of Youth Action is the right idea and I want to see it through. As soon as there is a person of color on staff who can take over, I will turn over the leadership. Do you think anyone on our staff is ready to do that?"

"No," he said. "I don't think any of our current staff could do what you do as well as you are doing it."

"Then," I said, "Can you agree to support me until there is such a person? There is no point in undermining our project in the meantime."

"Yes. I will agree to back you up. I'll tell the others."

He was true to his word, and that immediate crisis was over. However, sadly, I learned much later that the pressure on one of our black teenagers who had collaborated closely with me and as a result been called names and insulted, was so great she carried pain from the hurt for many years. Pressures within the black community regarding relationships with white leaders are a complicated reality to be named and understood.

In 1983 I made the move to turn leadership over to a person of color. By that time, we had moved into a huge building on the corner of 110th Street and Fifth Avenue, succeeded in getting separate funding for each of our community-improvement projects, and become a strong presence in East Harlem. By that time, we had an extremely wise and skilled deputy director, Milo Stanojevich, who was of Peruvian background. I announced to the staff and youth at one of our meetings, with his agreement, that he would become the executive director. Then I went to the board of directors of the Block Schools to let them know of my plans. The board continued to be entirely low-income black and Latino parents — pragmatic, deeply compassionate, and not ideological. Some were the same parents who had originally hired and promoted me years earlier.

They said, "No way." Ethel Velez, then chairman of the board, sat me down and said firmly and with great love, "Dorothy, you are thinking of leaving for the wrong reason. You want to turn this over to the deputy director because you are white and he is Latino. We have worked with you for almost twenty years in this community. We know you and trust you. We know you better than we know him, and we think you are more street savvy than he is. He's not even from East Harlem. We will not let you quit for the wrong reasons, just because you're white. Stay here. Stay in leadership. You're doing something important."

Once again, a wise head stopped me from leaving, from limiting my contribution based on race, and offered me a welcome to stay put, as a human being, in partnership with and subordinate to the community in which I had come to belong. The operative word here is subordinate. White people in communities of color can effectively contribute our full talents, as long as we make sure we are accountable to the community, responsive and subordinate to wise leaders within it, who will make sure that our judgments are accurately based in the reality they experience.

Ethel Velez and Carmen Maristany Ward at the 50th anniversary of EHBS, wise leaders forever

John Bell and Chantay Jones, lifelong friends from YAP

Reunion of YAP members at the 40th anniversary in 2018

CHAPTER 14

The Youth Action Restoration Crew
The First YouthBuild Program

One of the organizers we hired was David Calvert, son of the Reverend George Calvert, an East Harlem minister who had come to the neighborhood as part of a group of white ministers in the fifties, to bring increased resources for community development. George had created Hope Community, a very successful local agency focused on building affordable housing. David had been raised in the neighborhood, gone to Grinnell College, then abroad for a year, and now was ready to return to his home. He was 24 years old.

It's important to get to know David in this chapter, because 30 years later, he became the leader of the YouthBuild movement in

Mexico and Central America, bringing the same principles and ideals to impoverished neighborhoods and hopeful youth that he espoused at age 24. Still later, he returned to East Harlem to become executive director of the Youth Action YouthBuild program in East Harlem in its 33rd year, and after that he became coordinator of the New York City YouthBuild Collaborative to ensure ongoing funding to all the YouthBuild programs in the city. In 2023 he still serves effectively in that role, persuading the City Council every year to fund its YouthBuild programs. David's history is unique, but it also is representative of the life-long commitment many directors of local YouthBuild programs have made. Once they experience the deep satisfaction of making a real difference, implementing a philosophy and culture of love and empowerment, they tend to stay on the path.

David was hired to work with Chantay and Victor and their friends to do the gut rehab of a building at 2328 Second Avenue. He knew nothing really about construction, but he was a master at persuasion, connection, follow-through, and Hope.

He persuaded the city administration to let us officially use the building for a training site. Far from giving us the building for $1 as conventional wisdom had anticipated due to its being an abandoned building the city had no use for, when the city leaders realized we had a federal grant, they required $150/month rent for the training site. They saw a clever way to transfer some federal funds into the city budget.

David got the young people immediately to work as volunteers, gutting the building. He pulled the Renegades into the project — a former gang that had rebuilt a large tenement across the street and was one of the original sources of inspiration for Victor, who had been impressed as a boy by seeing older street kids reconstruct that abandoned building. There is nothing quite as good as having older boys serving as constructive role models on the block.

After a couple months of demolition, David and I were standing on the corner of 119th Street and Second Avenue, surveying the work done so far. "We'll have it done in no time," he said. "We just have to raise some money, get an architect, some contractors, teach the young people how to do the carpentry, and it should take about five months."

In fact, it took five years. But David stuck with it every step of the way. The city government took him through a complex rigamarole. The director of housing at the NYC Department of Housing Preservation and Development at the time, Joe Biber, told me candidly at the ribbon cutting ceremony in 1984: "We tried everything to get rid of David. We didn't think community-based housing development with teenagers doing the construction was a workable project. In general, we didn't have a lot of faith in community-based organizations doing housing. So, we gave him a lot of paperwork assignments. First it would be one thing, and then another. But every time, David would come back with a great written package of exactly what we had asked for, and it was clear he was not going away, and he knew what he was doing. So, after a year or two of that dance, we decided to give him some money."

This was an unusually candid admission of deliberate manipulations by well-intentioned but condescending bureaucrats aimed to derail what they considered an overly idealistic community-based project. It stuck in my memory.

Interestingly, what they gave us was not actually money. They did not have grants of that type to give. But once David had won the officials' respect, they found a way to provide resources.

This is often true of civil servants: they have ways to get around their own rules when they are convinced the virtue of a project warrants it. Since the city owned the building, the official put it on the city's list of buildings to be repaired, and then put up all the funds for the plumbing, heating, electricity, and roofing, and subcontracted with us to do it under the category of repairs. Only after the building was complete did the city transfer ownership of it to us.

This was a great lesson. Over and over again, we would learn that government officials could make things happen if they decided we were trustworthy, skilled, determined, persevering, and not attacking or embarrassing them in any way.

At the beginning, the young people doing the work volunteered after school. Some of them got paid with CETA funds. CETA stands for Comprehensive Employment and Training Act. It was President Jimmy Carter's big jobs program that allowed community-based agencies all across the country to hire local residents for all sorts of jobs. It was useful to us, although we only had a small number of CETA after-school "slots." There were in total about 200 youth who helped build 2328 2nd Avenue, most of them as volunteers. We had positioned this project as a voluntary community improvement activity for young leaders. Many of them were Victor's friends from the block. They named themselves the Youth Action Restoration Crew: "YARC", for short.

These CETA slots provided another lesson for me. Since we had only 3 slots paid for, but we had about five young people working steadily, we made an agreement among us to split the money among the five. The three would pick up their checks, and then redistribute it among the five. This seemed a good solution to a shortage of resources and an abundance of eager youth. But when the group of young people who had been persuaded to turn against me by the ideologues turned out to include one who was said to be prepared to report to the government that I was making the CETA workers share their pay, I realized the absolute danger of doing anything against government regulations even when it was in the interests of the people involved and was not a violation of the purpose of the program. Suddenly, because I had tried to figure out a way to help, I was vulnerable to attack by one of the people I was helping. I vowed never to make that mistake again.

There is always someone likely to be mad at the boss, so the boss needs to be impeccable in order to ward off attacks that can distract from the actual work. I decided then and there never to collude with anyone to violate any rules under which we operate, even if the action was entirely well intentioned. If there were rules that needed to be changed, my job would be to try to change them, not violate them.

Attacks on leaders will occur regardless, made up with rumors and false accusations, but they are less powerful when false than when true. Attacks on leaders are not always about their race or gender or class; sometimes it's just about deep resentment toward people with authority, often connected unconsciously to parents and transferred to bosses. I did find that attacks virtually disappeared after about three years, once I had weathered a few and had clearly established my resilience, my effectiveness, and my trustworthiness. Besides, from a practical point of view, if people see that they cannot actually succeed in getting rid of the boss through their attacks, it doesn't seem so attractive to engage in attacks and they fade away.

By 1981, three years into Youth Action Program, things had fallen into place. We had moved out of the East 111th Street basement into a large new building on the corner of 5th Avenue and 110th Street that had been given to the East Harlem Block Schools by Stella Saltonstall, a wealthy and generous supporter. We had developed the Youth Agenda for the Eighties. Attacks on me seemed mostly over, as far as I could tell. A few staff changes had been made. And factions among us had ended.

In 1981, out of the blue, Larry Kressley from the Public Welfare Foundation called me on my office phone and said, "The Foundation is interested in connecting youth in the 'underclass' to the workforce." He asked if we wanted to run an employment training program. I told him, "No, we're running a leadership development program. But thanks for asking."

I hung up and thought, "Now that was a pretty stupid answer. Here I have the unusual situation of a foundation calling me, and I can't think fast enough to realize that YARC could be framed as an employment training program." I called him back and said I thought we could figure out how to turn YARC into an employment training program without sacrificing the leadership development focus.

This was probably the first time that the question of how we defined the project to attract funds reared its head. Later, in 1989, after

YARC had been re-named as YouthBuild and replicated successfully with private funds around the country and we were developing federal legislation to replicate it nationally, I would write a two-page summary answering the question "What is YouthBuild and Where Does It Fit?" This was to respond to the staff director of the Senate appropriations committee who had said to me, "You had better decide what this is, and where it fits. It can't be all things to all people." Personally, I thought the power of its success was precisely in its comprehensiveness — it was an alternative school, an employment training program, a leadership development program, a national service opportunity, a re-entry program for ex-offenders, a crime prevention program for the community, and a housing program. In sum, it was a comprehensive community development program. It all fit together so well, doing so many things at once. It was highly efficient.

I have maintained this position for decades, but in fact some funding sources have been attracted to YouthBuild for just one aspect or another. For example: Gates Foundation chose us as a school, preparing students for post-secondary education; The US Department of Labor (DOL) funded us once as a demonstration re-entry program; The Corporation for National and Community Service (CNCS) liked us as a community service program; the Office of Juvenile Justice and Delinquency Prevention (OJJDP) funded us as a mentoring program to prevent crime.

Very few funders are set up to understand and support the power of a comprehensive combination of elements. When I looked at the workforce development system, the school system, and the service system, I saw that what each one lacked was what the others had, creating one-sided systems that did not respond in a balanced way to the needs and interests of the youth. Because we were free to create a program that was guided by the young people's needs and interests, we had the opportunity and the obligation to integrate all the aspects that they needed and wanted. We did just that, and continued doing it over decades, fitting the various funders into the package, but later passing legislation that defined the broader comprehensive scope as the definition of what would become the federally funded YouthBuild program.

Later, when the funding world named me as a "social entrepreneur," I realized that what I had done in partnership with the youth and community was create a new solution outside the existing siloed and often failing systems, and then created a funding stream to sustain it. The whole adventure worked!

It wouldn't have worked without David Calvert's persistent and loving energy. Here he is years later, talking with Antonio Ramirez, a YouthBuild graduate leader, on the steps of Capitol Hill after meeting together with elected officials.

Our Daughter's Heart Surgery

John and I had given birth to our daughter, Sierra (Rainbow) Stoneman-Bell, in 1976, two years after we had married. "Rainbow" is in parentheses because we did not put that on her birth certificate. We were torn between our hippy tendencies that wanted to include Rainbow as part of her real name, and our protective conservatism that thought we would somehow cause her harm by giving her a hippy identity. In those days it was radical enough to hyphenate her last name!

She was born in the heat of the development of the New Action Party. For the first two years of her life, I did not work full-time. I focused my attention largely on my baby girl, and the simultaneous birthing of the new political party. I had two consultant jobs to support us, and our family still lived in our communal home in Central Harlem at 212 W. 137th Street where our rent was minimal.

Sierra started going to early pre-school for three days a week at age nine months, at Bank Street College of Education. She loved it. John and I loved it. She made lasting friendships there. With a wonderful pre-school program available at such an early age for her, we were able to balance our lives between parenting, working, and starting the new Party.

In 1978, when John and I worked together on starting the Youth Action Program, as the beginning of the central action program of the New Action Party for a Human Society, Sierra was two years old. She participated in a lot of our activities, including coming to the first abandoned building that we started to rebuild on East 107th Street. Our family will never forget the little red rubber boots that we found in the abandoned building and took home for Sierra to keep. When Sierra graduated from college many years later, she returned to New York City, where she served as the development director for Youth Action Program in her first full-time professional job in the non-profit sector. Now, Sierra serves on the Board of Directors of the Youth Action YouthBuild Program that still thrives in East Harlem! Life's continuities are deeply meaningful and moving to me.

Unfortunately, Sierra's life was not without scary experiences while growing up. When she was 9 months old, her pediatrician raised an alarm. He told us she might have a serious congenital heart disease: coarctation of the aorta. This means the main artery taking blood out of her heart narrowed dramatically just outside the heart. He said it might require surgery when she was about 4 years old to prevent her from dying in her early twenties from inadequate blood circulation. He told us not to worry about it for a while, but to keep it in mind. We did.

Sure enough. When Sierra was four, in 1980, her doctor said surgery would definitely be necessary. We suddenly needed to turn a huge amount of our attention to this scary challenge in totally unfamiliar territory. We had to shepherd ourselves and Sierra through learning about her condition, preparing for her treatment, choosing and getting to know her new doctors, weathering a series of hospitalizations, and finally having her undergo serious heart surgery.

For two years, John and I carefully orchestrated this process. It occurred during a dramatic expansion of the Youth Action Program. I was stretched thin. I had succeeded in getting a $500,000 grant to expand Youth Action just as I was facing the need to gracefully guide our beloved four-year-old daughter through a potentially terrifying and traumatic experience for all of us.

We did it! She came out healthy and happy and without extensive trauma. This was such a complicated process that I kept very careful notes of every aspect of it just to help me stay sane. In 2021, I finally published the book that shares all the ups and downs, our thinking, our learnings, and the whole story that happened in the eighties. It can be found on Amazon, entitled *Our Daughter's Heart*.

The most important aspect of it was figuring out how to both collect the information about her illness and upcoming surgery for ourselves, and then share it with Sierra in a gradual and sensitive way, so that she wouldn't be scared, surprised, mystified, or traumatized. And then, we had to manage the medical system so that the professionals didn't scare, surprise, or traumatize her with unexpected and painful procedures.

There was one pivotal moment at the peak of the drama, when we had to reject the actual surgery at the moment when the nurses and aides had arrived at her hospital room door to take her to the operating room. Everything in the hospital had happened that morning in an unexpected way, 5 hours later than scheduled, with more shots than planned, in a rushed situation that would have caused Sierra to be taken from her parents and forced under anesthesia against her will.

We said, "No." The cardiologist responded by postponing the surgery. This was a huge decision. We went home and had to wait five months before the actual surgery was successfully performed.

For readers of this book who are interested in going deeper into John's and my approach to parenting, our efforts to include, respect, and inform Sierra in a way that minimized her fear, powerlessness, and trauma throughout scary medical experiences over two years, it would be worth reading *Our Daughter's Heart* (you can find it on Amazon). In this book, I have shared a very brief reflection because it is a key element of the backstory.

No matter how dedicated we are to our social change work, no matter how big our responsibilities, there will always be personal and family challenges that require a balancing act that is largely invisible, potentially overwhelming, and totally critical to our lives. Sierra's heart surgery was one of those challenges.

CHAPTER 16

Youth Action's Impact

and Winning City Funding through the Coalition for Twenty Million Dollars

The next few years of building up Youth Action Program's youth-run community improvement projects passed quickly. There was never a dull moment! When Youth Action staff would complain about how hard it was, I would ask, "Have you ever been bored?" The answer was always, "No, never bored." We had a roller coaster of exciting activities, relationships, and drama of various kinds.

Community Improvement Projects Created

We succeeded in creating several state-of-the-art projects:

We built a half-block **park** on 103rd Street after gaining ownership of five separate parcels of adjacent land from far-flung owners and persuading the church on the block to host us. We created a public land trust tucked between the railroad tracks and a crowded tenement block, and painted a big mural on the wall overhanging the park. The park and garden are still there.

We completed a **gut rehab of an abandoned tenement** building through the Youth Action Restoration Crew (YARC) after persuading the City to put up the funds. It took five years and 200 young people to do the work. Once done we continued the project and did the gut rehab of another 11 buildings over the following few years. The Youth Action Program still owns those 12 rehabilitated buildings with 124 units of low-income housing for East Harlem residents. This is the project that we later renamed as YouthBuild and replicated around the country and around the world.

We created a **leadership school** for 80 high school students after persuading the local high school principal to certify the Youth Action "We Are Somebody" Leadership School as an adjunct school. We housed it in our own large warehouse building on the corner of 5th Avenue and 110th Street. This project does not still exist, but in concept, like the East Harlem Block Schools, it was a precursor to the many charter and alternative schools that emerged later.

We revived the crime prevention **youth patrol** in Johnson Projects with Tony Minor, Billy Cox, and Kenny Cox at the helm.

Under the leadership of Rafael Flores, an East Harlem hero now deceased, **Hotline Cares** became a wonderful emergency support program for young people in crisis, with telephones "manned" by trained older teens. Hotline Cares had existed before Youth Action Program, but it joined our network.

We created a **Home Away from Home** for young mothers and their children who lived in the building we had rehabilitated.

Over-all it was amazing how well it worked to ask young people what they wanted to create and then help them do it.

To maintain our core practice of leadership by the young people, each project had members who served on the Policy Committee that in collaboration with the director had ongoing responsibilities for hiring, firing, and making policy. The young people who served on this committee tended to become long-term community leaders.

In addition, to support the young people's personal development we offered a healing support group led by John Bell and informed by the theory and practice of Co-counseling. Those with an interest participated.

I was surprised to discover in 2022, that a full 101-page report on these projects was in the archives at the Department of Justice, with enormous detail including our training curriculum, hiring processes, and impact. (This full report can be accessed by googling Community Anti-Crime Program of the LEAA Youth Action Program)

Five Policy Priorities in the Youth Agenda for the Eighties

Between 1979 and 1981 we organized three annual community youth conferences that attracted several hundred youth for a full day on a Saturday each spring. After gathering a broad set of issues and writing the Youth Agenda for the Eighties (see Appendix B) through these open conferences, the planning committee of 25 youth selected five priorities for action, toward which we would aim to influence existing government or elected officials:

1. Offering sex education for teenagers to prevent unwanted pregnancies and STD's;

2. Improving the public high schools and middle schools;

3. Holding local politicians accountable for serving the community rather than their own interests;

4. Creating real and meaningful jobs for youth; and

5. Changing federal spending priorities from weapons to people.

We decided to approach these priorities in the order of attainability, starting with those easiest to influence directly on the local level.

PRIORITY #1: SEX EDUCATION

The easiest and most direct step was to hold community-wide conferences for teenagers on sex and interpersonal relationships. The members of the Youth Congress brought in consultants to facilitate teenagers learning what they needed to know about how to say "No" to sex, how to use contraception when they had decided to say "Yes," how to avoid sexually transmitted diseases, and how to build stable committed relationships free of domestic abuse. This went very well.

PRIORITY #2: IMPROVING THE PUBLIC SCHOOLS

To tackle priority #2, "Improving the public schools," we held a neighborhood-wide student conference on how to improve the schools for teenagers. After we elicited their suggestions and facilitated their choice of priorities, two primary recommendations emerged: 1) student governments should be created to provide a real voice in policy for youth; and 2) "rap groups" (this is what discussion groups were called before "rap" became a music genre) should be set up in schools to allow discussion about the personal issues that could prevent students from succeeding in school. To implement these recommendations, we arranged with the principals in four local middle schools to create student governments and rap groups in their schools.

We couldn't do this simply, under our own direction, but we could build partnerships to gain access to the youth and schools. This worked reasonably well. We maintained student governments in the middle schools in partnership with the principals for several years. I don't recall whether there were specific ways that we succeeded in improving the schools, but we certainly did produce a nice flow of eager young leaders who were elected to their school's student government and then ended up joining the Youth Action Program to volunteer after school. It was worthwhile to have a pathway for them into leadership within the school, and then directly into community action and service in the neighborhood.

Arising from a different source, but also affecting the students in the public schools, was work we did in this same period in response to an invitation from Eugene Lang to help him create the I Have a Dream project. He was a wealthy man who as a child many years earlier had attended PS 121, an elementary school in East Harlem. In about 1980, when he was invited to speak at that school's graduation, he impulsively promised to pay for college for all of the graduates. Realizing later that they might very well not go to college without some effective mentoring as teenagers, he called me, at the recommendation of our donor, Stella Saltonstall (who had given us our building), to ask for help. I asked Johnny Rivera, one of Youth Action Program's outstanding young leaders, to become the organizer for that first cohort of I Have a Dream students. Johnny did home visits, convenings, personal mentoring, and provided the steady reminder to them that the man who had promised to pay for their college stood ready to keep that promise. As a result, many of them did go to college. Based on this success, Eugene Lang created the I Have a Dream Foundation and replicated this process across the country. He passed away in 2017, but the I Have a Dream Foundation continues. As of 2022, it had served 18,000 Dreamers.

PRIORITY #3: ACCOUNTABILITY OF LOCAL POLITICIANS

Priority #3 was much more complex. The issue of accountability of local politicians arose partly because of our history with some of our elected officials, creating deep feelings among our members. This experience is worth a diversion to tell the story.

In May 1983, a NYS official invited David Calvert to a private World Trade Center meeting to discuss a proposal we had written to the State Division of Housing and Community Renewal "Urban Initiatives" program for $40,000, the amount we needed to complete our first YARC (Youth Action Restoration Crew) gut rehabilitation project. John Sainz and Rosa Parilla, both teenagers in the project, went with David. We had been plugging away for four years on this project, short on funds and construction savvy but high on commitment, and we were determined to bring it to a successful conclusion in year five. The official, an associate of our local Assemblyman, Angelo DelToro, said that our proposal was the best in the state. They had never seen such youth participation and voluntarism, and we were to be commended; but before he could recommend that the proposal be funded, he had a request. With so many neighborhood youth engaged in our program, would we be willing to carry petitions for the Assemblyman's re-election bid? On the way home on the subway, they talked about how to handle this request and decided to have a meeting with the rest of the youth.

Meanwhile, I had also had a phone call from the potential State funder saying that we had a political problem with the Assemblyman because he wanted his brother's program, called Just Us! To be funded instead. The official suggested we put a friend or family member of the Assemblyman on our board of directors to build his interest in our program.

David and I took both those political requests directly to the young people, who soundly and passionately rejected the ideas.

We held a five-hour discussion with about thirty youth about how to respond to these requests. The practice of bringing the most controversial issues that would normally be addressed only by professional administrators directly to the youth for discussion always produced exciting conversations and good results. We sat packed in what we called the "hot room" because it had no windows and was next to the boiler room. It was definitely hot that night!

When one of our staff said that allowing our members to carry petitions voluntarily for the Assemblyman was a small price to pay to get the funds we needed, and probably would do us no harm, one of the leading teenagers, John Sainz, suggested that only youth should speak first. After every young person had expressed dismay at any compromise on our values, John spoke his mind. "If you make a deal with these politicians to buy them off, instead of making them do the right thing, you will never see my face in here again." He stood up, and tears began flowing down his face, as he added, "You taught me to do the right thing when it is difficult. If you are not going to follow your own teachings, then I am out of here." He was fifteen years old.

This moment set the standard for integrity that we would always aim to follow. It became vividly clear how important to young people is the integrity of the adults. They often expect the authorities who have power over their institutions to be corrupt and self-serving, or at least distant and uncaring, but when they see adults who are not, who remain true to idealistic principles, and commit themselves to the well-being of the youth and community, the young people embrace their values whole-heartedly and are heart-broken if they ever see those values violated. Everyone needs people and causes they can believe in and leaders who are truly trustworthy.

The whole group agreed with John Sainz. They said the politicians should do the right thing on the merits and that we absolutely should NOT get petitions signed for them nor put one of their friends on our board. A few days later one of the young people came to my office to say that we should get someone to run for the NYS Assembly against Mr. DelToro. I responded that we shouldn't do such a thing until we were in a position to win, or else we could risk our State funding permanently. I have often wondered if that was the wrong response.

Whether I was right or wrong to discourage an earlier effort from inexperienced and eager teenagers, in the longer run, ten years later, Francisco Diaz, the nineteen-year-old young man who had led the workshops on accountability at our community-wide youth leadership conferences and who held a seat with us in the "hot room" discussion, did run for the Assembly. After Angelo DelToro had passed away, Francisco ran against Angelo's brother, won the seat, and served with integrity for many years. This was an amazing unpredictable ripple effect of our organizing.

A few years later one of the other young men who was adamant about accountability and integrity in many contexts ran for the school board and won. He went on to become president of the school board, director of operations for Congressman Rangel in his

East Harlem office, and Democratic District Leader. This young man was Johnny Rivera, who also staffed the first I Have a Dream project. He had first demonstrated his own clarity about accountability when he was a teenager involved in YARC. He came to me and said, "Don't tell anyone I told you this, but you need to know that the new staff person who is supervising the construction at the Youth Action Restoration Crew is getting high on marijuana with the students at lunch." He went on to say, in a challenging tone, "Are you going to fire him? Or is this organization corrupt like all the other ones?"

That same week Johnny came to the meeting of the youth policy committee that had responsibility, along with me as director, for hiring and firing. He said, "We teenagers need leaders. We will follow them. Youth Action can't give us leaders who will smoke dope with us.... because we will follow them. Please fire him." One of the staff at the meeting said, "But the site supervisor is a community resident who needs a job, and we shouldn't fire him; we should just talk to him." Johnny said, "No, we shouldn't sacrifice the young people. He's a professional staff member and we need to hold him to the highest standards." We fired him. Johnny was clearly right. Johnny stuck with us and spent his entire adolescence taking on increasing responsibility as a young leader. He was the first East Harlem teenager I put on a plane by himself to go to Washington to represent his community. He made it there, made an impression, and made it home without any wavering. He became a long-term member of the board of directors of Youth Action Program in addition to the impressive roles I described above.

All our experience indicated that getting teen-agers involved directly in discussing policy issues, helping to make policy decisions affecting the program and its personnel, organizing their peers, and engaging or confronting elected officials, led gradually to the most outstanding young leaders moving into public leadership roles themselves. Nothing seemed more important or useful than giving young people the hope that the world could be better, and then offering them relationships with dedicated people they could trust, coupled with a close-up view of how policy was made, and how budget decisions were reached. They saw they could do the job better than some of the current leaders. Our goal was producing ethical young leaders for their communities. Deep involvement with decision-making about their own program and direct involvement with policy and politics within a strong value system was clearly the way to do it.

After the Hot Room discussion, our engagement with local politicians became very active. In order to win State funding without selling out, we decided during that tearful strategy meeting in the Hot Room that we would not only refuse to carry petitions or put a politician on our board of directors in exchange for funding, but we would fight for their support and to do so we would "walk softly but carry a big stick." We defined "walking softly" as always talking and acting with respect and never insulting or attacking the officials. We defined the "big stick" as making sure we had large numbers of people visibly behind us, organized and active, supporting our position.

A few days after the Hot Room meeting, we organized a visit to the office of Assemblyman DelToro with 40 teen-agers from all over the neighborhood who came to appeal to him respectfully for the funding to complete YARC's first building rehabilitation project. The group was roughly equally black and Latino. Normally East Harlem was somewhat divided between black and Latino, and teenagers were not involved in politics or advocacy of any kind, so our having a large and united group of active teenagers was surprising to him. He told us that he appreciated all the good work we were doing for the community.

However, a week later we learned that he had denied us the funding.

We immediately passed along this information to some NYC-based public officials, and David and the young people made plans to partially block traffic at East 119 Street during a community information session, with a stage on the sidewalk and a sound system, to tell our neighbors what was going down. During that event, while speaker after speaker took the microphone to tell the community about the building, the experience, and how we were being stymied by political pressure from the NYS Assemblyman, we noticed the arrival of Victor Alvarado, representing Manhattan Borough President Andrew Stein. After a while he strode to the platform and announced that the City government would deliver the $40,000 that the State had denied. We would have the funds to complete what would turn out to be the housing renovation project that inspired and informed the to-be-developed YouthBuild program, yet to be named and established. We had won the day!

Later on, when our East Harlem Youth Congress held a workshop on accountability of politicians, the Assemblyman's brother attended and spoke. He actually told the youth that politicians didn't make decisions on the merits; they made decisions based on who helped get them elected. "If you don't support us, we won't support you," was the message. The teenagers were livid. They again asserted, "You should support our projects on the merits! That's what you were elected to do." These interactions created clarity in the minds of the young people. Sadly, we had no reason to believe they changed that politician's assumptions.

PRIORITY #4: MEANINGFUL JOBS FOR YOUTH

By early 1983 we had done all of the above, but we hadn't found the right moment and method to start on policy priority #4: creating meaningful jobs for youth. And, of course, we had no idea how to tackle #5: "changing national priorities from weapons to people."

Suddenly, an opportunity surfaced to create meaningful jobs for youth. In 1983, at a conference on youth issues sponsored by the New York Foundation, I met Stanley Litow, then the Executive Director of Interface, a policy organization serving the City. His knowledgeable comments about a vision for youth employment caused me to call him a few days later to propose that we work together toward creating a citywide youth employment initiative. He informed me that Mayor Koch had just announced a $38M Jobs Program for Disadvantaged Workers through which workers were going to build housing for low-income people. I thought it was an opportunity for us to add a piece for disadvantaged youth.

I literally ran from my office, jumped in front of my young secretary, Sonia Texidor, who worked with me and the Youth Congress, and surprised her with the intensity of my reaction. "I've got it!" I cried. "We've got it! We've got a way to bring jobs to young people. The Mayor has a Disadvantaged Worker Program, and the East Harlem Youth Congress can propose that a component for youth be added! Let's go! We've got the way to do it!" Sonia has never let me forget that moment, which was the first day of the next ten years of her life, and mine.

I convened the leaders of our East Harlem Youth Congress to explain the situation. They were all in favor of taking immediate action. I also met with a group of executive directors from around the City who had previously been convened by the Fund for The City of New York and who had continued meeting to develop some policy recommendations for the City. We had come to trust each other. The Fund had previously convened a large group around possibly accessing some funds. When the funding opportunity disappeared, so did most of the directors, but a solid core of us continued meeting on principle, figuring we should find a way to affect policy with or without money immediately available. The group included Adina Johnson from Operation Crossroads, Bonnie Genevich from Good Shepherd Services, Tom Pendleton from The Dome, and John Bess from Manhattan Valley Outreach. We were soon joined by Getz Obstfeld from Banana Kelly Community Improvement Association. Trusting collaboration makes a difference.

We requested and somehow obtained a meeting with the commissioner of HPD, Joseph Shuldiner, to ask if he could include $8M in the City's initiative for jobs focused on youth rebuilding housing. After all, we had experience through the Youth Action Program's YARC project. We knew how to engage and train youth in housing construction.

He was firm and clear: "No." He told us that the administration already had a plan, a program, stakeholders, and was way too far along to even consider re-drafting their plans to include youth. "Sorry, but no way." He was not dismissive of our intentions, but he was absolute regarding its infeasibility.

After he left the room, we remained. We sat around that table, about a dozen of us, half young people and half adults, and discussed what to do. It was a similar turning point to the night in the Hot Room. We had experienced a direct relationship with a powerful public official, and had to craft a response, thinking it through together. We decided to respect his firmness about the mayor's program, not to inconvenience or criticize him in any way, and to write him a letter thanking him for the meeting, honoring his situation, but saying that he should not under-estimate our determination. We would be back. We promised to come back the following year with our own proposal for a job training program that would involve youth rebuilding housing.

Of course, we did come back the next year. We came back not only to Commissioner Joseph Shuldiner, but to the entire City government. Again, we were walking softly but carrying a big stick. We wrote a highly professional and respectful proposal for a Ten Million Dollar Program and delivered it carefully, one by one, to all the key players. At the same time, we organized a citywide coalition of 90 organizations to sign on to our recommendation, to show how serious we were, and to wave our big stick. We named ourselves the Coalition for Ten Million Dollars. In New York, that drew smiles. It was direct, down-to-earth, very New York.

Another key lesson was about to be learned. Ruth Messinger was a City Councilwoman from the Upper West Side whose progressive orientation was focused on grassroots involvement. She had a close relationship with Richard Murphy, then head of Rheedlen Foundation, a Harlem youth-serving organization that was the precursor to the now-famous Harlem Children's Zone. Ruth and Richard had decided to inform the community-based groups how to interface with the City's budget process. When they held a meeting to explain the process, the road map appeared clearly in front of us. The mayor produces a budget, gives it to the City Council, and the City Council holds public hearings in every borough. The City Council has the power to add items to the mayor's budget. But in those days, although 10 million people lived in the city, less than 600 people participated in the budget hearings to influence how to spend over 20 billion dollars! Hardly anybody paid attention or realized they could have an influence. The form and process of democracy was available, but the spirit, know-how, and essence of democracy was missing.

We decided to use those public hearings. What better way to get the voices of young people heard in New York City regarding what they needed? The Youth Congress steering committee began to have meetings every Wednesday night, to study the process of city government and to prepare both to speak at the budget hearings and to have small lobbying meetings with legislators. This went on for months. We practiced, and we practiced. Everyone took turns at the podium, reading from speeches they had written, speaking from notes, ad-libbing from their hearts, practicing until it became second nature to look at the audience, tell it like it is, and make their points in an organized and succinct yet passionate fashion.

We devised another strategy that would keep our voices soft but our "big stick" visible. We would get hundreds of young people to go to the hearings, all dressed alike. They would file into the halls in well-organized lines, taking up every seat one after another, filling a large section of the auditorium. When one of their members spoke at the podium, at the end of the speech they would all stand up and applaud, until the speaker had returned to his or her seat. Then they would all sit down, in unison. They were highly visible, highly polite, highly organized, and there were hundreds of them from all over New York City. Their T-shirts were bright orange with black letters saying, "The Coalition for Ten Million." On the back was printed, "Young People Want Real Jobs Rebuilding Our Communities."

It worked. It worked not just because we were visible and well organized, but because Ruth Messinger was our inside champion. That was another key lesson: an inside champion is absolutely essential in order to win any campaign for public funding. This lesson laid the groundwork for all my subsequent advocacy work.

This is the overall formula that emerged: A clear and well-conceived request + professional excellence + organized and respectful grassroots strength + the voices of youth + inside champions = success in obtaining funding for a good cause.

That first year the City Council added $5.4M to the mayor's budget for our proposals. But we had asked for $10M, not $5M. We were very disappointed! That was how we learned that even when you succeed, the government gives you only about half of what you ask for. Since we wanted $10M, not $5M, we took our letterhead and our T-shirts, placed a line through Ten Million and wrote Twenty Million above it, and went back the next year. This created additional smiles in down-to-earth New York City.

We increased our membership from 90 to 150 agencies, held training sessions for 14 agencies to bring their youth to speak at the budget hearings, and invited member agencies around the city to send groups of youth prepared to make various drama presentations on the steps of City Hall during the final budget deliberations that took place around the clock during the closing hours of the budget preparation.

I had learned the previous year, in 1984, through my experience standing in the lobby of City Hall for 24 hours while they went through their budget ordeal, that there was a real opportunity to influence what happened at the end through cheering on your inside allies and making final pleas to the Council people who were walking through the halls between meetings. I realized the origin of the word "lobbying." You stand in the lobby and talk to people!

I decided to bring young people with me for this amazing spectacle, to stand in the lobby with me for 24 hours and to offer something memorable to the Council people who were stuck there overnight. We scheduled songs, poems, cheerleading demonstrations, and short skits on the steps of City Hall, with one after another youth-serving agency bringing its youth at scheduled times to put on a performance. This was extremely well received by the Council people. They came out onto the steps, a few at a time, at various hours of the day and evening, and watched the enthusiastic young people perform. Ed Sadowsky, then president of the City Council, stood beside me watching. He said, "I can identify with their desire for jobs. They are very well behaved."

Mayor Koch had a similar reaction to the discipline and courtesy and large numbers of our demonstrators. In the afternoon that we were gathered outside City Hall, he drove up in his limousine, opened the door and stepped out, uncurling his very tall body. Members of the Coalition for Twenty Million Dollars were standing at attention in rows on both sides of the stairs leading up to City Hall. They all had on their orange and black T-shirts: "The Coalition for Twenty Million Dollars; Young people want real jobs rebuilding our communities." Mayor Koch looked tired. He didn't pay much attention as he walked up the stairs between the rows of youth who said, each in turn, "Good afternoon Mr. Mayor. Don't forget the Coalition for Twenty Million Dollars. Have a good day."

Two hours later he exited from City Hall. He walked back down the stairs through the lines of youth on each side of the steps who were again standing in dignified attention, who again said, "Good afternoon, Mr. Mayor." By the look on his face, it had not been a good afternoon for him. Somehow, it seemed the warm greetings penetrated his detached demeanor. He stopped a few paces away from the bottom of the stairs, turned and looked back, silent for a few moments taking in the lines of teenagers with orange T-shirts calling for Twenty Million Dollars, with the previous "Ten Million" crossed out. He cocked his head, smiled slightly, and said, "The Coalition for Twenty Million Dollars. ... Would you settle for ten million?"

That was a memorable moment! It reinforced our belief in the idea of speaking softly but carrying a big stick. Our steadfast, polite, determined, and very broad presence had penetrated the mayor's awareness.

That year, 1985, the City Council voted to add $12.75 million onto the mayor's budget for the Coalition's full set of initiatives. As we had built our City-wide Coalition, our agenda had expanded to include several distinct items, all of which were built into the funds provided by the City Council. The funds were delivered for implementation to the NYC Department of Employment (DOE) administered by Commissioner Ron Gault. The lesser amount that was reserved for the housing model required DOE to collaborate with the NYC Department of Housing Preservation and Development (HPD), administered by Commissioner Joseph Shuldiner.

Winning $12.75M of City tax levy funds for youth employment training that we designed was a huge victory which paved the way for everything we have done since. We had spread the love, and won the day!

To repeat the formula: **A clear and well-conceived request + professional excellence + organized and respectful grassroots strength + the voices of the people affected + inside champions = success in obtaining funding for a good cause.**

CHAPTER 17

Replicating Youth Action's Housing Model in New York City

and Defining "YouthBuild" for Future Replication

Of the $5.4M appropriated by the City Council in response to the Coalition for $10M in 1984, only $1M was for what was then called the Housing Model. The next year, in 1985, $2M was for the Housing Model.

One reason such a small amount of funds was appropriated for our model of youth employment in housing rehabilitation was that we had allowed other interests to pile their ideas onto our grassroots momentum. We welcomed this as a way of building even greater unity and clout. When they saw our momentum, they asked that their initiatives be included. The DOE Commissioner, the Mayor, the President of the City Council, and a City-wide advocacy group all added specific program designs they wanted to have funded.

They had seen that a dynamic train that carried the "big stick" of strong grassroots support was leaving the station and it would be wise to jump on board. We thought all these proposals had merit. There was no reason not to build greater unity around a wider variety of proposals. So, we accepted them all.

Actually, one side effect of our big tent approach was that once it was clear that City tax levy funds for youth employment would be added into the mayor's budget in response to our call, we had to fight very hard to even keep the Housing Model in the mix, even though it had been the core of our original proposal. The Commissioner had doubts about its feasibility, Interface had never loved it, and the conventional wisdom was that a program that required cooperation between two City agencies — the New York City Department of Employment (DOE) and the New York City Department of Housing Preservation and Development (HPD) — was doomed to fail.

However, City Councilwoman Carolyn Maloney (later to become Congresswoman Maloney) fought for our idea behind closed doors because she had witnessed its success in East Harlem. She eked out $1M for year one. This is another example of the necessity of having a champion on the inside.

Responsibility for implementation moved to Commissioner Ron Gault and Fredda Peritz in DOE, and Commissioner Shuldiner and Steve Norman in HPD. HPD Commissioner Joe Shuldiner said to me at that point, "Dorothy, this program is so complex that nobody can do it but you. The Youth Action Program should be granted the funds. Other community-based organizations don't have the capacity." I responded, "There is no surer way to destroy a coalition than to give all the money to the lead agency. We will not accept it, and we don't need it. We have a grant from the State Homeless Housing Assistance Program for this year, so we don't actually need any City funds."

The die was cast. A competitive RFP was put out by DOE. Five programs were selected to replicate what Commissioner Gault had named the "Housing Related Enhanced Work Experience" program. This name had no resonance, but we hadn't yet conceived of the name "YouthBuild."

We soon learned that although I had been right about not taking the funds because doing so would undermine the Coalition, Commissioner Shuldiner was right about how hard this program was to replicate, especially if there was no prototype defined and no technical assistance or training available.

Nobody was right that two city agencies were incapable of collaborating. DOE and HPD collaborated beautifully. Fredda and Norm stayed in close communication. They were both senior administrators committed to its success, and therefore had the clout to bring their agencies to the table.

But the replication largely failed within two years for lack of both a clear prototype and specific guidance to the new grantees. In years one and two, nine local non-profits were funded. Commissioner Lilliam Paoli, the new Commissioner of DOE who had succeeded Ron Gault, shut five of them down in year three. They had not been able to coordinate the education, the housing, the counseling, and the leadership development. I had overestimated the ability of other organizations to understand and replicate what we had done, and I had no understanding of the type of assistance they would need.

<u>This was a powerful and lasting lesson about replication of a complex program. It cannot be done without wise and careful guidance.</u>

Seeing this failure, we decided to write a handbook to guide new agencies. In addition to the Youth Action Program, the Banana Kelly Community Improvement Association had done a good job in the South Bronx under the leadership of executive director Getz Obstfeld. We brought together program directors from YAP and Banana Kelly, with Al Rodriguez as coordinator, and me as editor-in-chief, to produce the first edition of the implementation handbook for what would later be named YouthBuild. This handbook has gone through seven editions since the first one was completed in 1986. It still stands as the basic description of YouthBuild.

Since then, while expanding the replication of YouthBuild around the country, we also wrote full handbooks for each component of the YouthBuild program: education, construction training, leadership development, counseling, and graduate opportunities. Directors of later successful programs have said, "We just followed the book. It was all there." Of course, as replication occurred in the nineties around the country, we also learned how to train, guide, provide on-site training, coach the directors, and build unity and cohesion among leadership and staff.

The fact that Youth Action Program had no influence over the actual replication of the model it had created was a perfect set-up for failure. Distributing money to new entities, regardless of how well intentioned or well established, to replicate a new complex program without guidance or a roadmap, is a very bad idea and destined to fail in most cases.

Fortunately, we learned this lesson before we succeeded in getting the national YouthBuild program authorized in public law. When that occurred, I wrote into the law that 5% of the funds would be set aside for training and technical assistance given by "an experienced national non-profit organization." But I am getting ahead of the story... we did not create a national non-profit organization called YouthBuild USA, Inc. until 1990.

The Essence and Definition of YouthBuild

This seems like an appropriate moment to give a deeper description of the YouthBuild program for those readers who may not be familiar with it. While many readers may be YouthBuild staff from around the country, or YouthBuild graduates, I hope there are lots of young social entrepreneurs who are building their own projects and who are reading and using this book as a source of inspiration for their own persistence, methodology, and hope. They may not have any prior knowledge of YouthBuild.

As explained earlier, YouthBuild began as a community improvement project called the Youth Action Restoration Crew designed by teenagers who were still in high school and had a big idea of rehabilitating abandoned buildings to create housing for the homeless. They were only available to work on their project after school and on the weekends. It evolved over a couple of years into something very different.

It became the most comprehensive education, job training, counseling, community service, and leadership development program in the country that was designed especially for the most disadvantaged young adults: low-income 16- to 24-year-olds who had left high school without a diploma. This was a population with very little hope and very little opportunity anywhere in America. Once they had left high school without a diploma, their options were few. They were often pulled into street life, resulting in a criminal record. They were not welcomed back into the schools, nor into jobs. Their futures looked bleak.

The design modification was partly catalyzed by the phone call in 1981 from Larry Kressley, the program officer at the Public Welfare Foundation, asking if we might be doing job training for the "underclass."

Another catalyst came during the advocacy by the Coalition for Twenty Million Dollars. Some government officials said that we needed to limit the eligibility for the Housing Model not only to young people without a high school diploma, but also to those who were reading below the 8th grade level because that was the group not being served by any other initiative.

We changed the model. It became a full-time 11-month program, with half of the students' time spent on education and the other half spent rehabilitating abandoned buildings. We divided the students into two groups and alternated the groups back and forth each week.

One week they would be in the classroom with caring professional teachers who were preparing them to earn their GEDs. The next week they would be working on the construction site with skilled construction supervisors, building affordable housing. Classroom training resulting in construction certifications useful for employment would also be integrated into one or the other location. This balance worked extremely well.

They were paid minimum wage for their work on the construction site. Their travel and food costs for their GED week were also covered. The construction work was understood as community service, since they were building something of extraordinary value to their community, deeply appreciated and respected by their neighbors. The education component was their own investment in their own future.

We included three other essential components:

- **Individual Counseling and Peer Group Support**: Each student had a one-on-one relationship with a staff counselor. In addition, the students met in guided peer group circles of support to share their life experiences, challenges, and feelings. These would be organized to give each member equal time to speak with the full attention of the group. After speaking, they would be appreciated by the students sitting on each side of them. Safety for equal-time sharing, and ongoing appreciation, make an amazing difference.

- **Leadership Development**: Each cycle had a youth policy council elected by their peers who met weekly with the director to provide ongoing input on how to develop and improve the program. They also participated in staff hiring processes. Students had the opportunity to learn how to advocate for program resources from City and/or State government.

- **<u>Job and College Placement and Graduate Follow-up</u>**:
  Staff trained the young people in their college and job options,
  created relationships with potential employers, organized
  college visits, helped them prepare for applications and interviews, and supported students after graduation.

Even after defining the program components, we realized that
certain program qualities were just as important as the components.
If the components are not delivered in a spirit that integrates the
right program qualities, they could fail miserably no matter how
comprehensive or well-conceived in theory. We therefore defined
the program qualities distinct from the program components.

The qualities were designed to create an appealing and inspiring
program culture. Many low-income youth come to programs with
years of past negative experiences. Not only have they been raised
in families with insecurities and struggles on many fronts, but in
addition many schools and programs have been transactional, dismissive, disrespectful, racist, classist, and/or punitive. In contrast,
successful programs must deliberately create a culture that helps
students reverse these experiences. From the moment applicants
walk in the door, their experience should be dramatically different
from past experiences in other institutions. It should be the exact
opposite of the negative experiences they have suffered.

Students need to experience safety, respect, caring, and a sense
of community, with high standards and positive values coupled
with an inspiring vision of the future they can create for themselves.
They experience this as a loving family. I have heard many students
say something like, "I came here looking for my GED. What I found
was a family who cared about me more than anyone ever had."

Over time, we identified the positive qualities listed below that
have proven to create a particularly successful environment, incorporated into all aspects of a YouthBuild program:

1. Profound respect for the intelligence of program members.

2. Safety from harm.

3. A reasonable degree of power for them over their immediate environment (thus the importance of the youth policy councils, as a core component).

4. Meaningful and important work that provides value to the community and generates appreciation for the participants.

5. Real, patient caring for their development by caring adults.

6. Actual teaching of skills that will prepare them for future education and careers.

7. A firm and loving challenge to stop self-destructive behavior and change negative attitudes.

8. Family-like support and appreciation from peers and adults.

9. Caring support and resources for coping with extraordinary challenges.

10. High standards and expectations.

11. Inspiring and caring role models including individuals from similar cultural and racial backgrounds as the students.

12. Understanding of all participants' proud and unique cultural background, building a sense of unity and connection across racial and religious backgrounds.

13. Heightened awareness of the present-day world and their important place in it.

14. A clear and visible path to future opportunity.

15. Fun: opportunities for enjoyable social and recreational activities.

16. Real concern and action from the agency about changing the negative conditions that have affected them and their community.

This is a very brief description of the basic YouthBuild program that has been replicated across the country since we defined it in the late eighties. Of course, it has further evolved. For example, most YouthBuild programs now include additional career tracks. I won't try to describe the evolution here. At this point in the book, I just want to make sure the reader understands the basic description of YouthBuild that we were about to replicate city-wide and nationally in the late '80's and early '90's.

Helene Dorothy Nieschlag Stoneman, My Beloved Mother

Returning to Belmont to Care for My Mother

In 1985, John, Sierra, and I decided that we had to move our family back to Belmont, Massachusetts, to take care of my mother, who was suffering from Alzheimer's Disease.

We had been noticing her gradual decline in memory and intelligence since before my father's death in 1981. One memorable and telling moment was when we were home in Belmont to visit my father who was very ill. We spent most of the day with him in the hospital and returned home in the late afternoon. It was about 6:15 P.M., when a nurse called my mother to say, "Mrs. Stoneman, we need you to return to the hospital because your husband has just hit a nurse who was trying to help him. We can't handle him alone."

Her response was, "Oh, no. We are just sitting down to dinner." Fortunately, I had picked up the other phone, and was available to say, "I'm sorry to hear that. Thank you for calling. We will be right over." This was a dramatic indication that she had lost touch.

When my father died in 1981, my brother and his wife moved back home to care for Mommy. However, in 1984 they said it was too much for them. They had to leave. The choice was to put our mother in a nursing home, or for John and me to come and take our turn as caretakers.

Fortunately, my husband John's generosity of spirit made that move possible. Sierra was also willing. So, we did it. We left Harlem. We left New York City. We moved back to my parents' home in Belmont where I had grown up. I had been gone for 26 years. It was scary to return to upper-middle-class segregated white Belmont after 21 great years in Harlem and East Harlem. John and I had put down roots, found a communal home with colleagues, and built a deeply satisfying work life in support of education and community development in East Harlem. Sierra was happy in her East Harlem public "magnet school" with her multi-racial friends and in our neighborhood of Central Harlem where some of her school friends also lived. There was no reason to leave. But my mother needed us. So, we went to Belmont.

Meanwhile, my work in East Harlem had grown and my role in NYC had expanded. As a result, I had to commute to NYC from Belmont to manage both halves of my life. I left early every Tuesday morning, flew to NYC, worked there with total focus for three days and two nights, staying those two nights in our former home on West 137th Street in Central Harlem. I flew back home on Thursday nights to Boston Logan Airport where John would pick me up and we would drive home to Belmont.

This was hard for Sierra. She was only nine years old. Her mother was leaving every single week for three days. Every Monday night Sierra would be very sad. She knew I was leaving, and she couldn't stop me. She had to learn to suck it up, to be independent, to say good-bye every week because her mommy was busy and had to go away to work, to improve the world for the teenagers in East Harlem. This went on for three years, between age 9 and age 12. This dynamic probably caused her to internalize the idea that she had to sacrifice her own needs for the good of others. Nonetheless, she appeared to thrive, doing well in school, with lots of friends, and never intensely protesting or rebelling.

During that period, I wrote an article about what it was like to manage my mother's Alzheimer's disease. People facing similar challenges have found this article extremely useful and touching. I have therefore included it in the appendices. ("A Different Point of View on Alzheimer's Disease", written in 1985)

My mother, Helene Dorothy Nieschlag Stoneman, was a distinguished civic volunteer who gave her life to the League of Women Voters, as a local, state, and national official. She was an angelic sort of person, totally self-sufficient in a WASP (White Anglo-Saxon Protestant) sort of way, and gracious to all, never asking anything from anybody. She had been a wonderful mother who respected and trusted us profoundly. She very much deserved, but never would have requested, our care. She was the kind of person who would have probably preferred to drop dead unexpectedly the way her own mother did, without ever asking anything of anybody. It was thus a gift to us in many respects that we had the opportunity to care for her and surround her with love and enjoyable family activities in her last years.

Yet I still was director of Youth Action Program, commuting from Belmont to East Harlem every week. I did this from 1985 through 1988. What amazes me in retrospect is that we accomplished so much in East Harlem during those years of commuting, when I was really leading two lives.

My commuting was not only hard on Sierra. It was also hard on me. The weekly contrast between the insulated affluence of Belmont and the exposed poverty of Harlem gave me a headache. My head literally ached much of the time, which had never been the case before that period, (except when I was conflicted about whether to marry Leroy) nor any time since. Earlier in my life I had left Belmont Hill, and I didn't expect ever to return. I had loved living and working in Harlem for over 20 years. It had become my home. I was not drawn to the entirely white, mostly upper-middle-class, community of Belmont. In Belmont our home was down the street from Mitt Romney's mansion. In Harlem we were a few blocks from great big 20-story public housing apartments.

In Belmont John and I returned to the Unitarian Universalist Church where I had grown up, in part to test whether we could feel at home in Belmont and find a simpatico community. I stood up one Sunday in church to propose that the church become a "Sanctuary Church" for Central American refugees. When I did that, members of the church said this was very daring and bold, because it was a "very conservative" church. But they were wrong. After a year of meetings, the church voted by 85% to become a Sanctuary Church. We had been smart enough to adjust the definition so that the church members could provide sanctuary through giving funds for the refugees to get an apartment in Cambridge and then to attend our church, rather than having them live in the sanctuary of the church itself. That adjustment made it workable for Belmont. We had also been smart enough to meet with every committee in the church, gradually winning over the old timers and the people with influence.

After that, I decided to jump into the political life of the town. I took charge of organizing the town for Governor Dukakis's Democratic campaign for president of the United States. It was fascinating to notice that the activists in the town were much more focused on local politics than on national, so there was a void that I could fill. I had never participated in any aspect of electoral politics in New York City, despite the fact that I had imagined myself starting a new political party there.

Both these activities connected me to Belmont enough to put down some roots, to get comfortable in the liberal side of town, and make friends. It turned out to be fun to make political telephone calls to neighbors who would say, "Dorothy Stoneman? Are you related to Helene Stoneman? You are! What a wonderful woman she is! We're glad you came home." It was as if the stamp I had wished to have on my forehead in Harlem to validate me as a proven ally turned out to be automatically on my forehead in Belmont, as a townie, and as the daughter of my mother, who had been chair of the local League of Women Voters.

Interestingly, in the 1980's there was already an absolute divide between the Republicans and Democrats in Belmont. They simply did not relate to each other. This ideological divide struck me when I returned to Belmont as possibly harder to bridge than the national racial divide. Belmont had been the home of the John Birch Society, a radical anti-Communist right-wing organization. When my Girl Scout leader's husband, a professor at MIT, was interrogated as a Communist by the House Un-American Activities Committee in the early fifties, he was ostracized. When I was in sixth grade in 1952, only two of my classmates' families supported Adlai Stevenson for President.

When I returned in 1985, I was amazed. The town had actually become quite liberal, widely supporting Governor Dukakis. However, there was absolutely no cross-party communication that I could discern. This was a kind of warning of the political and ideological polarization of the country that was to take over the nation quite visibly at the turn of the century. For a short time, I served on the Democratic Town Committee, and then it occurred to me that if I were to get bi-partisan support for YouthBuild's expansion, possibly I should avoid a partisan identity. I resigned. Later, when I served actively on John Kerry's presidential campaign's fundraising committee, I similarly declined to have my name listed anywhere. These actions might have been based on an exaggerated fear.

Our daughter Sierra gradually put down roots in Belmont by attending the public schools and the Unitarian Universalist Church. When we adopted our son, David Lautaro, from Chile in 1988 (to be described in a later backstory chapter), I stopped commuting to New York, turned the Youth Action Program over to Sonia Bu as executive director, and launched the national effort to spread what we had done in East Harlem, using my mother's house as our office.

Bob Curvin, Ford Foundation   Bill White, Charles Stewart Mott Foundation

CHAPTER 19

The Movement Goes National: YouthBuild Spreads!

I t's almost magical how a good thing can be made to spread. Even though my original purpose had been to build a movement through creating a political party, building a central action program, and implementing a fifty-year plan to take power to eliminate poverty and injustice, by 1984 I had become extremely absorbed in East Harlem and New York City and was not connected to any national organizations or movement-building efforts. We had dissolved The New Action Party in 1980. I was not doing anything to push our work nationally. My field-worker psyche had taken over again, and I had no drive toward understanding or going to Washington.

New York City tends to have that effect on people. It is such a large city, almost the size of a country, that creative people can be completely consumed within it. I noticed when I moved to the Boston area that everyone in Boston who was doing anything interesting believed they should be influencing national policy; but in New York people could barely look beyond the bounds of our own city, no matter how interesting and effective their work.

Between the first success of the Coalition for Ten Million Dollars in 1984 and the creation in 1988 of the "National Replication Project of the Youth Action Program of the East Harlem Block Schools", the precursor to YouthBuild USA, the galvanizing factor was that our work was discovered by people who came to believe it should be replicated.

First of all, two national foundations discovered us: The Ford Foundation and the Charles Stewart Mott Foundation. Vinnie McGee, then head of the Aaron Diamond Foundation, brought Jon Blyth from the Mott Foundation and Gordon Berlin from The Ford Foundation to visit Youth Action Program. Jon and Gordon became funders, advocates, and advisors with enormous impact on our work for decades. Jon and Gordon also brought the boards of directors of Ford and Mott Foundations to visit our first program in East Harlem, resulting in lasting funding. Jon and Gordon remained thought leaders for decades in the areas of youth employment and poverty alleviation. I was very lucky to have them as allies throughout my professional life.

I will never forget calling Gordon on the day in 1985 when the Coalition for Twenty Million Dollars won $12.75M in city funds for youth employment programs. He said, from his seat at the Ford Foundation, "That's great. Now you need to make it the 'Coalition for One Billion Dollars' and go national." I was far from being ready to do that. But I never forgot his instructions!

In 1986 I was invited to go on a German Marshall Tour of youth employment programs in Europe with a distinguished group of funders, researchers, and practitioners, including Jon Blyth. I don't remember who nominated me, but it could have been Gordon or Jon. It was my first venture out of New York City to see what was going on elsewhere. While in Europe, Jon said to me, "Dorothy, you really need to take what you are doing at the Youth Action Program national, and when you do, the Mott Foundation will be happy to fund the effort." I was not ready, but said that if and when we did that, I would return to him.

At that time, in my awareness, there was no concept of "social entrepreneur" being touted, no idea of "taking a social innovation to scale," no Skoll Foundation, no intermediary organizations like New Profit, Inc. or Growth Philanthropy Network or the Edna McConnell Clark Foundation, nor the Social Innovation Fund, nor even Ashoka, to identify and assist "social entrepreneurs," and no roadmap for replication. In fact, if I remember correctly, the term "scaling up" for social programs was not yet widespread. Secretary Robert Rubin in the Clinton Administration had not yet said the government should find those programs that work and scale them up. (Of course, although often said in recent decades, this still has not been done by the government.)

It took me until 1988 to return to Jon Blyth to tell him I was ready to take Youth Action national. I wrote a list of 14 things we would have to do to successfully replicate across the country, took it to Jon, and wrote a proposal that met his specifications. (That list of 14 items is in chapter 21, "Dorothy Finally Goes to Washington.") Since the President of the Foundation, Bill White, and the board of directors of the Mott Foundation had already visited the Youth Action Program, Jon was able fairly easily to arrange to give us $200,000 in January of 1989. Meanwhile, the Ford Foundation had also given us $50,000 to build the National YouthBuild Coalition.

This crucial Ford grant was generated by a meeting with Vice President Bob Curvin. It was a classic expression of the power of including youth in key meetings. I had never met Bob Curvin, but he gave me a meeting because Gordon Berlin recommended it. Gordon had already brought the board of directors of Ford Foundation to visit Youth Action.

I arrived with about six Youth Action students. I hadn't thought to get permission in advance. The receptionist called upstairs to say there were six teenagers there and asked if they would be allowed to join the meeting. Bob Curvin always laughingly told the story of how this unexpected group of teenagers sold him on Youth Action and caused him to make the first grant. In that meeting I asked him for funds to support the National Coalition. In that conversation we made it clear that we were going to create a Coalition whether he funded it or not. He said, "Well, if you're going to do it anyway, I guess I might as well help you get started." That one $50,000 grant laid the groundwork for the next 30 years. Bob Curvin, a black man, was an early player among the Ford Foundation's role of uplifting philanthropic executives of color. In recent years Darren Walker has played a profoundly influential role as Ford Foundation's President. In 1984, Bob Curvin was delighted to have black and Latino young people from East Harlem speaking to him from their hearts in his downtown office. Much later, Bob joined YouthBuild USA's board of directors. Sadly, he passed away in 2015.

There had already been a great demand for information about how to do what we had done in East Harlem. People from around the country had somehow heard of it and had come to visit, to look, and then ask for help. Some of them had heard about it first through the young leaders that we were sending to conferences to talk about their experiences. It was clearly a model that other youth workers thought would be useful in their communities. This same pattern occurred internationally years later: people came to us from around the world to ask us to help them set up YouthBuild in their countries.

Once I had stopped commuting to Harlem, re-established my roots in Belmont, and obtained a grant from Ford Foundation to go national, we were off and running into the national arena. In 1988 I hired three full-time staff to join me in Belmont, and persuaded my husband, John, to come on board. He had left YAP in 1981 to become a professional folk singer, so we had not been working together for the previous seven years. But this was a new moment. He had just about reached the end of his run as a folk singer. He was choosing between our National Replication Project and working for Children of War, run by his close friend Judith Thompson, for whom he had played a key role as the half-time director of Leadership Development. He had totally loved his work for that organization, bringing teenagers around the world from war-torn countries together, helping them prepare and then deliver through speaking tours their inspiring and moving messages about the need for peace in the world.

Fortunately, John joined me. We would be work-partners for the next 28 years, along with being co-parents, husband and wife, co-counselors, and best friends.

At about the same time, in 1989, John and another staff member, Margherita Pagni, thought up the name YouthBuild. In 1990 we incorporated YouthBuild USA, Inc. as a new non-profit, funded by Ford and Mott, and a few other foundations we had met along the way. Leroy agreed to be the founding board chair. So, John and I, and Leroy and I, were consolidated in partnerships that leveraged all of our highest talents and strengths. This continued for the next 21 years, until Leroy passed away in 2011. John and I continued as work partners through 2015, when he stepped away from YouthBuild USA to give his full time as a Dharma teacher to the Buddhist community.

During those two+ decades, YouthBuild grew to over 250 sites across the USA, and another 80 sites in 20 other countries. About 200,000 young people built roughly 35,000 units of affordable housing in their communities while they worked toward their high school diplomas and prepared for either college or careers in construction. YouthBuild graduates are succeeding and contributing to the world in many wonderful ways. They have union memberships, homes, their own non-profits, small businesses, successful children... and some of them are running for office and winning.

Clarifying Note: YouthBuild USA, Inc. is a national non-profit that played a central role in the expansion of YouthBuild around the country and the world, and served as a contractor to the US federal government that administers the federal YouthBuild program. For the rest of this book I have omitted Inc. from its name. Just to be clear, the Department of Labor manages the federal YouthBuild program. YouthBuild USA has no authority over that program. (Editor's note: in October, 2024, YouthBuild USA, Inc. changed its name to YouthBuild Global.)

Jon Blyth, from Charles Stewart Mott Foundation, on a YouthBuild site visit

Sierra Welcomes Taro to our Family

CHAPTER 20: BACKSTORY

Our Family Expands!

Between 1985 and 1988, as described previously, our family was living in Belmont caring for my mother. I was commuting to New York City weekly to manage both the on-going Youth Action Program and the City-wide replication of our housing program. At the same time, other important stories were playing out.

John and I were trying to figure out how to give birth to another child. Not only did he and I want another baby, but Sierra wanted a younger sibling. She was already nine years old when we moved to Belmont. She was getting impatient for a sibling! Our efforts to get me pregnant hadn't worked. I was finally diagnosed with a blocked passage that prevented sperm from finding and fertilizing the egg.

191

John and I decided to adopt our second child. I had always been interested in adoption as a way of not overpopulating the earth and still having a full family. When I was about 14 years old, I remember telling my mother that I wanted to have one child and adopt a second one. It turned out that adoption is a demanding process in itself, although very different from pregnancy and birth. As we scanned the adoption world, there were a variety of reasons, including avoiding a long waiting period, that we chose to adopt internationally. We had to find a country with welcoming rules, find an adoption agency, pay lots of money, and work it out!

We did. In the summer of 1988, we traveled to Chile to meet and bring home our newly adopted son. He had been birthed by a full-blooded indigenous Mapuche mother. She was an artist and handicraft creator in Santiago. Our son's birth father was not identified. Based on Taro's appearance we always thought his birth father was probably a light-skinned Latino, but when Taro checked his ancestry he found his father was an indigenous person from Basque country. Our son had been given the first name "Christian" by his birth mom. He was four months old when we met him in late July 1988. He had been in a caring foster family since his birth in late March. We visited his foster family and first met our baby-to-be in their humble apartment. The family members cried a lot when we came to meet him and take him to the USA. He cried a lot too. We believed it was very important that we let him cry as much as he wanted during his separation from them and his transition to the USA. He needed to deal with the shock of leaving his foster family and landing in a whole different world where everyone was speaking a different language. The earlier loss of his birth mother was surely also deeply expressed in those many hours of tears that he shed in our arms. I believe that our welcoming his tears and holding him close while he cried fully, helped him become free of any apparent "attachment disorder." He was always very open and close with us. Later we learned much more about the trauma that being relinquished by a birth mother imposes on a baby. We'd been trained to think of adoption as a benign and wonderful thing; but it is more complicated than that, a very painful life-long trauma of separation, for the child.

We quickly re-named him. My Jewish father would not have wanted a grandchild named Christian. Neither did I. The father of one of the Children of War participants from Chile, whose family hosted John and me when we went to meet our new son in Chile, suggested we name him Lautaro, after the revered Mapuche leader of the indigenous resistance to the Spanish invasion of Chile. We did. His full name became David Lautaro Stoneman-Bell. We figured "David" gave him the option of having an easy American name, that could also be easily pronounced in Spanish. That way he could use David, or use Lautaro, or any combination, as he stepped into his adult identity. We didn't know if he would choose to live in the USA, or Chile, or where he would be as an adult. His nickname became "Taro" in our family and with his friends as he grew up. He did later adopt "David" for ease in navigating outside the family.

When Taro joined our family in August of 1988, I stopped commuting to New York City. Since we had started replicating nationally, it worked for me to move my office to Belmont full time. Our project became the "National Replication Project of the Youth Action Program of the East Harlem Block Schools." That's what we had to say when we answered the telephone: "Hello, this is the National Replication Project of the Youth Action Program of the East Harlem Block Schools." We definitely needed a new name!

With the funds from The Ford Foundation and Charles Stewart Mott Foundation, I hired a staff of four who worked out of our living room and basement and held meetings on our porch. Taro was a delightful presence for the staff. In 1990, we officially spun off from the Youth Action Program and incorporated our non-profit as YouthBuild USA, Inc. It was a relief to answer the phone saying, "Hello, this is YouthBuild USA." By 1992, with additional support from other foundations, there were 17 staff members working in all corners of our home, in the living room, dining room, upstairs in bedrooms and downstairs in the basement. They were parking their cars in the driveways of those of our neighbors who agreed to do it, since parking was not allowed on our suburban street.

During the same period, we crowded in a few more family members. Freddy Acosta returned. He had first joined our family in about 1980 when we lived in New York City. He was 13, participating as a wonderfully engaged founding member of the Youth Action Program. He asked his parents if he could live with us. He thought he would be better off with us, because his older brothers were having some significant mental health and addiction challenges and he wanted to distance himself. He took us to meet his parents and ask their permission. They said yes. As a result, he came to live with us, as his "second chosen family." Freddy was 12 years older than Sierra. He lived with us in Harlem for a few years, until he had to go back to his family to help take care of his ailing Dad.

This concept, of teenagers being free to choose a second family to live with, was one of the projects of the Youth Action Program. Freddy wasn't the only teenager who felt he would be better off with a different family of his own choosing during his adolescence. We started the "Second Chosen Family" project. Several of our teen-aged members went to live with Youth Action staff members. This initiative didn't expand very far, but our family definitely became Freddy's "second chosen family" for decades. In about 1989 he came to Belmont to live with us again, just in time to provide a lot of child-care for baby Taro. His loving attention was a great gift to us all.

During that same period, our godson Kwao Adams, the son of my college roommate Emmie and her Jamaican husband, asked if he could come live with us and go to school in Belmont. Things weren't working out well for him in Jamaica for various reasons, including the difficulty of being a light-skinned bi-racial boy. His mom said ok, so he came. He was one year older than Sierra. Then my nephew, Mark Shaffer, came to Boston from England for a year of graduate school. The family grew! Mark, Kwao, Freddy, Sierra, and Taro!

Over the years lots of other young adults, mostly YouthBuild graduates, would live with us for various lengths of time, supporting their transitions. Usually when a graduate came to work in our national office as a VISTA volunteer, he or she would live with us for the first month or for several months. Taro would later name our home "Hotel Stoneman-Bell." One wonderful example was Alexis Vasquez, whom I met in DC on an annual advocacy Hill Day. We were visiting elected officials together to encourage them to fund YouthBuild. While we were walking around the Capitol between office visits, Alexis shared that he was currently homeless. I invited him to come live with us, and he did! He came for a year, when he was about 18 and Taro was 14. He and Taro became loving brothers for life. More recently, Brandon Menjares, a graduate of Youth-Build Just-A-Start who had participated for a few years representing low-income youth of color in our Belmont Unitarian Universalist church group that was dedicated to bridging class and racial divides, needed housing. He and his girlfriend came to live in our home. They created a wonderful apartment for themselves in our base-ment. Brandon and Taro also came to relate to each other as loving brothers. There were others who stayed more briefly.

So, while YouthBuild USA staff members expanded into our living room, porch, den, and basement, so did our household of children, teenagers, and young adults spread throughout the rest of the house! It's amazing how complicated life can be! And amazing that it is possible to manage it all. (It helped to have a big house!)

The Family Expands in Another Direction and Location

When my father died in 1981, I inherited about $50,000... enough to allow John and me to buy some property in the Berk-shires, in Western Massachusetts. At that point we couldn't predict how much of our lives would be in NYC, and how much in Belmont, because my mother would clearly need more care in the future. John examined the map to define an area that was equidistant from both, asked realtors for available properties, and together we visited a whole series of them. One of them was beyond gorgeous, on a small lake adjacent to hundreds of acres of conservation land in Great Barrington. It had three houses on it! We immediately called all our best friends to see who might want to buy it with us to create a family-like community together. Two other couples with children roughly the same age as Sierra, bought in: John and Joan Kavanaugh, John's two best friends from Stanford; and Bob Harris and Ellen McTigue, a loving couple whom we knew from NYC. We named the place "Friendly Pond."

Our house had a big upstairs room that we turned into a dormitory full of beds and mattresses. We invited other friends to send us their children for the month of August, every summer for many years. We ran it like a family summer camp. Leroy and Kathy sent their two younger children, Agape and Camlo. Emmie sent both her children, Kwao and Paloma. My sister sent her younger son, Milo. Tom Roderick and Maxine Phillips brought their two daughters, Emma Rose and Anne-Marie. John Gallery sent his son, Wyatt. John and Joannie's daughter, Lisa; and Bob and Ellen's sons, Colin and Brian: all joined the party, sleeping in their own houses, but joining our crew all day every day. Altogether, it was about 14 children enjoying every August together. There were two groups, older and younger, separated by 5 to 7 years.

What a marvelous extended family this created! We swam, rowed boats, played volleyball, basketball, and tennis, explored the woods, cooked our meals, played endless board games, did the chores, planted flowers, cared for animals, cleaned up the goose poop, and ate and laughed together. For me it was a perfect antidote to the endless work at Youth Action and YouthBuild USA. A whole month of family fun in a gorgeous place every August, from 1984 to about 2000!

Those summers deepened the amazing on-going connections between the Looper family and the Stoneman-Bell family. At the end of this chapter is a photo of our two families celebrating together at Leroy's 80th Birthday party. We also came together in 1993 when Leroy received a well-deserved honorary Doctorate degree from St. Michael's College in Vermont.

Additional wonderful results include: Emmie's son Kwao and Leroy's daughter Agape got married and lived happily ever after in Jamaica. Leroy and Kathy bought a house across the street from ours in Great Barrington. Tom and Maxine bought that house when

Leroy passed away in 2011. The Kavanaugh's two granddaughters and their parents now travel annually to Costa Rico with Emmie's two granddaughters and their parents because the parents became life-long friends when they were teenagers on Friendly Pond. All of the children became godchildren of the other families. We've served various roles in each other's weddings, lots of them taking place outdoors by the pond. Tom and Maxine's grandson became Taro's godson. And so it goes! Family, extended family, never-ending connections, love and sharing. Shared land, shared family, surrounded by natural beauty.

I am not religious. If I "worship" anything it's nature. The miracle of life, the infinite unknown glory of millions of years of life on earth, of millions of fascinating plant and animal species, interconnected, alive, interacting with each other in ways beyond my comprehension. I am infinitely grateful for every day I get to be alive on earth. Having a lovely retreat on a beautiful small lake in the Berkshires with extended family including lots of beloved children enriched and balanced our lives tremendously.

Circling from upper left to right and back: John Bell, Bob Harris, Kwao Adams, Brian Harris, Emma Rose Roderick, Taro Stoneman-Bell, Fernando Aguilera, Sierra Stoneman-Bell, and Agape Looper Adams, with 3 of Agape and Kwao's babies in her, Sierra's, and Emma Rose's arms.

Members of the Looper and Stoneman-Bell-Aguilera families together for Leroy's 80th birthday.

Sierra and Freddy

Alexis Vasquez joins our extended family.

Kathy and Leroy

Great Barrington extended family

CHAPTER 21

Dancing into the Future

The YouthBuild Act is Introduced

Between 1988 and 1992, as mentioned earlier, our home office steadily expanded. We had started with four staff in the living and dining rooms. We ended with 17 staff spread throughout the house. We took over the basement, installing new carpets and electrical outlets; on the ground floor, desks replaced tables in every room; and finally, we crept up to the second floor and transformed two bedrooms into offices. Our staff meetings were often held on the patio in the sunshine, sitting in a circle of chairs. It was very helpful to our start-up organization that we didn't have to pay rent or parking fees. The restrictive town zoning rules forbade offices in our neighborhood, but I was both unaware of and uninterested in that detail, so it was four years before the town told us to end our unauthorized activities after some unwelcoming neighbors complained. By that time, we were ready to rent an office elsewhere.

During the richly filled four years in the home office, I was simply putting one foot in front of another, steadily pursuing the list of 14 steps I had laid out as necessary to spread YouthBuild around the country. One day Margherita, the coordinator of the Youth-Build Coalition, took a long walk with me on the nearby golf course during which she was interrogating me about our plans. "What," she asked, "is the actual plan? I don't understand it, and I need a plan." When we arrived back home after our long conversation, she said, "Now I understand. It's not exactly a plan, it's more like a dance. You are orchestrating a wonderful dance, moving all the parts forward in sync, and I have faith in it." For me, my list was the plan.

The Necessary Steps for National Replication

Here is the 1988 list of action steps which informed my dialogues both with Margherita about our plan and with Jon Blyth about funding from the Charles Stewart Mott Foundation:

1. Build a geographically diverse sampling of strong local programs committed to a common program design and a united national movement.

2. Build a broad constituency of community support through a national coalition.

3. Build a new national non-profit organization as the support center, to provide technical assistance, training, inspiration, evaluation, funding, national cohesion, and advocacy.

4. Obtain sufficient private support to fund the effort prior to federal funding and to compensate for any weaknesses in the structure and process of federal funding.

5. Gain bi-partisan political endorsement and several committed champions in the Congress.

6. Build strong partnership relationships with federal agencies which might administer and enhance the federal program(s), in particular HUD, DOL, and the Corporation for National and Community Service.

7. Obtain independent corroboration and documentation of the value of the program.

8. Develop young leaders as spokespeople to communicate the depth of importance of this initiative to them and their communities.

9. Obtain sufficient press coverage for a credible public presence and reputation.

10. Get federal legislation passed and appropriations made year after year.

11. Influence effective operation of the federal agencies.

12. Set quality standards and establish a strategy for inspiring and enforcing adherence to them at the local YouthBuild programs.

13. Provide the training and technical assistance necessary to all sites to meet quality standards.

14. Diversify the funding sources and build private sector support.

That was the plan. We did not have a consulting firm, did not have a "strategic plan," did not have a "theory of change." We just had a list of things to get done. Big things. Putting that list together cost us nothing and wasted no time.

Working to Get Federal Funding

One key item on that list was getting federal funding. Cliff Johnson, the policy director for the Children's Defense Fund under Marian Wright Edelman had visited our program in East Harlem. He was impressed. He decided he would do what he could to spread it nationally. He brought me to Washington sometime around 1989 to meet Braden Goetz, who was a staff member for Congressman Major Owens, a Congressman from Brooklyn. We talked through the possibility of writing legislation that would authorize a federal program modeled after what we had done. Braden said, "Well, it's a long shot. It has never worked before, as far as I know, for someone to come from a local community with a program model and get it written into law and spread it around the country. These things are usually initiated by someone with power in the federal government. But what the heck," he said, "It's worth a try. Let's write the bill."

And so we did! He told me to write the elements of the bill in an outline form (my favorite approach), and he would have legislative staff turn it into legislative language that we could then edit together. When the draft of the bill arrived in legislative language, I sat at my little desk overlooking the patio and my plants, on the telephone with Braden, tweaking the bill until it said exactly what he and I wanted it to say. I could not believe that this was happening. I had no idea how bills were written. The idea that I could sit at my desk, on the phone with a DC staffer, and get a bill written according to my specifications, was incredible. I figured hardly anyone in America knew that was how business could be done. Reflecting on it later, it was interesting and impressive that neither I nor anyone I knew had ever made a campaign contribution to Major Owens. Lobbying and money had nothing to do with this. It was all about spreading good ideas through legislation. Period.

The other surprise was that I barely met Congressman Major Owens. The work was done entirely with Braden. I didn't hobnob with the Congressman, and I didn't need to do so in order for him to introduce our bill. That was fine with me, because I still wasn't good at hobnobbing. The humorous irony was that Major Owens was the same gentleman in whose office I had camped in protest when he was running the anti-poverty program in NYC in the sixties and the East Harlem Block Schools had occupied his office to protest something (I don't remember what!). I was sure he had no recollection of that. It was more than twenty years earlier. One of the lessons in discovering that Major Owens would be the right person to sponsor the bill was that people stay in their work for a lifetime, and you never know when you will meet them again, in what positions, with what power over the issues that matter to you and your community.

Once the House bill was written, we needed to find a Senate member who would be its sponsor. This process took a while. First, we tried Senator Kohl from Wisconsin. He came close, but then chose not to do it. I was simultaneously trying to get the attention of staffers for Senator John Kerry, the junior Senator from Massachusetts, since I was his constituent. It proved difficult to get through to his staff. The key person in DC didn't follow through, didn't answer calls, and I began to give up on Senator Kerry. One key reason he was a good candidate is that he was on the Committee that governed authorizations for HUD.

I had, over time, chosen HUD as the sponsoring agency for YouthBuild for several reasons: its leadership supported the idea; its purpose was broadly to diminish poverty through community economic development and housing; and no other agency seemed appropriate. Rob Ivry of MDRC (then the Manpower Demonstration Research Corporation) had introduced me to senior staff at DOL. When I visited DOL to gauge its interest I was advised very directly and clearly by Rob's contact, David Lah, who had served there for many years: "DOL at this time is interested in short-term low-cost interventions for the young people most likely to succeed. The idea is to strengthen the workforce in the most efficient way possible. The comprehensive long-term intervention that you have created for the most disadvantaged youth does not fit the profile of our priorities. You would be better off elsewhere."

When I went to HUD, I got a different response. It was the era of George H.W. Bush. Secretary Jack Kemp was in charge. I had previously met Assistant Secretary Anna Kondratas at a conference where I had spoken about the importance of teaching responsibility to young people. She was attracted to that concept. She approached me after the meeting to say how much she appreciated my remarks. I followed up by scheduling a meeting in her office. During that encounter she said, "I am a radical conservative. I believe in democratic capitalism. I believe that we must find a way within democratic capitalism to diminish poverty." I responded by saying, "Well, I am a conservative radical. I don't care what economic system we have as long as we succeed in diminishing poverty. Let's work together." And so we did!

Anna came to visit both the YouthBuild program in the South Bronx run by Getz Obstfeld through the Banana Kelly Community Development Corporation, and the Youth Action YouthBuild Program in East Harlem that I had started. I went to visit both programs the day before her visit and warmed up the young people, getting to know them, informing them of the upcoming visit, listening to them, and making sure they were prepared for this critically important visit from HUD's Assistant Secretary. I usually try to do this before important visits from elected officials, so I can encourage the young people to speak from a position of comfort. It helps if I have knowledge of their individual stories, and if I have gotten to know them so they are not intimidated by me or distracted by the fact that they are excited to meet the founder of YouthBuild. I can facilitate the conversation better if I already know them. I remind them of what they said the day before and ask questions that draw them out.

The next day Anna Kondratas toured the awesome large apartment buildings rehabilitated by young people in both communities. Then we gathered together about 40 students from both sites in our cavernous East Harlem office building for a dialogue with Anna. She was blown away by their passion and sincerity, their apparent intelligence and good will, coupled with their painful histories. At the end of the day, she said to me, "This has been the most exciting day of my life at HUD. What you are doing is amazing. Let's work together to spread this." And so we did!

Meanwhile we had had a lucky break with Senator Kerry. Somehow, we had arranged for him to visit YouthBuild Boston, which was the first replication site outside of New York City. I still did not have a relationship with any of his staff, but there he was, visiting a constituent site in Roxbury. His reaction was the same as that of Anna Kondratas. He loved it. He said, "This is what needs to be spread around the country. This is what we need in addition to affirmative action — a real pathway out of poverty for the young people who will not benefit from affirmative action at the college and employment levels if they don't find a way to get out of poverty, get educated, and get work experience first." He agreed to sponsor the bill in the Senate.

Senator Kerry later visited several other YouthBuild programs: in East Harlem, Springfield, Fall River, New York City, and elsewhere. His love for the program steadily deepened. He later told me that part of its importance to him was that when he had served as a prosecuting attorney in MA, he had witnessed many young people being incarcerated whose lives would have gone in an entirely different direction if they had an opportunity like YouthBuild. When he ran for President in 2004, he publicly stated that if he became President, he would eliminate the waiting lists for YouthBuild by expanding programs around the country. He would "Open the doors to every young person knocking." That is exactly what needed to happen. Open the doors to every young person knocking. Senator Kerry remained our dedicated and active champion for the rest of his time in the Senate. His role was absolutely essential to the existence of YouthBuild as a federal program. Some of his staff members — especially Heather Higginbottom and John Phillips — also became friends and advocates for YouthBuild for decades.

While the original legislation was sponsored first by Democratic champions in the House and Senate, over the years the advocacy for on-going appropriations had a bi-partisan team in both houses of Congress who led the letters of support and negotiated with the appropriations subcommittees. Senator Mike DeWine (R-OH), Senator Kit Bond (R-MO), and Rep. Hal Rogers (R-KY) played key roles. Rep. John Lewis (D-GA) was a champion until he died, when his successor Nikema Williams (D – GA) took his place. She was joined by Rep. Don Bacon (R-NE). When Senator Kerry left the Senate in 2013, Senator Kirsten Gillibrand (D-NY) stepped into his shoes as the Democratic champion, joined by Republican Senator John Cornyn (R-TX).

Sen. Kirsten Gillibrand (D-NY) at a site visit in NY.   Sen. Mike DeWine (R-OH)

Aaron Jones, CoS for Rep. Hal Rogers, (R-KY) on a site visit in KY.

CHAPTER 22

Gomah Wonleh Speaks about his YouthBuild Experience

I t's one thing for me to tell the story of the negotiations with government that were necessary to create and sustain YouthBuild. But the most important thing going on all around the country is that YouthBuild was working to provide the conditions for young people to transform their lives. Nobody tells that story as beautifully as the students themselves. Elected officials were inspired to support YouthBuild by hearing directly from the students. Therefore, I must include in this book samples of their stories so you can understand that critical aspect of the history of YouthBuild. It is important to listen to the young people about their own experience and hear how their passion to make a difference is reliably unleashed by experiencing the power of love coupled with opportunity.

Only if the general public understands the force for good that is reliably unleashed, can we build the momentum to get full investment in programs that successfully empower the young people who are still being left behind, kicked to the curb, dismissed from society, all across America. We still need to fulfill Senator Kerry's vision of opening the doors to every person knocking.

Following is a talk given to YouthBuild students and graduates by Gomah Wonleh, a graduate of YouthBuild Providence.

"Good evening. My name is Gomah Wonleh. My story is not that different from any YouthBuild student or graduate here. There was a time when I made a lot of bad decisions and surrounded myself with the wrong people. I had no sense of direction, no aspirations, or long-term goals. I really didn't care about anything.

"I lost my father at the age of nine, eleven months after I had met him for the first time. See, I am originally from West Africa. I was raised by my grandmother while my parents left their home to pursue the American dream. A dream that many of you here can say your parents chased.

"After losing my father, being the oldest boy with two younger siblings, I had to grow up quick. My Mom was trying to make a man of me fast, while I was trying to adapt to a new country and trying to fit in with the cool kids. I got kicked out of almost every school in Providence because I was always fighting. I battled a lot of internal anger. Not only having to survive a civil war, but adapting to a new country, and losing my father, and the fact that I felt like nothing I ever did satisfied my mother, all made me an angry and confused child.

"My mother always spoke about education, but I really never knew the true value of it. I just did enough in school to get by and please my mother to some degree; but I didn't fully take advantage of my education. I graduated from high school and went to the Community College of Rhode Island (CCRI) where I was more focused on attending college parties than going to class. I continued doing the bare minimum and it caught up with me. I flunked out of CCRI and with no other real options I drifted. I had no money, no job, and I was about to lose my place to live. I remember I would go to my girlfriend's college and walk around the campus and wait until she got out of class. I was up there so much that people thought I was a student. It came to a point where I didn't want to be a pretend student anymore. I got tired of seeing other people working towards their goals. I had some of my own, but I wasn't sure about how to achieve them.

"A close family friend told me about a program that teaches you construction, where you can get your GED and get paid for it. While I already had a diploma, the prospect of learning something new intrigued me and it didn't hurt that they would be paying me. Little did I know that the program would change my life forever.

"The staff at YouthBuild were amazing. They helped a young man who had very few long-term goals, confidence, or sense of direction.

They believed he could make something of himself. The work was not easy, some of the basic tasks like being on time were hard for some of the students. YouthBuild was not only teaching us a trade, but also teaching us life skills.

"One particular staff member, Mr. Andrew Cortes, took me under his wing and believed in me. He convinced me that I had the quality to one day be a union carpenter and that I could be part of a tradition that's been around since the 1800's...the United Brotherhood for Carpenters. For someone who never believed he could really be anything, to have someone like Andrew believe in me was a wonderful feeling. Although we are now brothers in the same trade, I still look at him as my mentor and a good friend.

"Having the opportunity to join the Union has been and continues to be one of the best things that ever happened to me ...next to the birth of my son and graduating from YouthBuild. I get to help rebuild my own community! I've worked on schools, banks, hotels, and many other projects. I wake up every day proud to go to work as a professional. Being in the union has taught me many things and has helped transform my life. It has taught me to take pride in myself and my work and to be diligent in everything I do. I am getting benefits I never dreamed were possible: pension, annuity, medical insurance. I have skills that can never be taken away from me. Never once did I think that I would be worth almost $50 an hour! It's because of my career that I was confident enough to have our first child (Noah) a year and a half ago, because I knew that I could provide a future for him with the help of my beautiful girlfriend.

"I am very proud and honored to be a member of the United Brotherhood of Carpenters Local #94.

"My message to current YouthBuild students: If you have made up your mind that you are ready to change your life, YouthBuild is a great step forward. I wish you the best of luck, and when you reach a roadblock just remember there's nothing you can't do if you work hard. To all my graduates: I ask you to stay involved, use your experience to help the next person, serve as an example that this program works. I didn't understand the magnitude of YouthBuild until I attended my first Alumni Xchange. I was deeply moved to see young adults from all over the country come together for such a positive event. For the first time I felt like my voice could be heard.

"During my first Alumni Exchange my peers chose me to serve on the National Alumni Council. I vowed to do all I can to make sure everyone gets a chance at the same opportunity I have. I would do anything and everything I can for YouthBuild because they looked out for me. Thank You."

On his first site visit in 1992, HUD administrator
Roy Priest meets a YouthBuild Boston student

CHAPTER 23

Everything Comes Together in DC with HUD

then Everything Gets Complicated

As a result of our various relationships — with Braden Goetz in Major Owens' office, Senator John Kerry, and Anna Kondratas at HUD — we wrote legislation that placed YouthBuild in HUD. This Agency had a broad goal of diminishing poverty, so the comprehensiveness of the YouthBuild program was a good fit within it. Furthermore, Anna Kondratas, supported by Secretary Jack Kemp, wanted the program. <u>It is always important to have support from the administering agency, not just the legislators</u>.

At the time, our staff was still working out of my family's living room. After the legislation was written but before it passed, I found a wonderful lobbyist in Washington to help. His name was Bob Rapoza, a very good guy focused on affordable housing who worked with a lot of non-profits who did business with HUD. He charged us just $10,000 for his decisive first year with us. I don't remember how I found him. He stayed with us as a key player for many years.

The legislation passed in 1992, without discussion or amendment. It was part of a much larger bill governing HUD. It was replete with every single clause we wanted. It was signed into law by President George H. W. Bush. This is where the role of the champions is critical. Senator Kerry and Congressman Owens made this happen. They took personal responsibility for its success. They had visited and fallen in love with the program. There was a turning point moment for me after the bill had been introduced when I went to talk to Bruce Katz, who was the chief of staff for the authorizing committee for HUD at the time. He said to me, "Dorothy, don't get your hopes up. Senators introduce thousands of bills to satisfy their constituents but most of those bills go nowhere. This particular bill is going in the absolute opposite direction of the Congress, which is not passing new discretionary domestic legislation benefiting poor people. Unless Senator Kerry cares more about poor people than any Senator has ever cared about poor people, this bill is dead." I went home quite discouraged.

Two weeks later Bruce Katz called me. He said, "You are in luck. Senator Kerry cares. He called me and said it is my job to get this bill passed, so it might happen." It did. This was the beginning of 20 years in which Senator Kerry reliably promoted and defended YouthBuild behind the scenes at every turn, every crisis, every opportunity. He never got any public credit for it, but I am delighted to report that I made 600 calls to Iowa when he was running for president and told this story to everyone who answered their phone. I also served on his Presidential Campaign's Finance Committee which met every week for 22 months at 8:30 AM in Boston on Wednesday mornings at his brother's law firm. I learned a lot about what it takes to run a presidential campaign.

The process for passing a bill includes that it must pass through the authorizing sub-committees in both Houses of Congress; then the differences between the bills must be negotiated in Conference including representatives from both Houses; then it must be passed on the floor of both the House and the Senate; and then the President must sign it into law. After it becomes law, it subsequently goes through the similar appropriations process, through which appropriations sub-committees in both the House and Senate set a funding level for the coming fiscal year. If these levels are different, it must go to the Conference Committee that usually splits the difference between the two levels. Then the President has to sign the appropriations bill.

In our case Bob Rapoza, our lobbyist, somehow arranged in that first year, in consultation with Bruce Katz who was still the chief staffer for the process and still responding to John Kerry's desire to see it pass, for the authorizing committee to create a set-aside of $40M that superseded whatever the appropriations committee would do. This was an amazing sleight of hand that served us well, except that it made the staffer for the appropriations sub-committee so mad that he never forgave us. He did not like having his authority overridden. In subsequent years he tried cutting it a few times but never succeeded.

Getting the Right Person in Charge of the Administration of the Government Program

By the time that first appropriation of $40M was passed for FY'93, Bill Clinton was President, Henry Cisneros was Secretary of HUD, and Bruce Katz — who had previously been staff for the Senate sub-committee who had helped get YouthBuild passed, had become Secretary Cisneros' Chief of Staff. Roy Priest was the civil servant who was Director of the Department of Community Preservation and Development (CPD).

When Roy Priest read the legislation, he went to Secretary Cisneros and Bruce Katz and asked to be put in charge of the Youth-

Build program because it fit with the goals of his department and he really liked the design. He came to visit YouthBuild USA and YouthBuild Boston, to understand the program. Fortunately, by the time he visited, we had moved out of my mother's living room into an office in Somerville where we could host Roy Priest in a professional context. He loved the program on the ground as much as he loved it in the legislation.

When I asked former Assistant Secretary Anna Kondratas what she thought of Roy, she said he was one of the best administrators in HUD, who truly knew how to work the system. So, when Bruce Katz asked me if I had an opinion about placing it in CPD under Roy's leadership, I said I thought it was a good idea. Roy Priest became the key player in HUD. He did a brilliant job. He made sure that the regulations developed within HUD to govern the implementation of the program were appropriate and supportive to the mission. Later, a few years after he left HUD, Roy became Chairman of YouthBuild USA's board of directors and served in an extremely skillful and dedicated way through 2022.

Managing the Branding Issue

The moment the first YouthBuild appropriation was passed, several directors from among the 22 existing YouthBuild programs pulled me aside at one of our national meetings. Their spokesperson, Taylor Frome from Philadelphia YouthBuild, said, "Dorothy, you have made a serious mistake. You have given the government the YouthBuild name, and now organizations from all over the country, with no history with YouthBuild are going to apply, just to get the money to do what they do, but with no loyalty to our vision, no fidelity to the model, and no commitment to the movement. You have given away a name that we have spent our energy building with a positive reputation and a vision. We need to build a network that does have that commitment, in which there will be solidarity and a commitment to stick with it no matter whether they get funded from one year to the next. The political reality is unpredictable. We don't have confidence that we will always have federal funds."

This was a powerful statement. I had to figure out the right response. I suggested that perhaps we should convene the directors who had created the existing programs to figure out the solution. About 15 directors and I spent three days on a retreat on an island off the coast of North Carolina developing the first draft of program design and performance standards to which they wanted to hold themselves and each other and all future YouthBuild program directors accountable. This was the start of a very inclusive democratic decision-making process that served YouthBuild programs extremely well. In 1992 we formalized it as the YouthBuild USA Affiliated Network with a national Policy Council including equal numbers of elected graduates, elected directors, and appointed YouthBuild USA staff. I served as its chairperson. This council carefully revised the program design and performance standards, and all the guidelines governing affiliates, every 3 to 5 years.

Competing for the Role of Training and TA Provider

During 1993-94, YouthBuild USA had to compete to become the training and TA provider for HUD's YouthBuild grantees. According to the law as we had carefully written it, five percent of the annual appropriation was reserved for training and TA, to be given to "a qualified national non-profit organization." In the late stages of the competition, when we had submitted a full proposal and been identified as a finalist, we were summoned to HUD to be interviewed by the contracts department as part of the selection process.

Roy Priest took me aside before the interview and said, "Dorothy, you are at HUD now. Understand that HUD now owns this program and that YouthBuild USA must be subordinate to HUD as a contractor. Make sure you keep this in mind during the interview and are appropriately respectful and humble in order for them to choose you as the contractor."

This was very good advice. I was humble and respectful. No one could have guessed that I thought this program belonged to me. We were selected. Roy's wisdom and guidance held the day, as it would many times subsequently.

Part of what we had offered HUD in our proposal was the set of Program Design and Performance Standards that had been worked out through the Affiliated Network Policy Council. HUD said, "No thanks. These are too prescriptive for us. We have learned to let local programs set their own design and performance standards. You are welcome to run your own affiliated network, but it won't have anything to do with us. Hopefully, it will strengthen the quality of the programs, but we will not fund it, impose it, or oppose it." So, everything we had learned in our first 14 years was essentially thrown out, although not stamped out, by HUD. Therefore, we built the affiliated network on our own, and the DeWitt Wallace Reader's Digest Foundation funded it. This was a key part of the catalytic role of private funding, creating a more robust public/private partnership in which we maintained some independent influence.

The Role of the Private Foundations

Private foundations have played a key role at every stage, filling gaps, compensating for government errors and delays, and funding innovation. The moment that the appropriation passed, I called the Mott and Ford Foundations from a telephone in an airport as I was traveling to DC and said $40M had been appropriated and that we needed support to build our capacity to be prepared to manage the TA part of the equation. (After all, we had only just moved from my family's living room to an office in Somerville. I didn't mention that on the phone call.)

They both immediately gave us grants and we staffed up. But then, to our surprise, HUD was six months late in selecting the TA contractor, so we had to call Ford and Mott again to fill the gap. They both came through again...covering our beefed-up costs for those six months while we waited for HUD. This was an amazingly flexible and generous commitment to filling the gaps as we built the public-private long-term partnership. This is the kind of support from private foundations desperately needed by non-profits. Jon Blyth, our program officer and a creative genius, and Bill White, the wise president at the Charles Stewart Mott Foundation, together supported YouthBuild USA every step of the way. They made grants continuously from 1988 through the end of my tenure in 2016, and beyond. Both Ford and Mott gave major grants to us on our 20th anniversary to create an endowment. When we celebrated our 35th anniversary at the Ford Foundation, Bill White was named as one of the two "Fathers of YouthBuild." The other one was Senator John Kerry. Sadly, Bill White passed away in 2019.

Many foundations — too many to name — have played decisive roles at different points throughout our history, getting us over the humps, through the front doors, and down the road to our destinations. Without them, this story would have been impossible.

Shock Waves: The First Cycle of HUD Grantees

When HUD put out the first RFP for YouthBuild in 1993, it received 880 applications. Roy Priest was stunned. He said he had expected to be running a small "boutique" program, not something with this level of demand and capacity in the field. HUD funded only 30 of these applications for $1M of full funding, plus about 105 planning grants of $100,000 each.

There were 22 programs already operating around the country that we had supported between 1988 and 1993. To the shock and surprise of all of us, only four of those 22 existing programs were funded among the 30 HUD grantees. Furthermore, about half of the new programs were public housing authorities that had minimal experience with job training, and no experience with YouthBuild.

I spent a week on the telephone with thunderstruck, heartbroken YouthBuild program directors, one after another. This was a stunning moment of shock for us. What had we done? Directors were crying deep crocodile tears all over the country. I was standing in telephone booths listening to them, with incredible pain and grief. (This occurred before we all had cell phones).

This triggered a long four-page memo from me to the Secretary of HUD, explaining the background of YouthBuild and our vision and the problems created by these selections. My advisors told me the memo was far too long, but I sent it anyway. Fortunately, it caught the interest of the Secretary, Henry Cisneros, who passed it on to the Assistant Secretary, Andrew Cuomo, who called me in for a very useful meeting.

The next year there was a better balance in the awardees. Our original programs, by and large, survived the year and were funded in year two. They had never had federal funds before, so they kept on going with the local private and public funds they had raised. They had committed themselves through the Affiliated Network to being in it for the long haul, not just for the federal grants. They proved themselves sincere.

The "Revolution" and the Rescission

In 1994 the Congress changed hands from Democratic to Republican leadership with very different priorities. When Antoine Bennett, a YouthBuild graduate, and I met with Republican staffers for the House appropriations sub-committee in 1995 to negotiate for an appropriations level for FY'96 we were told, "There's been a revolution. You can forget about YouthBuild at the federal level. We are no longer funding federal discretionary programs for poor people. All the money is going to the states."

After that horrifying meeting Antoine and I looked at each other in the hallway and said, "Wow! We had better get to work at the state level, but there is no way we are going to forget about Youth-Build at the federal level."

Sure enough, the House zeroed out YouthBuild for 1996. Bill Clinton had also zeroed it out in his budget along with many other HUD discretionary domestic programs that were under attack. But John Kerry (D-MA) and Christopher Bond (R-MO) saved it in the Senate. Rep. Bill Goodling (R-PA), who had visited and liked the program in York, PA, actively supported their rescue operation by talking to appropriators in the House and Senate. The end result of this struggle was a 50% cut, from $40M to $20M for FY'96. That was terrible, but better than being zeroed out. It took several years to grow it back up, with incremental growth, helped by Congressman Jim Walsh (R-NY), who was chair of the House Appropriations Committee for HUD and had been a Peace Corps volunteer. He had visited a program in Syracuse, liked it, and already understood from his own Peace Corps experience that a year of service could indeed transform lives. First Lady Hillary Clinton also stepped in after she had visited YouthBuild Philadelphia. At that visit, the First Lady sat in a room with about 20 YouthBuild students, and about 30 photographers from the media. I was stunned by how little privacy she had, by the make-up she had to wear, by the media presence that had invaded our little office. I said out loud, impulsively, to nobody in particular, "Wow, what must it be like to have the press follow you everywhere!" The First Lady heard me, and turned to say directly to me, "It's terrible."

During that visit she had spontaneous and passionate conversations with the students. They impressed her. As she was preparing to leave, I stood by the door and explained what had happened to YouthBuild in the budget, and that President Clinton had zeroed it out in his budget without realizing its importance. Hillary went back to Washington and orchestrated a supplemental appropriation for YouthBuild in 1998 that brought it back to $40M. I was amazed and very happy that she stepped into the weeds in such an effective way.

At almost this same moment in 1996 when the House was cutting everything it could, the House forced a rescission of $10M to a $50M appropriation for '95 that YouthBuild had received the year before and that had already been bid out. Local programs had already submitted their proposals and been selected for funding by HUD and had been notified!

HUD's general counsel ruled that the only way to rescind $10M, since award letters had already gone out, was to simply lop off the last ten million dollars of contracts, based simply on which programs returned their signed contracts last. This was patently unfair because there had been no deadline for returning their contracts. This would have meant that 10 programs got unpredictably defunded.

Roy Priest, the HUD administrator, had a better idea. He called me, and we made a plan. At a YouthBuild conference of directors, Roy laid out the situation. He stated that if every single grantee that already had a signed contract would agree to take a 12% cut, that he could fund all the remaining selected grantees. He insisted that it would require voluntary agreement of every program that already had a signed contract, because he would not allow any one organization to be an exception. At that time nobody knew which 10 programs had not submitted their signed contracts and would therefore be eliminated. The leaders of the Affiliated Network spoke up in active support of this proposal, led by Taylor Frome, Executive Director of YouthBuild Philadelphia. Taylor and I had planned for this in advance with Roy. Within three weeks every one of HUD's more than 100 grantees had agreed to take the cut. The last program to agree was sponsored by a Native American tribal group that said, "No Way!" would it agree to the feds revoking money that had already been committed. They had experienced too much of the federal government taking resources from them. Fortunately, Roy persuaded them.

We viewed this amazing collective process as the pinnacle of solidarity. The HUD higher-ups were amazed… these programs already had signed contracts. It was unheard of for organizations to give back money when they didn't have to, just to help their peers who were actually in competition with them for the same resources.

This could not have happened without the leadership of the HUD civil servant — Roy Priest — who ran the program. It also could not have happened without the network of grantees being independently organized in the YouthBuild USA Affiliated Network to build solidarity among the program directors. It was a great example of a creative public-private partnership finding an unlikely solution to a challenging problem.

Some of the Many Dedicated YouthBuild Directors Across America

Patricia Bravo

Andy Delgado

Elijah Etheridge and Liz Morgan

Scott Emerick

Greg Flores

Taylor Frome

Bob Hennessey

Ditashia Kohn

Jennifer Lawrence

Joanne Munroe

Michelle Raymie

Simran Siddhu

Jim Smith

Ken Smith

Anthony Watson

221

Some of the Many Outstanding YouthBuild Graduates Serving as Young Leaders Across America

Jamiel Alexander

Kareema Barr

Mike Dean

Ely Flores

Jacob Gibson

Annette Goodrich

James Mackey

Brandon Menjares

Joel Miranda

Noe Orgaz

Sandra Quel

Antonio Ramirez

Julian Ramirez

Nina Saxon

Adam Strong

Jamie Turner

CHAPTER 24

Mikey Caban Speaks about his YouthBuild Experience

I am inserting another speech here by a YouthBuild graduate. In 2009, Mikey Caban was invited by Belmont Against Racism to Martin Luther King Day as the keynote speaker. Here are his remarks.

Mikey Caban, YouthBuild Lawrence Graduate

First, I would like to thank everyone in attendance for coming out on this special day to remember the late, great Martin Luther King Jr. on his birthday. I am honored to be here sharing my life experiences with all of you. Today is a special day, not only because we are recognizing one of the greatest people that has ever lived, but because I'm going to have the opportunity to educate all of you about a program which I believe is America's best kept secret. I will hopefully bring all of you into my life and share some of my stories with you about what the YouthBuild Movement has done for me.

YouthBuild is a national program that serves young adults between the ages of 16 to 24 who are growing up in some of America's poorest neighborhoods.

Students study for their High School Diploma or GED, while learning the carpentry/construction trade. We build low-income housing for homeless families and or first-time home buyers. Youth-Build consists of the following components:

- GED & or High School Diploma preparation
- Carpentry/Construction training
- Leadership Development,
- Counseling and Support Services,
- Alumni Services/ Career & Job Development.

YouthBuild was started in East Harlem, New York, by Belmont's own Ms. Dorothy Stoneman.

Today there are 273 programs nationwide and most recently we started going international. YouthBuild is a second chance for thousands of disadvantaged young adults who have dropped out or who have just basically "slipped through the cracks and have been forgotten about." Now I will be telling you about myself before the program, my accomplishments during the program, and most important …what I've been doing after the program.

I grew up in a home with a single mother and a younger brother. My father was an addict and was in and out of my life until I was about ten years old. From the age of five my mother had signed me up for sports and I was taught that teamwork, discipline, and hard work pays off. My mother not only talks the talk but also walked the walk. My brother and I had everything we needed, from clothes to a roof over our head, to having a cooked meal right after she got home from work. All this, while my mother was going back to school to complete her GED at the age of thirty-five because in her words, "I will not tell you to do something if I haven't done it myself."

Up until my freshman year in high school I excelled. However, due to the fact that my mother was working to provide for us and going to school, I had free time, and it wasn't very hard to get peer-pressured into things I shouldn't have been doing. When I arrived in high school I stayed involved as an athlete. However, I started meeting new people and was introduced to many other things such as drugs and alcohol, and how to make money selling drugs. After being introduced to the fast way of making money, I chose to sell drugs, not out of necessity but more so I could fit in with what was going on around me.

By the time I was seventeen years old I had my first son, Mikey Jr., with my elementary school sweetheart. I was only a junior in high school. With juggling school, sports, and being a young father, I was overwhelmed with all the pressure. To my mother's disappointment I dropped out senior year with just 3 months to go, to provide for my family. With some summer school I would have passed and really graduated, just not on stage with my class. Not one school counselor checked in with me to ask if this was the right decision I was making. (I will let you know why I said this later as I keep speaking.) But I left.

By the time I was twenty-one my 2nd son, Isaiah, was born, and I was still into making fast money, thinking this is the way to provide for my family. For a while I tried working wherever I would get hired, but at the end of the day I was tired of working dead-end jobs with no light at the end of the tunnel, so I kept selling drugs. There was one big risk factor in all of this, and it wasn't so much the fact if I got caught I would be in a lot of trouble, but more so that my girlfriend and kids were not benefiting from the instability in my life and also in theirs.

There was just a lot of partying, alcohol, and drugs. Fighting, shootouts, stabbings, and poverty are the norm where I am from, and the sad part is, that it still is. Eventually, at the age of twenty-three I was caught and charged with selling drugs, and I faced prison time. If convicted, I was looking at spending the next three to five years in prison. This would not have been good for anyone. But most important, my kids would have been just like me. Well, actually, if you think about it, up until then, I was doing the exact same thing my father was doing to his family, except I was not an addict.

This is what finally brought me to YouthBuild, and I will tell you up front I was not going there to change my life around. I was going to use it as a cover-up so the judge would believe that I was doing something productive and, yes, I was going to get paid for faking it through. This was perfect. Everyone would get off my back now.

Little did I know that this experience was going to completely change my outlook on life. After starting YouthBuild and realizing that there might be more to it than a GED and some basic carpentry skills, I started to slowly believe the message they were trying to relate to me. I began to feel the love that was being offered to me by the staff. Going back to what I said earlier about nobody caring if I was leaving from high school.... Well, here, they actually did care about me. This environment was new to me, but I was starting to feel comfortable. I excelled as a student. Not only did I receive my GED, but also my certificate in carpentry. But what impressed me most was the leadership development aspect of the program.

This is where I learned that having a voice, an opinion, or just wanting to be heard was actually OK. I was being taught to control my emotions and use them in positive ways to help not only my family and myself, but others around me who do not know or are not sure about expressing themselves. Again, my mother raised me right and I was always very sharp, I just had insecurities that made me worried about what others thought about me. I was starting to realize that through the trainings I received in YouthBuild, I was not only speaking for myself but thousands of others who were in my exact situation. This brought out a side of me that was unexpected, but that I see now. Leadership Development was for me.

Through YouthBuild I have been able to do many great things. I have done many speaking engagements like this one where I spread my story in hopes of others seeing that it is possible to make a change. I was elected by my peers at the National Conference of Young Leaders to serve on the Young Leaders' Council to represent the YouthBuild movement as a whole. After serving a year's term I was elected President of that Council. I was responsible for keeping the movement strong and on the frontlines of modern-day change for this world. I have been able to meet many great people of our time through YouthBuild such as the late Ted Kennedy, and most recently I met Martin Luther King III. When I leave here, I will write to him to tell him I had a chance to speak in honor of his father.

After graduating YouthBuild in 2005, I committed to one year of fulltime service while gaining hours towards my AmeriCorps scholarship, which I am using for my first semester at my local community college. I went to my first two classes this past week. After my one year of AmeriCorps service, I was hired at my program as one of the carpentry trainers. Since leadership development was my focus, YouthBuild gave me the tools and sent me to numerous trainings in order for me to take my skills to the next level. This is why YouthBuild is different. They see the potential in a person and help bring out the best. They push us to succeed.

For the last six years I have done many things to help make a difference in this world. My passion for helping others is very strong. How can it not be when you look back and realize those who came before us and the struggles that they went through for us to be here like Dr. Martin Luther King Jr. himself? I really do believe that there are many people out there that don't have a voice, who have gone through so many things and are so oppressed that they believe it is okay to live the way they have been living for years. This is not ok.

What I am trying do is a small piece of the large puzzle. I want to be out there speaking for them. Everyone needs a voice, and I have been blessed to be put in a situation where I can do this. This is about advocacy. I truly believe that I have a mission now in life and it is helping others. It's funny because one of my closest friends said to me just the other day that I am "a walking advertisement for Youth-Build." He made me realize that even on my off time I am speaking to others on how important it is to be positive people, regardless of our age, race, gender, or religion. We all need to be a little bit better so that the future of all our children looks that much brighter.

I feel in my heart if I can keep going in this direction of helping others and changing lives that things will be better. I have been through a lot. I know that through my experiences I can help others. This movement has given me a lot. It has opened my eyes to see how important life is. Now that I have learned as much as I have, I feel it is my obligation to give back. And again, I am a walking advertisement for trying to improve this earth we live on. I have been able to witness the importance of being in a leadership position and having to lead by example. I take this challenge with pride and dignity.

So much so that four years ago I finally found the courage to not be embarrassed about my past and I decided to do something I love. That is coach youth football and basketball in my community. About one year ago I was elected to the board of the Youth Football League where I coach. One of my main goals on this board is raising money so this League keeps running. In a city like Lawrence the families cannot afford it, so most of it falls on the board to try and raise money so these kids have better things to do with their time than be on the streets.

Again, I know firsthand what not having anything to do can lead to.

I've paid my dues and was given a chance at it. I will not look back. I have built relationships with many individuals who once saw me as a problem child. When I used to go to court and see my probation officer, he would call me by my name, but I was just another case for him. Now I go to the same courthouse to recruit potential students and he refers to me as Mr. Caban, the guy who runs Youth-Build. I laugh and shrug him off, but deep down in my heart I say,

"Hey that does sound good:

"Michael Caban, Director of YouthBuild Lawrence!"

I do not want to get away from the reasons we are all here today in honor of Dr. King, and that is Closing the Opportunity Gap & Supporting Programs that Really Work.

Well, if you cannot tell by now, YouthBuild is a Program that Really Works. If it wasn't, I wouldn't be here speaking to all of you today. The Opportunity Gap for me, has closed. Look at this opportunity just today. Imagine the opportunities for my future. They are endless. All because a program was in place that didn't judge me for what I had done, but that looked at me for who I can become.

This has been a journey that I am extremely proud of. Since I applied myself to making change, change has come. For many people, new adventures can be nerve racking. For me, I've welcomed it. I belong here. There were many people who thought I was going to fail, or who didn't want to see me succeed. Well, you know what? Maybe they should've received an invitation to this breakfast here in Belmont. Because look at me now, I'm doing just fine, and all of those people are my motivation to prove change is possible.

I want to thank my beautiful family for sticking by me through all these ups and downs. This year will be seventeen years with my elementary school sweetheart, who is here with me today. I am glad you have been my rock to help me get through all of this.

To my students who are in attendance: besides my family, you are a big part of me standing up here today in hopes that you see it is possible. All of you tell me all the time that I am your motivation. Well, let me tell you something: You are my Motivation.

I also would like to thank Dorothy Stoneman for starting this program and being the driving force behind thousands of youth changing their lives. Because of you, I have this opportunity to be here today. Dorothy, from the bottom of my heart and thousands of others, thank you for starting this wonderful program.

I would like to also thank those who put this wonderful event together. This has been an amazing opportunity for me.

And last but not least, I would like to thank Dr. Martin Luther King Jr. for setting the example of believing in change and fighting for it.

In closing, I would like to read a couple of quotes ...

> *Human progress is neither automatic nor inevitable... Every step toward the goal of justice requires sacrifice, suffering, and struggle and the tireless exertions and passionate concern of dedicated individuals.*

> *The means by which we live have outdistanced the ends for which we live. Our scientific power has outrun our spiritual power. We have guided missiles and misguided men. We need to build our spiritual power.*

Thank you all.

Our National Leadership Team

CHAPTER 25

Building the National Support Center at YouthBuild USA, Inc.

Chapters 21 and 23 took us through 1996 with a focus on our negotiations with the Federal government. Simultaneously, we were doing five other essential things at YouthBuild USA:

1. expanding YouthBuild programs around the country with private and local funds,

2. building our staff capacity and culture to create a strong national non-profit support center,

3. engaging students and graduates in national leadership roles,

4.   building a balanced and effective board of directors, and

5.   cooperating with an independent evaluation of YouthBuild to validate program impact.

The years between 1988 and 1996 were decisive for each of these elements. By 1996 there were 100 YouthBuild programs in the USA. At the core of everything was building a cooperative culture of love and respect for students and staff.

1. Expanding Beyond New York City

When the Ford Foundation agreed to support our replication and our coalition efforts, they said we should create five sites across the country and do an evaluation of their impact. I thought five sites would not be enough, because it seemed predictable that there would be a continuum of quality across the five. If one failed and another was weak, and only one or two were strong, we would not have decisive results. I decided that while Ford may only fund five, we would include as many as 20 in the expansion effort in order to get fuller information about the replicability of the program.

A number of organizations around the country had come forward with an interest in replicating YouthBuild. This had happened organically, partly in response to our active outreach to recruit members to the coalition we began in the late 1980's to create a federal funding stream; and partly in response to local leaders happening to hear YouthBuild graduates speaking out at various conferences. Individual leaders surfaced — like Taylor Frome in Philadelphia, who came to my office in Belmont and said she wanted to create a YouthBuild program in Philadelphia and would take it on by herself; and Tim Cross, in Boston, who had heard a graduate give a speech about her experience that inspired him so much he decided to launch it in Boston by convening a start-up group that organized the very first replication outside of New York City. YouthBuild Boston and YouthBuild Philly both became outstanding programs, still thriving today.

In response to the interest expressed, we held a national conference in New York City, on the 4th-floor walk-up of an alternative high school in East Harlem. Since we didn't pay their way, only leaders of very committed groups came for that training. John Bell and I, with other staff, presented all aspects of the work, deliberately emphasizing how challenging it would be. Our purpose was to weed out folks lacking resilient determination.

The results were good. Five sites emerged from that first training, ready to go home and raise the money to create a local YouthBuild program. They each succeeded. We did subsequent trainings for additional sites. We helped by raising philanthropic money and distributing it to them. We got an important grant from the DeWitt Wallace Reader's Digest Fund for this purpose, and from other funders, along with continued funding from the Ford and Mott Foundations. Each program also raised money locally.

We had learned our lesson from the first round of failed replication in New York City in 1984. As mentioned earlier, In 1985 Al Rodriguez and I, supported by Getz Obstfeld, had written the full program handbook. We simultaneously created the trainings needed for local leaders to understand how to put together all the complex pieces and cultural elements of this comprehensive program.

I also wrote a handbook in the eighties on Leadership Development. YouthBuild was never about minimal skills training for marginalized young people to survive and fit into the economy through dead-end low-wage jobs in the private sector. It was about personal transformation to become confident individuals who built their own future and who contributed to creating a better community.

Our letterhead said: YouthBuild, Rebuilding our Communities and Our Lives. The words on the back of the tee-shirt were: "**Young People Want Real Jobs Rebuilding Our Communities.**" The mantra became, "**Leadership means taking Responsibility to make sure things go right in our lives, our families, our communities, and our nation.**"

As a result of all this, the national replication of over 20 sites around the country prior to the federal funding reaching local communities, was nearly seamless. Many programs emerged that were effective, with determined and creative leadership, with fidelity to the philosophy, including both the qualities and the comprehensive set of components. Only two or three — those with weak leadership or inadequate funding — failed. Most were successful.

2. Building a National Non-Profit Organization as the Support Center for Local Programs

From 1978 to 1990 we operated under the Youth Action Program of the East Harlem Block Schools. In 1990 we incorporated Youth-Build USA, Inc. (YBUSA) as a separate nonprofit. Thus began the work of shaping a large nonprofit organization. By 2014, YBUSA had a staff of 118 and an annual budget of $32 million, not counting the millions of federal dollars that went directly to local sites.

Recently I reconnected with a YouthBuild USA staff member from the 1990's. Based on his heartfelt comments, I realized that I needed to add a section in this book about how in the world we created what he called "a loving, supportive work environment." Mike Walker was fresh out of college, a young black man with expertise in data management and technology, who came to work in the national office. When we spoke, almost 30 years later, he spontaneously and affectionately named virtually every staff member who was present during the five years when he was there. He strongly praised his supervisor, John Moukad, a white man who served as his kind and thoughtful mentor. He said the culture was one of love. He missed it when he left.

The creation of a cohesive organizational culture of safety, mutual respect, mentoring for people's individual development, and a feeling of trust in each other was needed not only by YouthBuild students joining the program to rebuild their lives. It was also needed by adult staff seeking their own purpose and building their own futures. These elements added up to what Mike and many others summarized as the "culture of love."

How does a leader create a cohesive, caring, community of staff dedicated to the success of a venture designed to create opportunity for others?

At the start we had defined the essential culture for the Youth-Build students as being one that was the opposite of their negative previous experiences. We summarized their past experiences as having been "dissed": disrespected, dismissed, discarded, disadvantaged, disdained, discriminated against. We named the opposite force as the "power of love coupled with opportunity." I was challenged occasionally by senior staff who thought it was corny or inappropriate to call it "love." As one senior manager put it, "Love is about romance. It is not appropriate for professional staff to talk about love as part of a program for young adults." However, most staff welcomed the idea of naming "love" as key to our success, understanding that love was a more deep, complex, and universal concept than romance. Either way, naming love as a key element of youth programming was somewhat controversial, and definitely not the norm when we got started. It is more common nowadays.

I described love in our context as showing that we cared enough to listen deeply and to go out of our way to take actions that were not convenient, to demonstrate that we truly cared about the students' well-being and would do what it took to help them be safe and get to their goals. We advised staff not to be constrained by the so-called "boundaries" professionals were supposed to create between themselves and their "beneficiaries," or "clients." This was not a transactional relationship. It was a full human engagement on behalf of the students' well-being. We encouraged staff to give out their personal phone numbers, to go to the bedsides (if invited) along with students tending to their parents in the hospital, to go with them to court and back them up in their probation hearings... to go beyond the expectations of the students, to surprise the students with their level of caring and involvement. This is a different way of describing love. Caring enough to step beyond the normal patterns of people distancing themselves from each other's needs.

It was actually a great relief to many staff members who yearned for the freedom to be generous and loving, to do what it would take to help someone through life's hard days. It made their own lives more fulfilling, their impact deeper. It also definitely made a difference for the students. They always said it surprised them how much staff cared about them. That was part of our goal: to surprise them, to open their own minds and hearts to new possibilities. The students often experienced this as the "family" they had yearned for. Hundreds of times I have heard students say something like this: "I came to YouthBuild looking for a job and a GED. I got those, but what I found that I didn't expect was a family."

Here is one of my favorite poems from a student expressing this:

> "Imagine a child captured in his rage.
> Anger, violence, it seems to be the only way.
> When he feels down... it's as if no one's around.
> When the world closes in on him,
> He only breaks down.
>
> To live in a world where ignorance nourishes a baby,
> Death is given by the handful,
> And sanity seems to be crazy,
> Searching and searching, It seems to never end.
> For what, no one knows until it's found, my friends.
> That's why I'm glad YouthBuild is made of family and
> friends.
> In an unstable world it gives me stability.
> YouthBuild, my extended family,
> I'll love you until infinity."

I used to tell our senior leadership that if we expected staff in the local program to give love to the students, we needed to make sure that love was flowing steadily out from the national support center to the local programs. I sometimes used the phrase "from the top down" since hierarchies were familiar constructs and power actually did exist in that dynamic. The idea was that our board had to love us, we had to love our staff, our staff had to love the directors, the directors had to love their staff, and their staff had to love the students. The result would be that the students would love themselves and their children, their families, and communities. The love would flow like a waterfall, it would cascade from the top throughout our network from every level to the next. It would be the opposite of the usual hierarchy of power providing constraints, punishment, rules, and rewards from the top down. It would be loving respect flowing from the top to every level. It would create an immeasurable ripple effect.

To create a caring context among the staff, we followed some simple but effective processes internally. We typically started meetings with everyone sharing good news, personal or professional, to build relaxed personal relationships within all our staff groups, and to set a positive and connected tone rather than a mechanical, transactional, business-like, get-the-work-done tone. We also built a process of mutual appreciation into our meetings. After a staff member gave any presentation to any group, we would invite a few appreciations from the listeners. At the end of meetings, we would sometimes close with a go-round where everyone would appreciate the person sitting next to them. When a new staff member joined us, after they had a chance to introduce themselves fully, we would invite the people sitting on either side of them to welcome them by sharing what they already liked about the new staff member. It's surprising what a difference it makes to invite genuine and open appreciations of each other in a work environment. (I often would assign the appreciators based on their seating arrangements, so the person being appreciated wouldn't have to wait for a volunteer to step forward and wonder why there was any hesitation, or why some people volunteered but others didn't; and so that everyone would learn to appreciate everyone else.)

Of course, we also built in accountability for good performance, thoughtful feedback in annual performance reviews, and sometimes processes we called "self-estimations" in which an individual would provide to their team members a verbal self-evaluation of their own strengths and weaknesses, and then be given constructive feedback from the group about their perceived strengths and any areas needing improvement. Doing this in a staff group is relatively rare. It can be a very useful process.

Of course, the key role of national staff was to provide information, knowledge, and on-going support to the leaders and staff of local programs. We had to systematically offer the local programs these classic resources:

- <u>handbooks</u> that both summarized key learnings and detailed the optimal implementation of every program component;

- regular on-site <u>technical assistance</u> visits by coaches dedicated to each program, capable of advising the program director and providing useful trainings to local staff;

- <u>group trainings</u> for every category of staff — directors, teachers, counselors, construction managers and supervisors, leadership and alumni coordinators, job placement coordinators;

- assistance in <u>managing data</u> about participants and program impact.

Over the years, wonderful initiatives emerged from the national office supporting local staff. John Bell and his staff in the training department created the <u>Academy for Transformation</u> to organize the many forms of training. The Academy provided training for YouthBuild staff and youth and also for the wider youth development field.

John also developed a stunningly successful <u>Directors Fellows</u> Program that selected and engaged, over a period of 18 years, a series of eight groups of about 14 directors in two-year fellowships. John always recruited and selected directors so that the majority would be people of color, to create a safe cultural space, to support the development of racially diverse directors across the country, and to build a collaborative cross-racial culture. Each group met three times a year, for three days, in beautiful natural settings — e.g. the Rockies, Puerto Rico, and the California Coast. They would lay out their own learning agenda, which always turned out to be equally divided between professional development needs like building a strong staff, fundraising, and program integration, alongside personal development needs like handling stress, work-life balance, and healing from trauma. They would pursue it over two years, with deep sharing and collegiality that built relationships that lasted a lifetime. Having this type of closeness with other directors around the country was profoundly valuable for every director. It also created a deeply cohesive spirit throughout the movement. Older directors who have retired are still holding quarterly meetings with each other on zoom.

3. Engaging Students and Graduates in Leadership Roles

The leadership development process is core to our purpose. It is never-ending. YouthBuild USA asked every local site to have an elected Youth Policy Council meeting weekly, if possible, but at least every other week, with the program director and executive director, so students could provide input into all key program decisions and know that the most powerful people in the organization took the time to listen to them. This is not easy to implement, because so many professionals have not been trained to include their participants in decision-making. New directors need to be persuaded, and sometimes mandated as well as trained, to do this. The young people always respond extremely well to being invited to advise the director, to assist in hiring staff, and to being informed on financial matters. They may not show up for every meeting, but when they do, it dramatically changes their viewpoint, their level of confidence in their own value, and their trust in the organization.

The members of the Policy Council get elected within their own program. They go through the process of developing a speech for their peers and getting elected. This is an unusual and useful experience for them. Running for office, being democratically elected, having to speak their ideas to a group... all of this is new for most of them.

We followed the same process on the national stage. Outstanding young leaders, usually people who were active on the local Policy Council, have been sent to Washington DC every year since 1988 (except during COVID), to attend YouthBuild USA's annual National Conference of Young Leaders (COYL). They fly on airplanes, usually for the first time in their lives. In DC they get to know other young leaders from across the country. They are always blown away by the fact that there are young people just like them everywhere in the country who have experienced and who care about the same issues. They realize they belong to a national movement with a purpose that they value. Toward the end of a three-day conference, some of the attendees run for office again, making a speech in front of about 100 of their peers from around the country, sharing their passionate priorities and asking to be elected to YouthBuild USA's Young Leaders Council. If elected, they serve for three years. They attend three 3-day conferences of their Council each year, giving input into national decisions. The relationships formed among them last a lifetime, and they develop a lasting identity as national leaders representing their peers.

Once the Young Leaders Council was formed each year, it elected its own leaders, and then it also elected representatives to serve on the YouthBuild USA Affiliated Network Policy Council, alongside directors, staff, and alumni, chaired by the CEO. This Policy Council would have the authority to develop the Program Design and Performance Standards for local programs. This is a high level of responsibility. Young people who make it to this level of leadership are on a lifelong path to leadership.

Everyone who attends the Conference of Young Leaders (COYL) also participates in civic engagement training and Hill visits where they meet with elected officials about their experience in YouthBuild, and the challenges they faced prior to YouthBuild. Being on Capitol Hill, navigating the corridors, talking with Senators and House members and their staff, is life-changing. At the local level, many programs do the same thing with their City and State legislators, taking all their students through a similar educational and impactful process, often with a State YouthBuild Coalition or a City-wide YouthBuild Collaborative.

In order to extend the leadership development opportunities beyond the students' time in the program, YouthBuild USA began to sponsor regional alumni gatherings around the country, and a National Alumni Council. At the regional gatherings alumni elected representatives to the National Alumni Council, who then elected some of their reps to the Policy Council of the YouthBuild USA Affiliated Network. They served with the Young Leaders Council members, national staff, directors, and the CEO. The Policy Council included six young leaders, six directors, and six national staff, including the CEO who chaired the Council. This gave equal voice to each essential group.

As CEO of YouthBuild USA, I attended every moment of every meeting of both the Young Leaders Council and the National Alumni Council. I also joined them for every meal. I did this to demonstrate that the CEO considered them important and was deeply listening. I also did it because I learned a lot from listening, enjoyed getting to know them, and it kept me grounded in the real experience and priorities of our students.

The spirit of leadership is well expressed by this poem from Porschia Johnson, a 2003 graduate of YouthBuild Gary, who was a member of the national Young Leaders Council.

VOICE

> What is an idea if you don't have a plan?
> What is taking action if you don't make a stance?
> What is trying if you don't take a chance?
> Nothing. You have a voice,
> let it be heard.

What is seeing things in your own perspective if you don't
have a positive scope?
What is trying to deal with life's problems if you don't
know how to cope?
What does wanting to become a leader mean if you just
don't have hope?
Nothing. You have a voice,
let it be heard.

What are dreams if you don't have goals?
What is being strong if you don't play the role?
What does wanting to be positive mean
if you cannot feel it in your soul?
Nothing. You have a voice,
let it be heard.

What is coming together if we cannot rejoice?
What is making a decision if you don't have a choice?
What is changing a situation if you don't have a voice?
Nothing. You have a voice,
let it be heard.

What is trying to sail through life smoothly if you don't
have a boat?
What does passing the message mean if you don't send the
note?
What is a fair election if you do not get to vote?
Nothing. You have a voice,
let it be heard.

What does the day mean without the night?
What does victory mean without the fight?
What does freedom mean without the right?
Nothing. You have a voice,
let it be heard.

What is an enemy if you can't make a friend?
What is starting a new beginning if you're stuck at the end?
What does it mean to be successful if you can't harness the power within?
Nothing.

You have a voice
I have a voice.
We have a choice:
BE HEARD!

The Alumni Council

Emerging from their experiences within YouthBuild, many graduates have moved on into public leadership roles. Some now either run a local YouthBuild program, have started their own non-profit organization, or have been elected to public office, all serving as a force for good. (For a deeper dive into youth leadership development, strong staff building, and integration of program components, see *YouthBuild's North Star: A Vision of Greater Potential*, written by John Bell, available on Amazon, or for free download on his website, www.beginwithin.info).

Moved by the talent he saw in YouthBuild, David Abromowitz, formerly YBUSA's Chief Advocacy Officer, started a new initiative when he left YouthBuild called New Power, which lives within New Politics, Inc. It is dedicated to supporting young adults raised in poverty who emerged with skills and passion for making a difference, giving them the resources they need to run for office and take public leadership in local communities around the country. The participants are not limited to YouthBuild graduates, but they are included. If you know great potential candidates to recommend to New Power, you can find them at www.newpolitics.org/new-power.

4. Building a Balanced and Effective Board of Directors

I continued to act on my conviction that accountability to a board comprised of people who represented the constituency and communities served was the correct power dynamic informing the board structure, not only on the local level but also the national level. I was not interested in a board filled with funders, or to be more blunt, a table of primarily upper middle class or owning class white men who held the purse strings. I believed it was my responsibility to raise the money, and it was the board's responsibility to hold me accountable to the values and programmatic priorities wanted by our constituents. Throughout my tenure as leader, the three individuals who served in sequence as chairman of the board of directors were black men. I wanted the largest group of young people participating in YouthBuild — young black men — to see that the top person in our hierarchy looked like them. I wanted them to know that even though the staff leader was a white privileged woman, her boss was a black man who understood their lives and priorities and cared personally and deeply about them.

Leroy Looper served as board chair for the first 14 years from 1990 to 2004. Charlie Clark served for about a year before he joined the staff. Roy Priest served from about 2005 through 2022. As you know, Roy had served as the director of YouthBuild inside HUD and was totally dedicated to its integrity and success. Him serving as board chair was a gift to the movement. The wisdom and good judgment of these three men, as well as their passionate commitment to our mission and dedicated support to me, guided me throughout my tenure. The love was definitely flowing from the top.

The rest of the board was made up of a majority of people of color, including 3 to 5 YouthBuild graduates. It included community activists, pro bono legal advisors, skilled financial managers, non-profit local leaders, and other dedicated folks from various walks of life. It was a cohesive, attentive, and effective board, with no conflicts or stresses that I recall. There was no time limit to service, so members once committed could stay on as long as they liked. At least three of them over the years moved from the board into senior management positions.

We did not have program directors on the board, nor local or national staff, nor current members of our graduate leadership councils. I wanted to avoid any weird power dynamics between myself or other senior managers with our affiliates or constituents.

As described earlier, in order to get democratic input on key programmatic decisions we created a different structure: the **YouthBuild USA Affiliated Network**. This Network was made up of all the programs that chose to formally affiliate with us. None of the local YouthBuild programs have ever been owned or managed by YouthBuild USA. They have all been independent non-profits or local public entities. YouthBuild programs funded by the federal government were not required to join the YouthBuild USA Affiliated Network. They got the money and the right to use the name from the government, independent of us. They joined the Affiliated Network only if they wanted to be part of the national movement.

The board delegated to the Affiliated Network Policy Committee the programmatic decisions regarding program design priorities and performance standards. Membership on this Policy Council included equal members of directors, graduates, and national staff — 6 of each. I chaired it. The directors and graduates were elected by their peers, and the staff were appointed by me. The program director of the Affiliated Network, Anne Wright for many years, was not a member; she provided staff support for the Council and oversaw implementation of all our membership processes and various innovative initiatives available to affiliates.

This Policy Council structure complemented the board of directors, created another layer of accountability and grassroots input, and was a well-respected democratic process. I strongly recommend comparable democratic decision-making structures to other national non-profits managing a network of affiliates. If you google "YouthBuild USA Program Design and Performance Standards", the complete 2013 version will come up as an example of what can be produced.

5. Managing an Independent Evaluation to Validate Impact

When we began the national replication, prior to getting federal appropriations passed, urged on by Ford Foundation and supported by several other foundations, we launched an independent qualitative evaluation led by Professors Ron Ferguson at Harvard and Phillip Clay at MIT, in collaboration with Gary Walker at Public/Private Ventures. Our program officer at Ford Foundation, Karen Fulbright, introduced us to them. The evaluation lasted from 1991 to 1994. They selected five sites and evaluated the sites' first and second years of replication. They tracked outcomes and held deep interviews with students and staff. The purpose was to determine the replicability and the positive impacts of this new model.

They did an extraordinary job. It was superb, wonderfully useful for our learning process. Enormous guidance emerged about what made a difference at each site. The full study is available online if you google "YouthBuild Evaluation by Philip Clay and Ron Ferguson." For current YouthBuild directors and other youth development practitioners it would still be extremely useful in the 21st century.

Fortunately, it had positive results that gave crucial credibility to our expansion. A short quote from the introductory summary is here:

"Chapter two identifies five nationally known programs that have undergone evaluations and serve the same general population that YouthBuild serves. The YouthBuild Demonstration Project surpassed all but one of the others for average length of stay and had the highest GED completion rate for the GED. The data show that compared to the other programs YouthBuild serves a much higher than average share of minority males. Generally, evaluations show that young minority males are a difficult population to serve. Hence, YouthBuild compares well with the other programs in the rates of retention and GED completion that it achieves, particularly for minority men." It also reported that more than half of the participants in those five sites had been court involved. A little later, on p. 8, another summary paragraph said "... we conclude that the YouthBuild model is replicable and appears to be most effective when sites are most faithful to the philosophy and substance of the core YouthBuild model."

Below are a couple quotes from the research (p. 307). These are from students who were asked to compare how they viewed life before YouthBuild compared with "now," after YouthBuild:

STUDENT #1:

Before: "I probably would tell you I couldn't give that answer because I would probably be like, 'Right now, the way I feel I don't care a fuck about nobody but me. What happens to you I don't give a fuck. Not care.' I couldn't help you. Not without helping myself."

Now: "I know where I want to go, what I want to do. I got a heart now, patience. You can come to me for help, advice, or for anything. I'm willing to listen to you, good or bad, and be able to give you advice on it."

STUDENT #5:

Before: "People looked at me like I was a dope dealer. I used to sell dope ever since I was 15 years old, but I knew I had to change 'cuz' I didn't want to see that penitentiary. It was a few people here I was a friend with, but I got more friends now."

Now: "I'm a role model to people now. I ain't selling drugs no more. I go to church. Sing in the choir. We talked to the young people...they started to realize that ain't the way to go... now I got more friends... everybody's my friend. I'm just a nice guy."

Here's one more quote from the research, from a student at YouthBuild Seattle, (p.408)

> "YouthBuild not only gives US a chance, which we desperately need, but it gives SOCIETY a chance...to realize people can change. Society needs that."

The Role of Evaluations:

That first independent evaluation was absolutely essential; but it was just the beginning. From 1996 to 2018 we cooperated with numerous national evaluations implemented by governments, universities, research corporations, and professors. A list of *twenty-two* of them can be found in the appendix. This is a never-ending process for organizations aiming to prove impact, demonstrate cost savings, learn from their experience, and advocate for increased funding.

Be prepared!

Testifying before a Senate Subcommittee

Being a Woman in National Leadership

In response to a 2017 commentary in the NY Times about sexism in the corporate sector entitled "Why Women Aren't CEO's, According to Women Who Almost Were," I was moved to write about my experience as a female CEO in the non-profit sector. This chapter is derived from that essay.

It's easiest to become a female CEO if you are the founder of an initiative and you build it from scratch into a sizable organization. No men have the authority to decide if you are ready to be the CEO of an organization you have created.

As the founder of YouthBuild USA, that was my reality. As I described earlier, I had created the original YouthBuild program within the East Harlem Block Schools (EHBS), an organization that I had previously led as Executive Director. I had been appointed as Executive Director by low-income parents, mostly women of color, who served on the board of directors of the EHBS. At that time, in the federal Anti-Poverty Program, "Maximum Feasible Participation" of local community members was the guideline. As a result, low-income women of color had the unusual power to hire me as a teacher in 1965. Those same women promoted me to executive director in 1969. They granted me their trust, gave me the freedom and authority to build their organization in collaboration with them, and with accountability to them. As a result, I gained skills and confidence. I have no idea whether any group of men in 1969 would have appointed me executive director. But probably not.

Ever since 1969, I have been the "boss" in one or another organization. It's been a full and satisfying life with the freedom and autonomy to create wonderful things benefiting large numbers of people, with accountability to those same people. Without the backing of the women of color on the board of directors of the East Harlem Block Schools in the sixties, I might have had a very different life.

During the '60's and '70's, given that I was rooted in the Civil Rights Movement and the Anti-Poverty Movement, I did not put a lot of attention on the women's movement. I felt that racism was much stronger and more damaging than the sexism experienced by the white women who were then leading the women's movement. They had every right to claim their own oppression, but my proximity to people of color raised in poverty gave me a different perspective. As a privileged upper-middle-class white woman, I felt no amount of sexism directed at me and my peers could in any way be equivalent to the racism that was directed at all black people, and other people of color in America.

It is nonetheless useful to understand the various forms that discrimination against all sub-groups takes. So, I'll share a few reflections on sexism as I did and did not experience it.

I had not experienced much sexism directed at me in my professional role in East Harlem. I mostly had to figure out how to navigate people's feelings about me as a white person. It was clear that I should transfer my leadership role to a person of color as soon as workable. It seemed that it would be ok to be a white person in a leadership role on the national stage, but that it wouldn't feel right for any length of time in a predominantly black, Latino, or indigenous community where the work should be led by local people, even if I had played a catalytic role in starting an important project designed by community residents.

When I was leading in East Harlem, I didn't play much of a role in New York City's downtown white male dominated scene. My memories of the sexism that occurred when I entered the downtown scene for advocacy purposes are vague, although I know I wasn't taken seriously until I brought very large numbers of young people to testify at public hearings. I have clearer memories of what happened on the national stage.

An illustrative story occurred in 1996. HUD was having an all-day meeting about how best to work with youth in the housing projects. They had invited expert advisors. Roy Priest, then HUD's YouthBuild administrator, noticed that I hadn't been included and he requested that I be invited. He was told, "OK, Dorothy can attend, but she will have to sit with the staff on the sidelines, observing. She must not sit at the table with the guest experts."

The day before that meeting, the MacArthur Foundation announced its MacArthur "genius" Fellowship awardees of the year. I was among them. This is one of the most prestigious awards in the nonprofit and public sectors. I was called away from the HUD meeting for a TV interview. When I returned to my seat on the sidelines, a facilitator at the podium said, with a tone of respect in his voice, "I understand that Dorothy Stoneman is in the room, and that she just received the MacArthur Genius Award. I would like to invite her to sit at the table." I chuckled to myself, got up and waved a humorous good-bye to the other people sitting on the sidelines, and took my seat at the table. I nonetheless stayed rather quiet, aware that I hadn't actually been invited to sit there originally. During the lunch break, a senior official at HUD with whom I had worked closely when he was a Hill staffer, said to me, "Dorothy, congratulations! What is it like to get that amazing award? Has anything changed in your life?" I responded, "Didn't you notice? I was invited to sit at the table." He said, "Yes, you're right. I have never really taken you seriously until today. I thought you were just some kind of well-meaning do-gooder." He said it with complete warmth and friendliness, unaware of how sexist this comment was. I found it quite shocking.

I realized then that awards helped overcome sexism. In fact, they might be necessary to get a seat at the table and respect from the professional men. It was helpful that I unexpectedly got the Points of Light award in 1999, the Independent Sector Award in 2000, and a few others thereafter. But by 2006, when I was approaching age 65, a new dynamic had set in. I was not only a woman, but I was getting older. Soon ageism would be in play, coupled with sexism. I decided I needed another significant award in order not to be dismissed as an aged-out irrelevant old woman. I competed for the Skoll Award for Social Entrepreneurship. Fortunately, I won it. This gave me another ten years of relevance, of attention, of respect. I couldn't be written off yet. It made a huge difference. By that time, there were an expanding number of women in leadership roles in the philanthropic sector. Sally Osberg was president of the Skoll Foundation. She was profoundly gracious and welcoming! Times they were a-changing. There are now many women in national leadership roles.

There was another interesting perception about sexism that influenced my behavior in a funny way. At the time when John and I got married in 1974, when I was 32, I thought it would not be useful to me, in the male dominated world within which I had to raise funds, for the men with the money to know at first glance that I was married. This was an odd concept. I was never a beautiful woman, so I didn't depend on my looks for any relationship development. I had only once dated someone in the funding world when I was single, so there was no pattern or expectation there. Nonetheless, I was a likeable and warm person, definitely female, and I thought it would be better if men with power did not know my marriage status in the first five minutes. So, I didn't have or wear a wedding ring. However, when I was approaching sixty, I decided it would be better not to be perceived in the first five minutes as an "old maid," so around that time my husband and I bought two pretty rings in a convenience store (for $2.50 each) and started to wear them as wedding rings. This may seem ridiculous to you, and in retrospect it seems quite ridiculous to me, but it is interesting that a young woman in leadership, and then an aging experienced woman in leadership, would even think these thoughts and act on them. Either I was crazy, or it was an indication of the pervasive presence of sexist attitudes that had to be managed somehow. Every woman in leadership probably has her own unique stories about how sexist attitudes affected her or how she imagined she needed to manage them.

I did not socialize, play golf, go to bars, share a beer, or hang out with men who had money and power. White male CEOs in the non-profit sector may possibly have done so and may still do this with potential benefactors and funders, although I do not know for sure. In any case, I didn't aspire to those relationships, so I was not aware of missing anything. For me, the main expression of sexism was simply men with power not taking me seriously until or unless I did something truly extraordinary or received a noteworthy honor. I'm not sure whether sexism actually undermined my work, but I was aware of it and felt I had to manage it.

I happened to carry a kind of timidity toward powerful men, probably developed in response to the aspect of my father's personality that was critical and demanding. I never fully overcame this. So even when I developed meaningful relationships and mutual respect with powerful men, I tended not to pro-actively sustain those relationships. I think that was a real loss for me. There are a number of men I admire, love, and am grateful to for their decisive support at key moments. But I have typically not maintained pro-active contact with them over time, assuming that I was not important enough to warrant their attention.

Now, as an 80-year-old woman looking back, I think I benefited deeply from the fact that I spent my life working to counteract the effects of racism and classism and didn't get absorbed by the struggle against sexism. The black, Latino, and Indigenous communities as I experienced them never seemed as sexist, classist, individualistic, or competitive as the white European American community. I have generally been respected for my commitment to justice and equality regardless of my gender. Yes, in the early years people were suspicious about the motives of this "white girl in the ghetto." My motives and actions were tested repeatedly. In each new context over the years, I had to demonstrate that I was trustworthy. But there was also a cumulative trust that attached itself to me that I believe flowed from my living the lessons I had learned in the Harlem Action Group and the East Harlem Block Schools about how to create a structure through which I was accountable to, and in collaboration with, the people most greatly affected by YouthBuild.

In more recent years, the public culture has changed somewhat in the national arena. White folks in leadership in the national non-profit social justice and faith-based sectors — both men and women — are often given the message that they should step back, defer to leaders of color, and not take initiative to start and implement new projects because this is an unconscious expression of their privilege and their power that crowds out people of color. Millions of people are working on creating a new reality that expresses none of the classic forms of discrimination. This is a healthy evolution. Nonetheless, it is sometimes awkward for white people who are eager to use all their talents, privileges, and status to exercise their creative initiative, but who get the message not to do so. The message is, "Wait." "Go slower." "Let people with lived experience lead." "Let the people with proximity to the problem solve it. Not you." It was easier for white folks in the earlier days when it definitely worked to create a structure of direct accountability to the people with lived experience, creating boards of directors with a majority of people of color who said, "Please move as fast as you can with us, and for us, to solve this problem! Please go ahead and invent solutions, just let us know and get our input before going full steam ahead. Then we will have your back."

The goal of working together for a good society is profoundly more personally satisfying and more beneficial to humanity than the goal of gaining power and/or wealth in a corporation that values profit as its bottom line. This is probably as true for men as for women. I strongly recommend it to the next generation. Society needs more social change activists who are clear that our current one-rule economic system that values profit above all else is not producing a healthy society and is a profound threat to our and other species' natural habitat. We need to create a new economy that works well for everyone.

CHAPTER 27

The Faith-Based Redistribution Outside the Beltway

During the period in HUD, YouthBuild USA had to compete every couple of years for the contract to provide training and technical assistance (TA) to YouthBuild grantees. There was never any earmark or set-aside. We regularly won that competition between 1993 and 2002. But in 2003, when HUD issued the request for proposals (RFP) for the TA contractor, we were stunned by the content: it did not ask for a national provider. It called for ten regional providers.

Roy Priest was no longer at HUD. I called the Deputy Assistant Secretary, who was a political appointee under George W. Bush and very friendly to us. I asked what they were thinking. He explained very candidly that the White House had realized that over $2B of discretionary TA funds for large federal programs were being distributed to large entities inside the beltway. They had a focus on supporting faith-based entities. They had therefore directed all agencies to re-structure their TA for all programs in such a way as to spread these funds to small faith-based community organizations outside the beltway that were not strong enough to compete for national contracts. I pointed out that the coherence of the national YouthBuild program depended on a national TA provider communicating consistently the essence of the program and the factors that made it work. He said, "You're right, this directive should not apply to YouthBuild. We'll withdraw the RFP."

True to his word, the next day he withdrew the RFP and we breathed a huge sigh of relief. When the new RFP came out a couple weeks later, it called for a national TA provider ...AND ten regional providers! I called him again to ask what they were thinking now. He stated that they had to comply with the White House directive at least to that extent, but they had decided to add a national provider to allow us to compete for that coordinating role.

We decided we would compete not only for the national contract but also for every single regional contract. Our affiliates agreed not to jump in to compete for the regional contracts because it would create chaos. This was another wonderful example of solidarity. We proceeded decisively. Can you imagine the scene in our office as we prepared eleven competitive proposals, culminating in the submission one morning of these eleven proposals, each in its own enormous box with ten copies? This was before electronic proposal submissions.

Happily, we won in all ten regions. However, shockingly, we did not win the national contract! Another national organization underbid us by $1.5M and HUD was obligated to choose them. HUD officials apologized profusely, and then they managed the roll-out and subsequent management of these contracts in the best way possible in order to damage us as little as possible. That is, they postponed announcing and starting the national contract until we had begun our regional work, to position us as strongly as possible.

Unfortunately, this other organization worked alongside us for the next 8 years as a competitive TA provider, repeatedly winning a subset of the contracts through 2009. YouthBuild had been transferred from HUD to DOL in 2007 (that story to be told in the next chapter). In 2010 DOL decided it would be more efficient to have only one contractor. We won the 2010 competition. We had not enjoyed sharing the space with the other provider, but over-all it did no harm and finally we were re-instated as the only national contractor.

We were grateful that there were caring and responsible leaders at HUD who orchestrated this required change with as much consideration as possible. And fortunately, the leaders at DOL made the rational decision to have just one unified process under one contractor providing training and TA.

Once again, it is worth mentioning that the public officials who work in the government are typically deeply committed to doing the best work possible in the public interest. There can be bureaucratic complications, and occasionally political complications, but I always experienced the public servants in government as having the best intentions, deep knowledge, and a genuine openness to learning.

Senator John Kerry with YouthBuild students

CHAPTER 28

The Complicated Transfer of YouthBuild from HUD to DOL

In December of 2003, the White House Task Force for Disadvantaged Youth put out a report. The report recommended that the YouthBuild program be transferred from HUD to DOL because it was, ultimately, more aligned with DOL as a workforce development program than with HUD as a housing program. Never had any representative of this Task Force spoken with me or any member of our network.

In other contexts, the Bush Administration was also recommending the transfer of several other programs out of HUD. We were not sure of the ultimate intent. We did not know if we should resist, or yield. Other HUD programs were resisting any such transfer, thinking it meant their demise.

I called the same Deputy Assistant Secretary who had advised me how to handle the break-up of the national contract into 10 regional contracts. I asked what in the world were they thinking now? He said, "Dorothy, we have to obey the White House, but we love YouthBuild at HUD. It's up to you whether you fight it or not, but we have to go along with the White House report." This was clearly an invitation to fight it.

Then I called the Deputy Secretary, Roy Bernardi, also a good friend to YouthBuild who had helped us manage the prior political vagaries. He said, "Dorothy, we have to follow the lead of the White House. We love YouthBuild and frankly would rather keep it. But I suggest you assess for yourself what the future would hold for YouthBuild in DOL, and weigh whether you want to use your political capital fighting to resist the President and keep it in HUD, or use it fighting to expand YouthBuild in DOL."

This struck me as good advice. Then followed two-and-a-half years of negotiations with DOL, both Houses of Congress, and our constituency, with Senator John Kerry protecting us through every step of the very complicated process.

I wrote a long memo to the White House regarding the pros and cons of moving, describing all the strengths and weaknesses under HUD, and outlining what would need to be the case under DOL to warrant a move. I walked the draft around to key HUD and DOL officials, talking it through with each of them. In this process I made friends with the DOL folks who had decided they wanted YouthBuild and had persuaded the White House to give it to them. The key player in this process was Deputy Assistant Secretary Mason Bishop. He had served on the Task Force, and had encouraged the transfer to DOL.

Mason deeply appreciated that I had brought him a draft to talk through before sending it to anyone. He said, "If everyone in Washington behaved with the respect that you are showing in this process, it would be a completely different city." This began a long conversation, based on the trust created by the fact that I had not over-reacted and gone public before talking with him. Mason also told me in that conversation that he sincerely believed YouthBuild would have the opportunity to grow and flourish within DOL, and if it remained at HUD, it would continue to stagnate as a non-priority for that federal agency.

In the end I never sent the memo to anyone, because the conversations were more valuable than any mailing would have been. I had a similar conversation with Roy Bernardi at HUD about the draft memo and made some changes to it based on his advice.

While talking with the administration, I opened up similarly complex conversations with the YouthBuild USA Affiliated Network's National Directors' Association. We needed to get virtually unanimous consent from our constituency about whether or not to cooperate with the Administration in the transfer to DOL, or to oppose it. My memo about the pros and cons was studied by directors. They discussed it at length in our national meetings. In the end, they decided that if we could get agreement on our key points, the risk of moving was counteracted by the potential promise of expansion in DOL as espoused by Mason and others. After all, if DOL really wanted YouthBuild as a signature program for the most disadvantaged youth, it could expand dramatically. We thought it would never be more than a small "boutique" program in HUD, whose core purpose was housing. We aimed to become what we called the "in-community analog" to Job Corps, which was a residential program located outside of local communities that had an appropriation of about $1.3B/year in DOL and was enrolling about 60,000 young people each year.

All of these conversations were accompanied by complex moves on the part of the Administration. First of all, because the Administration was recommending a move from HUD to DOL, there were no dollars in the President's budget for FY'04 for YouthBuild in HUD. And because YouthBuild was not yet authorized in DOL, there were also no dollars in the President's budget for YouthBuild in DOL. This was an obvious danger that made me very nervous about the ultimate goal at other levels of the Administration, even though I trusted that Deputy Assistant Secretary Mason Bishop, and his boss, Assistant Secretary Emily DeRocco, were sincere in their desire to bring YouthBuild to DOL as a signature program.

During the spring of 2004, DOL submitted transfer legislation to Congress. We had not seen this legislation in advance. It is not DOL's practice to share the details of its legislative moves with advocates.

Fortunately, Senator Kerry refused to let it go through unless I agreed with it. There were elements of DOL's version that we definitely did NOT agree with, and furthermore, it was submitted so late in the process that it almost caused YouthBuild to miss a whole year of appropriations while the HUD appropriations committee said they no longer had jurisdiction and the DOL appropriations committee said they didn't yet have jurisdiction. Straightening this out took some fancy footwork.

There were two peak moments in the negotiation related to the transfer.

In the spring of 2004, 6 months into the negotiation, DOL decided to give YouthBuild USA a sole source grant of $18M for a re-entry program at 34 YouthBuild sites. "Sole source" means it would be given to us without any public announcement of funds available and without any competition from other providers. This idea had originated in a conversation between me and Lorenzo Harrison, who was then the Director of Youth Programs in the Employment and Training Administration at DOL. He and I had conceptualized a program behind the scenes that met DOL's goals and that would enable them to spend down, on time, some money that had been appropriated by Senator Specter (R-PA) but had not yet been spent. Lorenzo was not a political appointee. He was a civil servant whom I had known for years and who had healthy knowledge of YouthBuild on the ground. He was not involved in the transfer process. He didn't have the power to fund the sole source grant, but he encouraged the idea.

Other folks at DOL, especially Mason and Emily, approved this grant, as a demonstration of support for the program and how it could flourish within DOL. In fact, no sole source grant could have gotten through the bureaucratic process without Mason and Emily's support as the political leadership. Mason and Emily had also publicly announced that YouthBuild was one of three national models they wanted to support as achieving results for disadvantaged young people. But by early July, although they had made the decision internally and had officially obligated the funds to us prior to a June 30th deadline, they had not announced it publicly nor closed the deal either verbally or in writing with us.

Meanwhile, John Kerry was running for President, promising to expand YouthBuild enough to "eliminate all the waiting lists and open the doors to every young person knocking!" He was also planning to feature a video of his role in YouthBuild at prime time in the Democratic convention at the end of July. In addition, he planned to have a YouthBuild student nominate him at the convention! His campaign asked me if they could put a large number of YouthBuild students on the stage with him in prime time when he accepted the nomination, but I said I thought that would be politically unwise. I had similarly declined a highly visible role at the Democratic Convention when Bill Clinton was nominated, since YouthBuild was designed to live beyond any particular president's term of office and would always need bi-partisan support.

In early July I got a call from Mason, still Deputy Assistant Secretary at DOL: "Dorothy," he said, "I just read in USA Today that John Kerry is the founder of YouthBuild. Is that true?" "Yes," I said. "It wouldn't exist without John Kerry. But it has also been supported by Senators Cochran, Bond, and Specter." (These were leading Republican supporters still in office in 2004.) Then I added, "But that doesn't have anything to do with this grant award, does it?" I was referring to the pending $18M award. I will never know if this comment was foolish or wise. It was quite impulsive. My comment was followed by a short silence on the other end of the phone. Then came the answer: "No, it doesn't." Phew! I had my heart in my mouth on that one. To their credit, DOL leadership never politicized the transfer or on-going funding to YouthBuild.

We got past the Convention with no reversal of the grant. I worried that perhaps Karl Rove would see the link between Kerry and YouthBuild at the Convention and ask why in the world DOL was investing $18M in YouthBuild USA. But as far as I know, nothing like that happened. In September, DOL announced the $18M grant to YouthBuild USA. This was the largest federal grant we had ever received. Since it was "sole source," we had not won it through an open grant competition, but, instead, because senior officials had noticed and supported our unique model that served youth like no other program. I am proud to share that the results of that grant, through the creation of the "SMART YouthBuild" program (SMART stood for "Start Making A Real Transformation") which specifically served young people coming out of prison, were superb. The demonstration sites dropped the recidivism rate to 1% within a year of completion. The report can be found by googling "Life After Lock-up — YouthBuild."

The negotiation about the Transfer Act continued unabated. DOL, and Mason in particular, included for-profit organizations as eligible entities to run YouthBuild programs in initial bill language drafts. I did not want for-profit organizations included. Senator Kennedy's staff had told me I would have to give in on this because it was such a critical ideological point for the Republicans. Senator Kerry's staff said the same thing. One of them suggested that we just yield by putting a 15% cap on the grants that could go to for-profits. I imagined the authorizing committee's meeting in which a Republican official would notice that cap and suggest raising it or removing it. It seemed too dangerous to open that door, because it could destroy the essence of YouthBuild. I preferred not to have any language in the bill that would bring anyone's attention to the fact that there was an explicit limitation on for-profit sponsors. So, I held my ground and said No.

In one meeting with Mason and other staff at DOL, I tried to persuade them to drop the proposal to add for-profits as eligible entities. I said, "It would be counter-productive to include for-profit organizations because, truly, the reason YouthBuild works is due to the power of love. The young people invest their own energy in their own transformation because they perceive that for the first time somebody cares about them. If the young people thought for one second that the adults were in it for money, not for love, it would re-inforce their belief that all adults are corrupt, and it would diminish the power of love that is the transformative agent." Mason listened closely, with some apparent openness.

Mason smiled at me and said, "You know, Dorothy, the differ-ence between for-profit and nonprofit organizations" — he then paused — "is the way they categorize earnings." He then proceeded to say, "Dorothy, maybe the greatest love of all is capitalism." I met his enthusiastic eyes and smiled. I couldn't think of anything to say. He went on to suggest that maybe we should just have a subset of for-profit corporations run YouthBuild programs as an experiment, to compare them, to see what would happen. Maybe they would sur-prise me and do a great job. According to Mason, still to this day, this conversation and negotiation was very meaningful and enjoyable.

A month later, after more negotiations, in an open meeting with key players at DOL and several of the leaders of the YouthBuild Co-alition, Mason closed the deal: "Dorothy, I am not going to fall on my sword over inclusion of for-profit organizations. Since you feel so strongly about it, we'll take it out."

I was ecstatic. That was a huge victory. It was perhaps the great-est achievement of the entire negotiation. I have profound distrust of the profit motive intruding into programs designed to be in the public interest and especially in the interests of poor people. More broadly, I think the steady efforts to privatize, or profitize, the public sector is a huge political issue that is not being properly ad-dressed. Through Mason's and my gradual trusting friendship, and our patient, candid conversations, in the end, Mason came around, outside his deep ideological convictions, to resolve the issue in a way that respected our convictions. This was a truly beautiful and deeply reassuring result. Honest negotiations could lead to desired results, even against the odds.

It must also be acknowledged that Mason was encouraged to yield partly because John Kerry had made clear that no bill would pass without my agreement, so Kerry's judicious use of his power was as critical a factor in the negotiation as the development of Mason's and my genuine friendship, coupled with my principled, or stubborn, refusal on this point. I will always carry infinite gratitude to John Kerry and Mason Bishop.

Another moment of drama came at a different point. Our negotiations with Senators Enzi (R-WY) and Kennedy (D-MA), the chairman and ranking minority in the Labor/HHS authorizing committee, were stalled. At that point John Kerry jumped the gun and introduced his own transfer bill that had everything in it that I wanted, and nothing that I didn't want. His staff had previously asked me to make very clear to them what bill would be acceptable, but we did not collaborate on the introduction of his bill. I didn't know that he planned to do it. He just abruptly did it, as his way of putting a stake in the ground to make clear that YouthBuild was still his program. In the end he would have to agree to its passage, and there were some non-negotiables on which he would hold his ground. His role had already been made clear to DOL by other Senators when DOL first went to the Senate to propose the transfer.

Even though the Senate was under Republican leadership at the time, in 2003, DOL was directed by that leadership to Senator John Kerry as the person who would have to agree with a transfer of YouthBuild from HUD to Labor.

When Kerry introduced the bill, the other negotiators were temporarily furious, including the Democrats. He seemed to have seized their prerogative. It seemed to throw the negotiations between the Senate and the House into disarray. The committees were negotiating internally, separately with DOL on the one side and with me on the other, and then with each other, trying to balance our different emphases and requirements. Then suddenly Kerry, who was not on the authorizing committee, threw his monkey wrench into the process, making clear his priorities.

The combination of Kerry's political stand and my negotiating relationships somehow, miraculously, worked. Mason and I both realized we needed to agree on every word in the Transfer Act for the transfer to occur, and that if we did agree, but only if we did, we could actually get agreement from both House and Senate. So, we went through that process together, agreeing on every word, and took it back to Congress. John Kerry and both committees in both Houses accepted our final version once they had verified that Mason and I, representing DOL and YouthBuild USA, genuinely agreed.

We nonetheless faced a cliffhanger. At the last minute, Senator Coburn (R-OK) blocked the bill. Since it required unanimous consent as a technical transfer, one Senator could stop it. He said he wanted a 25% non-federal match to be written into the bill. I refused to go along with that because I thought the pressure on local programs to raise that money would be excessive, and I believed the federal government should pay the full amount for YouthBuild, as it did for Job Corps. I got a call that evening asking me to agree, but I said no. Kerry's staff and I turned to Senator Mike DeWine (R-OH), one of our Republican champions, to ask if he could persuade Senator Coburn to remove the block and yield on this point.

It was the last night of the Senate session for the year. It was 9 PM when Mike DeWine pulled Senator Coburn aside in the Senate coatroom and asked him to withdraw his block on the YouthBuild Transfer Act. We believed Senator DeWine asked him to do it as a favor, because he was in a tight Senate race and YouthBuild was important to his constituents. But Senator DeWine might have done it simply because of his respect for Kerry and YouthBuild. The issue was still the 25% non-federal match. Coburn withdrew his block at 9:30 PM.

At 11:50 PM, on September 22, 2006, the Senator in charge announced the unanimous passage of the YouthBuild Transfer Act. I was watching on C-SPAN. It was announced without fanfare, in the blink of an eye. It took 30 seconds. Thirty months of negotiations, done, just like that. There was no allowance that for-profit organizations could sponsor YouthBuild programs, and there was no 25% non-federal match. It was done, and I had won on these key points. It was unbelievable.

Little did I know that something else had transpired in the coatroom. Senator Coburn, being just as stubborn as I was, had called DOL and gotten an informal agreement that they would use their own power to impose a 25% non-federal match, even if it wasn't written into the authorizing law. Someone later told me about it. DOL has implemented that requirement ever since through its regulations and competitive funding process. It hasn't seemed to do harm; rather, local programs have built useful non-DOL support that helps sustain them in years when they may not receive the DOL competitive grant.

The over-all process of this complicated negotiation and this victory was an unforgettable lesson of how to manage government relations in partnership with inside champions, through careful and honest negotiations with all players, with fidelity to core values, and inclusion of all key stakeholders. It was tough. But, overall, we won what we most needed to win.

DOL Secretary Hilda Solis welcoming YouthBuild to DOL

CHAPTER 29

The Real Impact of the Transfer

The transfer of YouthBuild from HUD to DOL occurred in September 2006. For the next three years, we struggled to adjust to DOL's style of bureaucratic micromanagement. HUD had never had more than one staff person focused on YouthBuild, did not believe in overly prescriptive approaches, and therefore let us run the technical assistance and training almost entirely according to our own judgment. In contrast, DOL was accustomed to directing every detail of every process, training, TA event, handbook, and meeting. This required a radical readjustment.

Two dedicated senior DOL program administrators, not the political appointees who had arranged the transfer, called me in during the first month for a start-up meeting. One said, "Dorothy, we need to change the culture in the YouthBuild field. Directors are used to going to YouthBuild USA with all their questions. From now on, every local director who approaches your staff with questions must be re-directed to DOL. The local Federal Project Officer (FPO) must be the one who answers all the questions. Furthermore, we don't want you to ever mention the YouthBuild USA Affiliated Network in your role as DOL representatives because that would represent a conflict of interest."

Soon DOL's Director of YouthBuild began to give us detailed directives on how to do every single thing: what hotels to hold conferences in, what speakers to invite, what subjects to cover. Our suggestions and experience were discounted consistently. She also established a team of about six full-time staff members and put them in charge of each of the areas of work and subject areas including education, counseling, construction, and leadership development. Although these staff had substantially less experience than our staff in these areas, they were put in charge and expected to call the shots.

The details of this adjustment absorbed our attention and emotions for quite a while. It was terribly difficult for my staff to give up their role as the primary supporters and contacts for the local programs, and even more difficult to give up their role as the creative leaders of the planning for all trainings, handbooks, events, and on-site TA. Suddenly we were in a subordinate contractual relationship with people who understood YouthBuild less well than we did, and whose style was top-down and over-controlling. The explanation from DOL was that the Employment Training Administration (ETA) is driven by performance and metrics, and the federal agency is responsible for managing the program and the funds. The contractor, in this case YouthBuild USA, does not have that responsibility.

Tensions rose, tears flowed, staff morale plunged. Sometimes even senior staff were in my office in tears, offended by the disrespect they were experiencing. Staff roles had to be reorganized. YouthBuild USA staff with the deepest knowledge and investment in certain approaches had to be moved off the contract because DOL could not tolerate their confidence and leadership and because our staff couldn't tolerate the condescension from DOL. Two of them left YouthBuild USA.

At the same time, DOL's staff showed enormous passion for and commitment to YouthBuild and great determination to make it work. They simply were not very respectful and were inadequately informed. Their deep engagement was in stark contrast to HUD's approach. There were pros and cons to both methods. It was fascinating to see how different and deeply embedded were the internal cultures of two federal agencies, quite independent of the political leadership of any particular administration.

Another source of enormous tension was that in the competitive process through which we became the lead contractor for DOL, they also selected another contractor to do part of the work. They had decided early on to divide the TA contract into three parts. We competed for all three but only won two. The other contractor was not as competent as YouthBuild USA, yet its staff insisted on playing an equal role. This slowed everything down. There was constant competitive tension with them, even as DOL tried to present us to the field as a three-way collaborative, controlled by DOL.

Now, fast forward to the fall of 2011, five years after the Transfer.

I was attending a training for YouthBuild grantees that we had organized in collaboration with DOL that took place inside the DOL federal building. DOL had brought representatives of ten other federal agencies to help YouthBuild directors access additional federal resources to enhance the YouthBuild program. Every official at DOL — the YouthBuild director, ETA Youth Director, Deputy Assistant Secretary, Assistant Secretary, and the Secretary, all attended the event. They all said exactly the right things. They all inspired the attendees. The Secretary, Hilda Solis, shook the hand of every director present.

I sat in the audience, thinking that this total embrace of Youth-Build by the federal government that I was witnessing was the amazing payoff for the long march of negotiations, relationships, legislation, and difficult adjustments we had made.

YouthBuild was by then deeply embedded in the Department of Labor, as a central aspect of their work. It was embraced, beloved, surrounded by all the power and influence they had. It was an awesome moment of realizing that YouthBuild had a life of its own, fully owned and embraced and enhanced by both the political and the professional leadership of DOL, who were bringing other federal agencies into the mix to strengthen the program.

By this time, we had also reorganized internally and had put just the right people in charge of all aspects of our DOL contract. Our Chief Program Officer, Sangeeta Tyagi, had a perfect combination of enormous respect and appreciation for the passion of the DOL YouthBuild Director, and confidence to manage the relationship in a way that she could never be disrespected. It was hard to describe, but she simply took charge. As a result, the relationship had evolved to a positive place, with trust and collaboration the dominant mode. Meanwhile DOL had decided that having two contractors was a mistake. In the next competition they sought just one contractor for all aspects of the work and chose YouthBuild USA as the sole contractor through a competitive process. This entire transition took from September 2006 to September 2011, but we had made it to a good place. It was another miracle of wise, gradual, honest collaboration between a national non-profit and dedicated public officials.

Alongside this progress came a threat not realized until later. The election of 2010 had swept large majorities into both houses of Congress for the Republicans. In 2011, the House Appropriations Subcommittee over the Labor Department was quietly considering funding cuts — including complete elimination of YouthBuild by "zeroing out" the program.

By this time, the YouthBuild appropriation had grown from about $65 million since the transfer to DOL to $80 million at the time the House considered eliminating the program. I found out later that the House Subcommittee staff were consulting with Asst. Secretary Mason Bishop on recommendations for budget streamlining. Senator Harkin's (D-IO) appropriations staff member said that the House did not eliminate the program because Mason gave a strong recommendation and proactive endorsement of YouthBuild.

The lesson learned — in Washington, DC, bipartisan trust and support can be achieved through working with people, getting to know the views of all sides, and standing for principles.

Of course, the negotiations will go on, ad infinitum. That's the nature of the public-private partnership that we have created. But for me, and for the young people across the country and their communities, I believe the results are well worth the ups and downs, unpredictable changes, struggles over the details, philosophy, design, and delivery of everything. The impact is much greater than we could ever achieve without the power and resources of the federal government. In case that is not true, in case we could have found equal resources from the private sector somehow, the way Habitat for Humanity has done, I would still have chosen to work with the government.

Our government has responsibility for the health and well-being of people in our society. We need to use our own power to influence it to exercise that responsibility wisely. Investment in opportunities for low-income young people to get educated, trained, employed, and prepared to be productive citizens is a public responsibility. Persuading the government to do it is the responsibility of active citizens. Leading the charge is the responsibility of elected officials dedicated to the common good. Demonstrating programs that work is the responsibility of social entrepreneurs, non-profit social service organizations, and local public entities. Figuring out how to build workable systems to implement good policy and programs is the sacred responsibility of career public servants and political appointees who work in the government agencies. Working together, we can create opportunity systems that eliminate extreme poverty and inequality in America.

CHAPTER 30

The Breakthrough and Setbacks

In 2006 I had decided I needed to step back, take a deep breath, and decide what was next for me. I thought maybe some big new idea would take over and I would decide to leave YouthBuild USA. The YouthBuild program had been ensconced in the federal government for 14 years already, there were about 143 YouthBuild programs around the country, I had a strong senior management team, and so maybe YouthBuild didn't need me anymore and I should think of something bigger.

I set aside three months, from April through June, in 2006, for a short sabbatical. I asked Tim Cross, who was the COO at that time, if he would take over while I was out. He was delighted.

During those three months I tripled the time I spent hiking and biking and swimming, restoring my connection to nature, and to the woods near my home. Exercising up to two hours a day instead of half an hour felt good. I separated myself from the daily work at YouthBuild USA, and I tried to open my mind to new possibilities. I spent more time with my family.

However, nothing surfaced except more YouthBuild. First of all, during that period I did have to continue the negotiation with the government regarding the transfer of YouthBuild from HUD to DOL. As described in previous chapters, that was a very consuming process. Second of all, that transfer gave hope for a breakthrough to full scale. I had by then defined "full scale" as reaching either the limit of the need, or the limit of demand from beneficiaries, or the limit of capacity of providers to deliver quality programs. Given the potential for DOL to expand YouthBuild as a signature program, and given my deep frustration from our turning away thousands of young people each year, it seemed that I needed to re-commit to what I called a Breakthrough Strategy. I wanted to break through the glass ceiling on YouthBuild's growth, and reach full scale.

The Breakthrough

I re-committed to growing YouthBuild enough to open the doors to every young person knocking, to eliminating all the waiting lists, as John Kerry had said he would do if elected president. I returned to YouthBuild USA after those three months, refreshed, with a new commitment to the Breakthrough Strategy.

During the next period Charlie Clark, one of our vice presidents, joined me in creating a business plan that had YouthBuild doubling in size in the next five years. We did this quite efficiently, in collaboration with Shirley Sagawa and Deb Jospin, two long-time allies from the national service movement, and with Growth Philanthropy Network, led by Alex Rossides, who had launched a new effort to help organizations scale and amass capital for doing so. I had always held the view that elaborate strategic planning processes led by outside expensive consultants was a waste of time and money. I generally felt I knew what needed to happen, and in collaboration with our internal leadership we could make a reasonable plan. And so, with a little help from our friends, Shirley and Deb, we produced a formal and acceptable-to-funders plan covering 2008 to 2013.

At the same time, I calculated what a "Full Scale" expansion would and could look like, based on the fact that there had been 1600 organizations that had applied to HUD between 1992 and 2006 to bring YouthBuild to their communities. This level of demand, and the obvious capacity shown by their ability to create complex proposals, caused me to estimate conservatively that at least half of them would be capable of running a decent program if guided by our handbooks and trainings. I therefore projected the optimal growth over five years would be 800 programs in as many communities, engaging 50,000 YouthBuild students. This was a growth of five times, well beyond the doubling projected in the more conservative and attainable business plan that we were going to use to assure foundations we had a solid plan.

I thought we always had to plan on several paths: one for maximum growth, one for reasonable growth, and one for radical loss of federal funding in an unpredictable political environment. We had lived through the near elimination in 1996, never to be forgotten. The business plan was reasonable growth. The Breakthrough Strategy was for maximum growth.

The wisdom of having more than one plan in hand was proven in 2008. I was attending a learning retreat of our Directors Fellows when I got a phone call from Heather Higginbottom. Heather was the staff member who had served John Kerry as Senator and in that role had supported getting other Senators to support YouthBuild's annual appropriation for many years. She was a very young junior staff member when we first met in the early '90's. But now she was the director of domestic policy for Senator Barack Obama's emerging campaign for President of the United States.

She described a conversation she had just had with candidate Obama. At his request, she had brought him a plan for the expansion of national service.

He read it with interest, and then asked, "But what about the inclusion of low-income people in providing service to their own communities? That seems to be missing."

Heather said, "Do you mean something like YouthBuild?"

Barack replied, "Yes, that's exactly what I mean."

Heather said, "Well, I know YouthBuild very well, and I know Dorothy Stoneman, and I could call her to see if they have a growth plan."

"Yes," Obama said. "I also know Dorothy. I know her from the Saguaro Seminar convened by Robert Putnam a few years ago. Call her and see what she's got."

So, Heather called me and asked what I had. That afternoon I sent her the plan for the breakthrough strategy that was in my back pocket (in my computer's flash drive), including a chart showing the precise projected growth of the federal program for the next five years.

Heather and Barack reviewed it, accepted it, and in the twinkling of an eye it was part of his plan for growing national service. Within days our growth projections were put up on his campaign website. This was before the Iowa caucuses.

Wow! This was at their initiative, not mine. But fortunately, I was ready. This was the first expression of Barack's commitment to engaging poor people as service givers, not just service receivers. This would inform his relationship to the service movement throughout his presidency. This perspective would be reinforced by various advocates, especially Jonathan Greenblatt who served as Director of the Office of Social Innovation and Civic Participation (SICP) in the United States Domestic Policy Council under Obama, and Paul Schmitz who was then head of Public Allies. We worked together to promote the idea that residents of low-income communities should be engaged in AmeriCorps as service givers, generating a positive force overcoming poverty in their neighborhoods. The prior perception of national service had been emphasizing privileged people giving a year of service to benefit low-income communities.

True to his word, when Barack was elected, he more than doubled YouthBuild's DOL appropriation in the FY 2009 budget, including an increase to $102.5M in the regular appropriation and $25M more in the ARRA stimulus funds. The appropriation went from $60M to $127.5M in one year. The breakthrough had occurred! I was ecstatic. I was glad I had ended my three-month sabbatical by making a commitment to another round of advocacy toward a Breakthrough.

Doubling the size of YouthBuild's federal appropriation did not produce a huge challenge. We were totally ready. All the materials for all the handbooks, all the trainings, all the coaching, had been well prepared over the previous decades since our original failure in 1985, when we tried unsuccessfully to replicate in NYC without the proper materials in hand. But twenty years later, we were more than ready. Furthermore, there were more than enough organizations at the local level that were ready. Jubilation roared through the field.

That's worth repeating and imagining. Jubilation roared through the field! Every year, every YouthBuild program applying for a grant goes through a fearful period of suspense, waiting to see if they get funded.

Some do. Some don't. When the announcements are made the winners are elated. The losers are depressed and heartbroken. The whole field shakes with deep emotion. But this year, the funds were more than doubled. The field was ecstatic!

By this time Jane Oates was the Assistant Secretary at DOL. She had been Senator Ted Kennedy's staff person who had helped guide the transfer to DOL. She built on the moment of growth to change the structure of the grant programs, with each grant committing two full years of funding at $500K/yr. plus $100K for a third year of follow-up. This would all come out of the appropriation for that year, rather than depending on annual appropriations to carry on the commitment.

The Government Accounting Office (GAO) had previously done a study of YouthBuild in HUD in which they concluded that the unpredictability of funding from year to year, the need to re-apply and re-compete every year, was a source of instability that under-mined quality. The change under Jane Oates' leadership in DOL to a full two-year grant cycle was an improvement that reflected these conclusions and the GAO's recommendations.

There were no negative repercussions from doubling the appropriation.

The Setbacks

Unfortunately, this marvelous breakthrough was short lived. In 2010 the Republicans took back the House of Representatives, and Obama's control over his agenda was over. In 2011 the YouthBuild appropriation was cut back to $79M, a cut of 37% when the ARRA cut was included in the calculation, and 23% if only the regular appropriation was included. President Obama had requested $120M for FY 2011, but he didn't get it. Subsequently President Obama backed off and requested level funding for YouthBuild for the rest of his presidency. Whatever the Democrats and Republicans agreed on each year is what he requested in his budget for the following year. While the appropriation increased slowly and steadily back up to $84M, given steady support from Congressman Hal Rogers (R-KY) who was chairman of the Labor-HHS appropriations committee during that period, and continued support from our bi-partisan champions in both House and Senate as well as many bi-partisan supporters who had YouthBuild programs in their Districts and States all over the country, we were basically back at the stuck place with a glass ceiling, turning away hundreds of communities and thousands of young people.

Congressman Rogers' support was not happenstance. His chief of staff, Aaron Jones, had joined me on a visit to a YouthBuild program in rural Kentucky. He met with the students and observed them building a home. He fell in love with the whole thing. This informed Rep. Rogers' support. Aaron remained a strong advocate ever after.

President Obama's retreat to level funding was a disappointing mystery. Given his later creation of My Brother's Keeper, and his commitment to apprenticeship programs, and given the fact that many people very supportive of YouthBuild cycled through both the White House and OMB between 2010 and 2016, I never understood why he gave up on at least promoting steady expansion of this program that was decisively helping young men of color and also helping the rural white poor, Native Americans, Asians, and all low-income young adults. Nobody in the Administration ever answered my question about why ... other than the fact that the Republicans were conservative about spending. I had all sorts of guesses and speculations, but none of them were ever confirmed. My most lasting speculation was that the one time that President Obama went to visit a YouthBuild program, it seemed not to have been well handled by the host organization. I guessed that President Obama did not leave with the same profoundly positive impression of the power of YouthBuild that John Kerry, Mike DeWine, Anna Kondratas, Rep. Walsh, Aaron Jones, Roy Priest, and many other champions received from their site visits. The site host had not welcomed me to join the visit or to prepare their students for something so overwhelming as a visit from the President. <u>Important lesson: unprepared students can be very hesitant to speak. Fearful students do not win the hearts and minds of powerful politicians.</u>

Another decisive move that President Obama made was that when he doubled the YouthBuild appropriation he also mandated a random assignment evaluation of the program to be done by MDRC, the foremost research organization in the country focused on youth programming. President Obama set aside the funds to do it. In the end this would cost over $15M to study 75 randomly selected local YouthBuild programs with a study group of over 4,000 students. This step reflected his deep commitment to evidence-based decision-making. The study was planned to take place from 2011 to 2017.

During that period, the officials at DOL responded to every advocacy request for expansion of YouthBuild by saying, "We look forward to the results of the random assignment evaluation." But those results were not due until after the end of Obama's administration. The interim results reported in December 2016, were positive. But it was too late to influence the Obama budget requests between 2011 and 2017.

These years were discouraging for me. I was deeply sad that we were stuck, that the breakthrough had been temporary, that the field was suffering from lack of funds. I began to feel that it was my fault, that perhaps someone else could have leveraged relationships with the decision-makers better than I could. In any case, I had shot my wad, and the situation with the federal government was static.

The Essential Role of Philanthropy

However, during the same period, relationships with foundations continued to grow. Philanthropy has always played a critical role supporting the innovations and resilience of YouthBuild, locally, nationally, and internationally. I earlier referenced the key roles of the Ford and Charles Stewart Mott Foundations. It would take another whole book to describe the myriad relationships over the years with other traditional foundations and corporate philanthropy. Gates, MacArthur, Skoll, Casey, Kellogg, Lily, DeWitt Wallace Reader's Digest, California Endowment, Fund for the City of New York, Robert Wood Johnson, Irvine, Hilton, Public Welfare, Rockefeller, Kresge, Wallace, Edna McConnell Clark, Meridian, Robin Hood, Schultz Family, Walmart, Home Depot, AT&T, Starbucks, Saint Gobain, and many others gave decisive important support. Some gave at key moments, some over many years, some for innovation, some locally.

The dynamics were similar to those with elected officials. Foundation leaders would visit a YouthBuild program and be profoundly inspired by the students' passionate stories of finding respect, hope, love, skills, community, and opportunity. I'll tell just one story:

Melinda Giovengo was the director of YouthBuild in Seattle. She had become well connected to Starbucks and the Schultz Family Foundation (SFF). Melinda brought Sheri Schultz, chair of the SFF board of directors, to visit the Youth Action YouthBuild program in

East Harlem. We sat together in our little office space for a couple hours with staff, students, and graduates. They all spoke deeply to Sheri about their lives and program experience. Sheri was deeply moved. Afterwards she said, "I want Howard to have this exact same experience. I am going to bring him here as soon as possible." She did. We arranged not only for Howard and Sheri to re-visit the East Harlem program but also Abyssinian YouthBuild in Central Harlem. Howard was similarly moved and inspired to take action. He himself had grown up in the housing projects in Brooklyn. He knew the challenges. Sheri and Howard went on to pour philanthropic dollars not only into YouthBuild USA but into other initiatives serving Opportunity Youth. They soon launched the 100,000 Opportunities for employers to hire Opportunity Youth.

Above: Sheri and Howard listening to YouthBuild students at Abyssinian.

Below: Sheri and Dorothy celebrating the launch of the Hundred Thousand Opportunities.

Reflections on Raising
Our Children

While doing all the complicated and demanding work related to YouthBuild, John and I were also raising our two children, Sierra and David Lautaro (aka Taro). Except for describing their participation in the wonderful summers on Friendly Pond, they have rarely been mentioned in the chapters covering the 22 years from 1988, the year when I stopped commuting to NYC every week and we adopted Taro, through 2010 when the YouthBuild breakthrough strategy stalled. Working, parenting, and leading are on-going balancing acts for most families, especially now that women work full-time and even lead in lots of spaces. Overall, John and I thought we were doing fine, but we learned later that we had missed some very important things affecting our children.

Sierra and Taro were twelve years apart in age. They were similar in some ways, and very different in others. They were both loved deeply by our family. They both had great talents and friendships. They both grew up with financial security and a general sense of safety. They both had interesting cross-race and cross-class experiences. They both suffered to various degrees and in different ways from having parents who were so busy we missed some key aspects of their lives. On the other hand, they had totally different school experiences. In addition, the one big difference between being born to parents who looked like you and shared your DNA, and being adopted by parents from a different heritage, had lots of effects.

Sierra spent her first nine years living in Central Harlem. Starting in kindergarten she went on a school bus from Central Harlem to a public "magnet school" in East Harlem that was multi-racial. Many of her friends were black or Latino. When we moved back to Belmont and she entered 4th grade, she had adjustments to make. She was in a very different all-white community. She missed her friends in Harlem and wanted to merge the two worlds somehow. She sadly faced that there was no way to do that at age 10, with hundreds of miles of separation plus deep gaps in cultural awareness between Belmont and Harlem. She even said to us after about 6 months in Belmont, "I'd like to take my friends here to meet my friends in Harlem, but I don't think it would work. They would only notice the trash on the streets." Later, as a teenager, when she wrote her biographical letter of application to Brown University, she wrote that she had learned her values in Harlem, and her academic skills in Belmont. I found this a profound commentary.

The lucky thing for Sierra was that she was essentially at home in both worlds. In Belmont she excelled in school, did fine in sports and social life, and graduated from Belmont Public High School in 1994 as valedictorian, just as my father had wanted his three children to do (but remember — none of us did). When Sierra went on to Brown University, she gravitated toward a multi-racial friendship group that she has sustained ever since. In addition, because her little brother Taro had been born in Chile, during college she took a semester living in Chile and met Fernando Aguilera, a Chilean man with whom she fell in love. He followed her back to the USA, where they later married. They are now raising their son in Queens, NYC, within their deliberately bi-lingual family, and he is attending a bi-lingual public school. They are working daily to bridge the cultural divides between white Americans and Latino immigrants. Sierra's professional life has also been focused on social justice opportunities that bridge divides. Her first major job out of college was working as the development director at the original Youth Action YouthBuild program in East Harlem. She has remained ever since in the non-profit sector as an advocate, fundraiser, and program developer, obtaining educational and vocational opportunities for low-income and immigrant people in New York City.

Taro's story is very different. According to the social worker, Taro was relinquished at birth by his Chilean Mapuche mother. Then he was taken from his Chilean foster parents at four months of age and brought to Belmont by us – new, strange, English-speaking, different-smelling, adoptive parents bringing him into a totally different world. The maternal relinquishment needs to be understood as a primal trauma. Adoptive parents are not adequately informed of the deep pain their adoptees lived through at birth. Separated from their mother, they enter the strange new world alone. They are not able to nurse naturally within their mother's warm embrace. They have to look around at the world without the profound foundation of loving connection, belonging, and safety.

Despite this trauma, Taro was a delightful baby and toddler. He bonded deeply with us. He enjoyed active preschool. His first four years came during the period from 1988 to 1992 when our home was filled with expanding numbers of very busy but friendly Youth-Build staff, and lots of family. Freddy was living there and did a lot of babysitting with Taro. Everything seemed fine. But when Taro entered first grade in our local public school, he really didn't like it. He didn't like sitting still behind rows of desks. He struggled with the academic work. In first grade he asked us to come and spend a day with him in school so we could see how boring it was. But the principal wouldn't let us.

Taro attended the Belmont public elementary school through grade 4. He never liked it. We tried a private neighborhood school in grades 5 and 6. Then we tried home-schooling for grades 7 and 8 with a hired at-home teacher. When it was time for high school, we talked with the Belmont public high school counselor, who said Taro would be better off in vocational school. Taro liked the idea of a more practical study with hands-on learning of how to do real things, so he went to the local Minute Man Vocational School through high school and majored in auto repair. The vocational school was largely serving low-income black, Latino, and white students who hadn't done well academically in other schools. They became his social group, with whom he hung out, drank, and used drugs. He didn't want most of them to know he lived in an upper middle-class home in a white family in Belmont. He learned to code-switch and hide his two worlds from each other. He never got in trouble in school or with the police. He graduated proudly from high school with his class. He made several life-long wonderful friends. But he mostly didn't bring his social group home to our house, and we had no idea how he was spending his time after school. We were very busy working, and we believed whatever he told us.

Doing poorly in school, for a child adopted into a family with a history of school success and an older sister who was first in her class, caused ongoing shame and distress. When he was in 5th grade he said to me, "Mom, you have no idea what it's like to go to school and not get it." I realized he was right. This helped me not to judge him or pressure him unfairly. He especially struggled with math. We tried tutors and remedial classes, but nothing worked to overcome his challenges. He was diagnosed with ADHD, but neither he nor we wanted him to get dependent on the prescribed medications, so we skipped that. When he went on to community college, he passed all his classes except math. Three times he tried to pass the required math class, and three times he couldn't. As a result, he was not allowed to receive his AA degree, even though he had earned all the necessary credits. This produced more shame and humiliation. Over time he internalized a deep sense of being a "loser." He didn't tell us how deeply he felt this until much later.

Being from a different race, in a white community, was another ongoing source of pain and anxiety. It took various forms: being stopped by police when he was old enough to drive, and being asked constantly by everyone where he was from. Just feeling different, looking different, and not wanting to explain it or have it noticed, was a daily reality.

While their experience in school was drastically different, both Sierra and Taro suffered from having parents who were extremely busy and focused on improving the world. Sierra internalized a feeling of needing to sacrifice what she wanted from her parents in order to free them to serve the welfare of other people. This pattern of self-sacrifice has followed her all her life. Taro developed a kind of envy of the YouthBuild students and graduates whose successes we touted, and whom we welcomed to live in our home when they needed housing. He wanted to be equally worthy of being celebrated.

One of the take-aways for me of the suffering Taro experienced through school is the exaggerated emphasis our capitalist culture puts on competitive school success. There is no reason why children should have to feel inadequate, inferior, or to put it bluntly, stupid, because they can't do math as well as other students. Who cares? Why is math success essential for self-respect? Why does every child have to value himself or herself based on grades in school? How was this competitive academic system invented, and for what purpose? It's certainly good to have universal public education where all children can learn to read, write, think, and do basic calculations. Remember, there was a time when it was illegal to teach black children to read! Getting access to good free education should be a universal right, but why should children be ranked, compared to one another, graded and valued based so much on academic success? It's very hard to get over the deep feelings of being inferior that are imposed on probably three quarters of all school children. Maybe the system does this so lots of adults will be willing to be underpaid for the work they do that enriches the owners and shareholders of the businesses where the underpaid workers land.

Being unsuccessful in school, on top of being relinquished as a newborn, plus coming from a different racial heritage than your family and different from the dominant culture, makes growing up very challenging.

Taro was very successful in getting along with everyone in his vocational school. He was voted the most friendly student. He always had a wonderful girlfriend, and always had male friends eager to hang out with him. He graduated proudly from high school with his class. He stayed with his lovely high school girlfriend, Jillian Lea, for fifteen years after graduating and is still with her. But sadly, the teen-aged hanging out life was filled with alcohol and drugs. Taro was extremely skilled at code-switching, at living a double life, at hiding his lives from each other. Since his parents were both so busy at work, all day every day and often traveling around the country, it was pretty easy to hide what was going on in his teen-aged life. He lied to us very skillfully. He became an alcoholic. But he never had hangovers, never seemed drunk, and never got arrested for anything. He just drank a lot of alcohol all the time in his social life and to help him sleep at night. We didn't have any idea of that. Then suddenly, in his early thirties, he got hit with alcohol-related liver disease and landed in the hospital with his life absolutely in danger.

What struck him when he learned about the impact on his liver of his drinking, was that nobody had ever warned him that by drinking he could be killing himself. They warned him never to Drive Under the Influence. That was the way people thought one might die from alcohol. But they didn't warn him that alcohol could cause his liver to fail, and that could kill him. He began to imagine ways of warning other teenagers about this danger.

We were stricken with guilt and shame that we had been so unaware of this aspect of his life. How could we not know? How could we be so stupid? How could we have allowed ourselves to be so fooled? Were we out of our minds? There we were, successfully working to provide pathways out of despair and poverty for thousands of young men and women, and meanwhile our own son was mired in a self-destructive and deceptive life of alcoholism. He seemed to be focused on college and work. He even held a good job for several years while attending Community College. We had no idea he was drinking steadily around the edges of his life.

When I attended the alanon meetings that are designed for family members of alcoholics, they taught me to say this statement: "I can't control it, I didn't cause it, and I can't cure it." Of course, I thought we should control it, must have caused it, and should be able to cure it. But no. Life is more complicated than that. Our son is now a recovering alcoholic, committed to being clean and sober. He is working every day toward that end, struggling with all the challenges faced not only by himself, but by the millions of people who fell into alcoholism and had to identify themselves as recovering alcoholics, often for the rest of their lives. We're doing our best to support him.

Taro is an extremely intelligent and caring person, who is very handsome, very likable, and very skillful at managing all sorts of relationships. He has many friends and family who love him dearly. He also has some friends who are recovering alcoholics or recovering addicts who are offering wise support. Hopefully he will find his pathway to the proud and fulfilling life he is meant to live.

One thing I have learned while facing Taro's struggle with his addiction is how widespread is the reality of people having family members and close friends who are struggling with nearly insurmountable physical or emotional problems. They are often under cover, invisible, hidden behind the family's general commitment to success and respectability. But in truth, pain of all sorts is remarkably widespread. In our case, it was even hidden for a long time from ourselves within our own family.

Fortunately, despite the challenges we didn't realize at the time, we have a loving, cohesive, resilient core family. Sierra, Taro, John, and I are all doing well in our own important ways, now healthy and well, contributing to the common good, supporting each other and each other's loved ones, and participating in other communities of extended and chosen families.

Clockwise from upper left: Sierra, Fernando, Taro, Dorothy, John and baby Antu

Tim Cross (left) and I with South African Delegation

CHAPTER 32

YouthBuild Goes International

Starting in 2001, YouthBuild began to spread to other countries. Prior to 2001, whenever representatives from other countries asked for help bringing YouthBuild to their communities, I declined, saying they were welcome to use our ideas, but we had no capacity to assist. That all changed after 9/11 in 2001.

About a week after al-Quaeda attacked the twin towers in NYC, we had a meeting with representatives from South Africa at the Youth Action YouthBuild program in East Harlem. Led by Malose Kekana, head of the Umsobomvu Youth Fund (UYF), the group had toured the United States seeking models of good youth development programs. When they found YouthBuild they felt it was a perfect fit for hundreds of thousands of young people in South Africa.

Sitting around the table in East Harlem, hearing their vision, and having been emotionally impacted by the shocking bombings a week earlier, I decided we had no right to hoard our knowledge any longer since the larger world was suffering in so many ways. I was of course also drawn to South Africa due to my history of wanting to work in the Congo and of traveling to Africa with Leroy. In addition, all over the developing world, the majority of the population was under age 20, and without opportunities for work and livelihood, lost youth were a recruiting ground for violent extremist groups like al-Quaeda.

Malose asked if we would please send a delegation to South Africa at his expense to teach his staff the principles and practices of YouthBuild. I said yes. And so we did. I flew there and had a profoundly moving experience meeting young people in South Africa who almost perfectly mirrored the YouthBuild students in America. Various staff members, including John Bell and Helen Whitcher at the start, plus David Burch, Tanya Cruz Teller, Peter Twichell, and Caroline Hopkins over time, dedicated themselves to training and program development in South Africa, working with various local leaders. A few years in, the South African government embraced YouthBuild and spread it around South Africa with government funds, closely resembling the USA funding process. Two of our staff members moved to South Africa and stayed for many years.

During this same period, David Calvert was in Mexico City, where he had moved with his wife who was working for UNICEF. In November 2002 he met with Dr. Pablo Farias, the local director of the Ford Foundation office and pitched the idea for a Mexican version of YouthBuild, where unemployed and out of school youth would renovate crumbling sections of the Historical Center of Mexico City. With a verbal go-ahead from Dr. Farias, David found a viable nonprofit sponsor, wrote the proposal, and obtained $100,000 to launch the first Latin American YouthBuild project. It would be called *Jóvenes Constructores* — YouthBuild, in Spanish — and David would be its director for the next three years. A few months later, David convinced officials of the Mexico City government to match the Ford grant with $120,000 worth of youth stipends, trainer wages, and training materials. He found a great local staff leader — Paco Almanzo — plus the perfect building to work on, and hired a staff group. On May 3, 2004, David and Paco were invited to make a 60-second promotional announcement at 7pm at a local Spanish language rock station. The next morning, incredibly, 500 youth arrived for the 9am rendezvous! Due to budget constraints, they had to trim the cohort to 100 members. What resulted was a transformative, wildly successful project for 100 young Mexican students.

A few months later, Tim Cross, Malose Kekana, and I traveled to Mexico City to join David and see what Jovenes Constructores was doing and to feel the energy and spirit. Then we moved on to the coastal city of Veracruz for an international youth employment conference. During that week, the four of us held a meeting that ended with an agreement to form YouthBuild International.

Meanwhile, with a major grant from the Kellogg Foundation, under David's leadership Jovenes Constructores (JCC) branched out to other sections of Mexico City, to the State of Mexico, to Chiapas, Tabasco, Monterrey, Ciudad Juarez, Tijuana, and Morelos. David left in 2007 to launch YouthBuild in four Central American countries, and then on to Mozambique. Paco succeeded him as executive director of JCC. Before long YouthBuild Mexico was created. That on-air minute at the radio station between David and Paco jumpstarted a process that has transformed the lives and experience of many thousands of Mexican youth.

In 2007, Tim Cross stepped forward to lead our international work. He had been in various leadership roles within YouthBuild USA for several years, in addition to having successfully launched YouthBuild Boston back in 1988. He was eager to go full steam ahead, fully in charge of movement-building on the international scale. We formed YouthBuild International (YBI) as a department inside YouthBuild USA, Inc., with Tim as its President. This worked beautifully.

Tim and his dynamic staff team carried the work forward, country by country, with exciting challenges, relationships, successes, and rare failures. Tim won support from many funding sources who hung in with him over many years. He served as President of YBI until January 2022, when he left to become Senior Advisor to Aspen Institute's Global Opportunity Youth Network. In 2022, YBI was working with 56 programs in 17 countries.

I am not equipped to tell the full international story; and even if I were, it is much too long to fit into this book. Hopefully Tim will write it one day. I just want you to know, it happened, and it created great results. It happened because the need was enormous, David responded brilliantly to that need in Mexico, Malose was searching for solutions and found YouthBuild, and Tim Cross's leadership skills and energy were perfectly on target.

This is another lesson worth naming: when competent and ambitious staff show leadership energy and vision, offer full support and let them do their thing without excessive supervision, bureaucratic requirements, time-consuming demands, or other distractions. Create the conditions for them to have the freedom to create!

President Roosevelt famously named the "Four Freedoms — Freedom from Fear, Freedom from Want, Freedom of Speech, and Freedom of Religion." Let's add a fifth sacred freedom: **The Freedom to Create.**

The first National Council of Young Leaders, 2012

CHAPTER 33

The Launch of Opportunity
Youth United

In 2012 I turned some of my attention to the creation of a collaborative movement of national organizations who would sponsor
young leaders emerging from poverty who would themselves build
a new movement to increase opportunity and decrease poverty in
America.

At YouthBuild USA we had been scratching our heads about how
we could use our commitment to leadership development to take the
whole field of youth programming to a new level. We had sustained
leadership councils in the YouthBuild movement since 1988 — the
YouthBuild Young Leaders Council, the National Alumni Council,
the VOICES Council for higher education, and the Rural Youth

Bringing Hope to Life

Council. We had done this with private foundation funding, with unrestricted individual donations, plus ongoing support from one individual donor named Mike Lyons who had been very impressed by graduates whom he had met. As a result, he wanted to support the graduate programming. Finding funding for leadership development was always a struggle, but it was always core to our purpose. I made sure to protect this item in every annual budget.

However, our practices had not spread to the whole field of job training and national service beyond YouthBuild, and our resources had not expanded enough to create a robust movement of Youth-Build graduates on the ground. Then I got another one of those wonderful out-of-the-blue exciting phone calls. A program officer at the Gates Foundation called in May of 2012, to say, "Patty Stone-sifer, the former President of the Gates Foundation, has asked the Foundation to make grants of $250,000 to each of seven organizations which will continue the work of the White House Council for Community Solutions which is about to issue its final report on what should be done for Opportunity Youth in America. Youth-Build USA is one of those organizations. Please think about what you will do with those funds. Let us know in the form of a proposal."

The White House Council on Community Solutions had been appointed by the Obama Administration about a year earlier. I had not been appointed to it, but various colleagues including Paul Schmitz of Public Allies, Patty Stonesifer from Gates Foundation, and John Bridgeland of Civic Enterprises had served on it. Unfortunately, they had been instructed by the White House not to include federal spending recommendations in their conclusions. Otherwise, they had a lot of good ideas.

This was the beginning of the widespread use of the term "Opportunity Youth" to define 16- to 24-year-olds who were neither in school nor employed. There have typically been close to 5 million of them in America over the past decade. About half of them grew up and are still mired in poverty. We would always say to explain the term, "They are both seeking opportunity and they offer an opportunity to our nation if we would invest in them."

This phone call offering $250,000 was the catalyst for me to step into gear to convene the seven grantee organizations that Gates Foundation had selected and to create a National Council of Young Leaders that would be made up of young leaders emerging from those organizations who would then advocate for their peers. We did that. Starting with The Corps Network, Jobs for the Future, Public Allies, Youth Leadership Institute, The Aspen Institute, Year Up, and YouthBuild USA, we launched that council in August 2012. I facilitated a three-day retreat in partnership with Abrigal Forester, a YouthBuild staff member at the time who later became Executive Director of Teen Empowerment, and James Mackey, a YouthBuild graduate active in leadership in Boston.

During this retreat the young leaders who had been recommended for the Council from these seven organizations produced a draft platform called "Recommendations for Increasing Opportunity and Decreasing Poverty in America." I worked with them for the next few weeks to finalize it through endless phone calls getting every member's input and agreement on every word in the document. The National Council of Young Leaders presented their final platform in a dynamic session including 500 young people at the Opportunity Nation launch in Washington DC on September 19, 2012. It was a stunning and proud moment.

We had also put together a high-level Circle of Allies and Champions with Jeff Skoll as the Honorary Chair, that included Patty Stonesifer, John Bridgeland, Melody Barnes, and many other influential leaders. (These Recommendations, updated in 2020, can be accessed by googling "Recommendations for Increasing Opportunity and Decreasing Poverty in America. Opportunity Youth United.)

During the next two years the Council members bonded, built a cohesive core, became the well-respected youth voice at numerous public gatherings and for several national coalitions. At the end of two years, they decided it was not enough to be a Council. They wanted to build a movement. They changed their name to Opportunity Youth United. We expanded to include 15 sponsoring organizations and raised some additional private funds from the Schultz

Family Foundation, Marguerite Casey Foundation, Blue Haven initiative, Annie E. Casey Foundation, Skoll Foundation, and others. Soon we began to organize local Community Action Teams designed to uplift the voice of young people in local policy and politics. By 2020 Opportunity Youth United had 20 Community Action Teams (CATs) on the ground. During 2020 we received and distributed to those CATs over $1.5M from the Carolina Fund, created by Theresa DelPozzo, a 1960's SNCC member. These funds were designated for local non-partisan voter mobilization during the Presidential election. The CATs worked to increase voter turnout among young people in their communities.

I saw Opportunity Youth United (OYUnited) as a natural next step for building a national movement of young adult leaders who had been raised in poverty, had transcended those conditions with the help of effective programs like YouthBuild, Service and Conservation Corps, Public Allies, National Guard Youth Foundation's ChalleNGe program, and others, and who were deeply committed to giving back, to doing everything in their power to end poverty and injustice.

The original Council included Jamiel Alexander, Lashon Amado, Gilbert Bonafe, Ramean Clowney, Ryan Dalton, Ladine Daniels, Francisco Garcia, Megan Gregory, Timothy Gunn, Tekoa Hewitt, Shawnice Jackson, Julie Jent, Deon Jones, Dominique Jones, Jarrett Jones, Humberto Palacios, Kimberly Pham, Teresa Rivera, Adam Strong, Philan Tree, and Shanice Turner. They were an awesome group, deeply talented and dedicated.

In March 2020, Lashon Amado became the director of Opportunity Youth United (OYUnited). Lashon is a YouthBuild graduate from Brockton, MA, who earned his Master's degree from UMass Boston, and served on the National Council for a number of years before becoming OYUnited's director. The story of OYUnited will play out over the next decade. I served as assistant to the director for three years after Lashon took the reins, and stepped off the staff at the beginning of 2023.

CHAPTER 34

My Departure from YouthBuild USA

In 2016 I had decided that it was time for me to leave YouthBuild USA. It no longer needed me. YouthBuild had become a stable institution both in the federal government and at the grassroots. YouthBuild USA was also stable and filled with wonderful leaders and staff in every department. I was approaching age 75. My attention was increasingly attracted to the movement-building of Opportunity Youth United.

I decided that when I left YouthBuild USA, I did not want to maintain responsibility for it through board service. I knew that if I stayed on the board, I would continue to feel 100% responsible. I had remained chair of the board of the Youth Action YouthBuild program in East Harlem since 1988 so I knew how seriously I took that responsibility and how consuming it was, even for a small local program.

I told the board of YouthBuild USA, still led by our highly effective and trusted chairperson, Roy Priest, that I did not want to serve on the board, and I also did not want to choose my successor — that would be the board's responsibility. We worked together throughout

2016 to implement that plan. The board chose John B. Valverde as the new CEO. He had not previously been connected to YouthBuild, but he emerged in the board's selection process as a charismatic, passionate leader whose prior work was relevant, whose style was magnetic, and whose vision was inspiring.

I spent the week after Christmas by myself in my long-time office in Davis Square, sorting and packing up all my papers. I left on New Year's eve with my car packed full. The rest is history... history that is still in the making.

YouthBuild lives on in the United States with steadily (although slowly) expanding federal funding with bi-partisan support, fabulous leadership in local communities throughout the country, passionate young leaders who graduated from YouthBuild and now serve their communities on a variety of levels, devoted career staff at DOL, dedicated and skilled staff and leadership at YouthBuild USA all supporting the national network of local YouthBuild programs and staff and perpetuating the culture that deeply reflects the power of love coupled with opportunity. The international expansion has been continuously supported by YouthBuild USA, with a variety of global events bringing folks together. On October 1, 2024, YouthBuild USA announced that it had changed its name to Youth-Build Global, to reflect the unification of its work around the globe.

One wonderful thing I have noticed is that not only do the YouthBuild programs and graduates across the country continue as healthy contributors to our society, but there is another unexpected ripple effect. Former staff at YouthBuild USA moved on to leadership roles in other important contexts. Hartford Community Foundation, Boys and Girls Clubs of America, New Power, New Profit, Blue Meridian, AmeriCorps, the Plum Village Community of Engaged Buddhism, Emerald Cities, Aspen Institute, Teen Empowerment, Mothers Out Front, and other wonderful organizations have embraced and benefitted from professional leaders previously engaged in the YouthBuild network.

I get to smile and relax and take pride in the results of 38 years leading the YouthBuild movement. Sometimes I feel regret that I did not create the New American Party for Truth, Justice, and Joy — or fulfill the 50-year plan of the New Action Party for a Human Society to build the movement and win the power we needed to totally transform society, as I had envisioned in 1974. But hopefully someone more charismatic and powerful than I, some incredibly brilliant and passionate and honorable group, some broadly united movement, will lead that transformation in the future. When Amanda Gorman brought forth her poetry at the inauguration of Joe Biden and Kamala Harris, she spoke of "Justice and Joy." Maybe the idea is organically rising in the national consciousness. I hope so! Then I can sleep well in my eighties without regret or grief, with just pride and joy, peace and happiness, for a life fully lived with beloved family, friends, and colleagues, all empowering people previously oppressed and excluded, who step forward to work together as best we can for a loving and just world.

Of course, during my eighties I am still engaged in a variety of ways to support efforts to bring inspiring opportunities to young people in hard-pressed communities; to empower and support people uniting toward ending all forms of injustice; to share healing methods with activists working hard for human liberation; and to join conversations about how to transform our society into one where both the economy and our democracy are working to benefit all people and to protect the planet from destruction.

CHAPTER 35

Some Lessons Learned

As I bring this book to a close, I'd like to summarize some of the lessons learned. Below is an edited excerpt from a speech I made at Harvard in 2011 when I received the Robert Coles Call to Service Award. This is not a precise summary of all the lessons in the previous chapters, but it covers many of them.

Summary

1. **Decision.** It matters what you decide to do. Nothing big ever happens unless you decide to make it happen.

2. **Persistence.** Nothing important happens if you give up.

3. **Support.** Friends, family, colleagues, and all forms of communities of support matter — you can't build a positive force alone. You may be able to write a paper or a convincing proposal alone, but you can't build any movement for social change alone.

4. **Partners.** Both work partners and lifetime personal partners who support your vision make a world of difference.

5. **Awareness.** We live in an unjust society where racism, classism, sexism, heterosexism, ageism, ableism, and adultism suffuse our lives and experiences. Everyone's experiences and worldviews are influenced profoundly by these dynamics and stereotypes. We must work to understand the impact of them. We must step outside the limits of our own experience to learn about the world from many points of view. A key learning experience is to embed yourself in a community totally different from your own for at least a year, or many years, or in several different communities, long enough to internalize a new viewpoint, including through deep and lasting inter-personal relationships as well as through community engagement, to realize how limited your previous viewpoint was and to expand it decisively.

6. **Accountability.** Anyone aiming to produce something that benefits any community needs to set up a structure that makes yourself directly accountable to the people in that community. And of course, once we get government and philanthropic dollars, we need to be accountable to produce what we promise.

7. **Integrity and reliability.** Never lie, never do anything you would have to lie about, and always do what you say you're going to do. This is what builds your reputation and the trust of other people. Without their trust, nothing gets done.

8. **Kindness and respect.** To build an organization that holds together, where people care about each other and the mission, and are empowered to give their fullest and best, they need to be treated with kindness and respect at all times. Even when you have to fire someone for good reason, fire them in a way that does not de-value or humiliate them. It's also important not to talk negatively about any people behind their back. They will always hear it. It will always create pain and drama and be disruptive to what you are

trying to do. Deliberately pass along the positive feedback. Avoid any negative gossip. Build a safe and caring working community. Give your staff the freedom and support to use their passion to create what they envision that will benefit the mission.

9. **Diversity.** If you're building an organization, pay attention to getting a variety of perspectives to the table at every level of the organization. The result will be better decisions and a healthier culture that counteracts the distorted dominant views and habits of the larger society.

10. **Champions.** Find people with greater power than you who will act as champions for your initiatives. If you are advocating for public policy or public dollars, you absolutely need champions on the inside, both elected officials and leaders within relevant public agencies

11. **Negotiations.** Trust that if your work is having a truly beneficial effect on other human beings, you can win support and collaboration from people from all walks of life and all different political viewpoints. They can become real partners in figuring out the right path to adequate resources and correct policies. Treat everyone as a potential ally. Treat nobody as an "enemy."

12. **Personal healing and self-management.** We all come to this work with emotional weaknesses, attitudes, and behavior patterns that are rooted in past distress and are counterproductive. We each need a system for dumping painful emotion and emerging from limiting and self-destructive ideas and irrational or reactive patterns of behavior. Find a system that works for you.

13. **Mentors.** Pick the smartest, most generous people you admire the most, and try to learn from them. Ask them if they would be open to being your mentor. They will be honored to be asked. Include people from different class, racial, and cultural backgrounds to guide you through complicated terrain.

14. **Humility.** Be aware how little we actually know. Listening to other people is key. Cool out your ego. It's not about you. You're a servant of the people, a servant of God if you wish, a servant of the sun, whatever you believe you're a servant of, but don't let it become about you. It's easy for ego to sneak in. Try to resist. Forget about your "career." Think about your purpose.

15. **Defy conventional wisdom.** Don't believe what conventional wisdom says about what's possible or necessary. Use your own best judgment about what would create an optimal situation and what contradicts the injustices we are accustomed to. When I started the first YouthBuild program in 1978 the officials said, "Don't bother. It won't work. Those youth can't build a building. They're high school dropouts. They have no discipline, no skill, no perseverance. Forget it." They were profoundly wrong.

16. **Resist materialistic pressures.** When I first got funding for the Youth Action Program in 1978, a young man named Tony Minor, who was 14 at the time, said, "Oh, I get it. A bunch of people are going to get salaries — they'll get rich off our poverty — and we're going to stay poor. That's how these things work." I told Tony I wouldn't let that happen. I stuck to my word. When I read the Chronicle of Philanthropy report recently that a number of CEOs of nonprofits are paying themselves $500,000, I found it very disturbing. The unofficial rule I followed at YouthBuild USA was that the top salary would be no more than 5 times the lowest salary. When I started the Youth Action Program in 1978, we

made all the salaries equal. Surprisingly, the federal agency that gave us our first grant told me we couldn't do that: the director had to be paid more. My board later told me the same thing in 1990. Salary inequality is deeply embedded in our culture. Limit it as best you can. Do not believe the expanding pressure on non-profit leaders saying they must pay competitively high salaries to get talented staff. The best talent is often the most committed to the public mission, not to personal gain.

17. **Provide guidance.** When mobilizing others to replicate your initiative, give them guidance through handbooks, trainings, and on-going mentoring. You know more than you think you do. Be sure to organize the sharing of it.

18. **Offer the Freedom to Create.** Use whatever authority you have to help other people step fully into their own passionate desire to create solutions to problems and to give wonderful experiences to other people.

19. **Manage your disappointment** about the inevitable gap between your big vision and the reality you have created. This is the sad part. Over time, nobody achieves their full vision. When I realized that all my heroes must have had pain regarding that gap, I decided to start taking joyful pride in what I had created instead of being disappointed for failing to bring my whole vision to reality.

20. **Spread the love.** Love is not about romance. It's about safety, respect, appreciation, forgiveness, deep understanding and empathy, profound commitment to the well-being of every person, all groups of people, all life, and our planet. It's about caring deeply about the well-being of people and nature. It's an abiding force for good. It lives in all of us. All people need it, are drawn to it, and want to spread it. If you give your colleagues the chance to spread the love, they will do it. It gives irresistible beauty and meaning to life and creates immeasurable ripple effects.

More on the Need for Personal Healing

In 1972 I found my personal healing system in something called Re-evaluation Counseling (RC), or Co-counseling. It teaches that we are all born brilliantly intelligent and profoundly good, but that interpersonal and societal hurts impact us in ways that create distress patterns resulting in behavior that is not fully intelligent. "Intelligent" is defined as being attuned to the actual reality before us and able to think clearly and act rationally to make the situation as good as it can be. "Intelligent" means that we are free of the reactive behavior caused by similarities of present experiences to our past hurtful experiences that evoke painful emotions that trigger rigid and reactive behaviors that don't serve our real goals.

Re-evaluation Counseling teaches that we can heal from all past hurts through emotional release of the stored pain, and that we can heal from new hurts the same way in present time. It also teaches that we can make deliberate commitments to manage our attitudes and actions in direct opposition to the behavior patterns produced by past hurts, and we can create new capacities within ourselves. It sets up a system of peer counseling in which people become trained in how to offer each other the safety and support to go through that healing process, to take more intelligent actions in present time, and to set new commitments for our attitudes and actions, free of emotional confusion caused by early hurts.

I have practiced this since 1972 with co-counselors met only through the RC Community as well as with family and friends who learned the theory and practice with me and then we built it into our ongoing relationships. It has been an essential tool for acting rationally, and for not burning out. The work we all do can be exhausting and the obstacles we face can be painful, causing burnout if we don't have a way of releasing the stress. I make sure to cry — and release other deeply held feelings of fear or anger — at least an hour a week with a trusted co-counselor. Sometimes when things get rough I do it several hours a week. I have never taken any medication for moods or feelings. I have never been pulled down by depression. Co-counseling gives me a way of facing, releasing, and healing from negative feelings. The process has been reliable for me and produces no financial burden because we are exchanging time and attention, not money. You can find out more about Re-evaluation Counseling at www.rc.org. I currently teach RC classes to young social activists and entrepreneurs reaching for their most rational and resilient selves. I recommend finding a system that works for you.

In Closing

The greatest reward of all is knowing that my life has made a difference. I hope that you will win joy through your own life of service and struggle, loving humanity and our planet.

Epilogue

I hope this book serves as a source of inspiration for social entrepreneurs, change makers, activists, public servants, servant
leaders, elected officials, young leaders, non-profit leaders, community leaders, philanthropists... whatever we choose to call ourselves
and each other. There are huge numbers of people who devote their
entire lives to improving the conditions of humanity. There are millions of us. That's why the arc of the universe bends toward justice.

I hope these stories reassure you that using your best judgment,
trusting your heart, putting one foot in front of another, taking
direction from people impacted by the oppression you aim to eliminate, working with people you trust, and finding champions and
allies everywhere, will empower you to make a difference. It may
never be the full difference that you would wish. Most of us wish we
could eliminate evil and injustice, and then spread love and hope,
opportunity and community, everywhere.

Sadly, none of us achieve our highest aspirations and fullest vision.

I realized one day, listening to Thich Nhat Hanh, the Vietnam-
ese Zen Buddhist leader of the Plum Village Tradition, that all the
people I admired the most had been forced to live with a HUGE
gap between their vision and reality. Even our superheroes that we

nearly worship, like Mahatma Gandhi, Martin Luther King Jr., and Nelson Mandela, had to be deeply pained by the gap between what they aimed to achieve and what they did achieve. I realized that experiencing the gap between my vision for change and the reality I could achieve would be a never-ending source of sadness. But realizing it was sadness shared with all my heroes, lightened my heart.

The other side of the story is that we get to take delight, enormous pride, and deep satisfaction from every success we have had in liberating any single person from any form of oppression or misery or isolation. Let us enjoy every step. Let us delight in every success. Let us persist as long as we live. Let us share and rejoice in every victory, for the rest of our lives. Let us not underestimate the never-ending ripple effects of spreading love and respect, freedom and justice, opportunity and community, in every direction.

In solidarity,

Dorothy Stoneman
December 31, 2023

With YouthBuild Graduate Leader, Bea Sweet

THE ESSENCE of YouthBuild
Quotes from Students

"YouthBuild is like the Statue of Liberty for the Inner City."
Greg Mason, Minnesota

"YouthBuild is like a trampoline — it has vaulted me over so many obstacles!"
Anthony Turner, East Harlem YouthBuild (NY)

"YouthBuild is like a windshield wiper. For the first time in a long time, I am able to see where I am heading."
Tyra Johnson, CCEO YouthBuild, Gardena, CA

"YouthBuild is like an extraction machine — it finds the gold among the garbage."
Jeanette Abdul-Saleem, Bloomington, IL

"YouthBuild was like a drive-in package: everything I needed in one place."
Edgar Galvez, Fresno, CA

"YouthBuild is my key to unlocking a world of possibilities for my future as well as my children's."
Candice Stewart, YouthBuild Columbus (OH)

"Please, someone get me a cot, so I can sleep at YouthBuild. I don't ever want to leave."
Patrick Sheffield, San Diego BCA YouthBuild (CA)

"YouthBuild changed my life forever. I built housing for homeless people and earned my GED. Now I'm chairman of the homeowners' association in my inner city neighborhood."
Anonymous

"YouthBuild shines a ray of light into the dark places of the community where hope is very dim and limited, giving second chances and helping down-and-out youth realize the importance of their lives."
Justin Taylor, YWCA YouthBuild Springfield (MA)

"YouthBuild is a place where we know we're welcome and we know there's knowledge waiting for us."
Raymond Morales, Moreno Valley YouthBuild (CA)

"Because of YouthBuild, I can now walk the streets with my head up. I used to sell dope. Now I'm giving hope."
Anonymous

"YouthBuild sheds light and gives drive to those who once walked a dark road."
Trevor Daniels, Youth Action YouthBuild (NY)

"I grew from dirty, muddy soil and blossomed into a beautiful rose because of YouthBuild."
Shandrika Shipp, Space Coast (FL)

"I used to be a menace to my community; now I am a minister to it."
Antoine Bennett, YouthBuild Sandtown, Baltimore (MD)

Advocacy Principles of Youth Action Program and YouthBuild USA, Inc.

The set of attitudes and principles that have made our approach to community organizing and policy advocacy effective have been as follows:

1. We have organized people on the basis of vision, caring, and responsibility, not on the basis of anger.

2. We have motivated people toward the common good, not for self-interest.

3. We have encouraged people to propose solutions, not to protest wrongs.

4. Our objective has been to win, not just to be morally right.

5. Our approach has been consistently to persuade and win over ever more allies, never to identify so-called "enemies" or to attack or embarrass the opposition.

6. Our advocacy work has had people who benefit from the campaign, such as youth in low-income communities, in the forefront of speaking and lobbying as well as participating in planning and policy making.

7. We have organized for broad diversity, bringing as many relevant perspectives into the thinking as possible.

The result has been that we have produced no enemies. We have attracted extremely responsible people who are able to sustain their energy over time, and we have achieved many of our objectives so far. We have followed these principles since the early 1980's, when we developed them in the Youth Action Program.

APPENDIX 3

The YOUTH AGENDA
for the Eighties

(produced and distributed by the East Harlem Youth Congress in 1982)

"There's nothing you can't have if you want it, so don't ever let anybody tell you that you can't do this because you're Red, Black, Hispanic or whatever. You can do whatever you feel you want to do if you work hard to achieve it."

Tony Minor, Steering Committee Member

This YOUTH AGENDA is made up of recommendations from the workshops and dialogues at the 1982 East Harlem Youth Leadership Conference, along with some recommendations from the 1980 Youth Conference.

There were a total of over 500 people putting in their ideas at these two conferences: about 400 young people and 100 adults. The adults were representatives from the business community, the Board of Education, the Police Department, the military, youth programs, other community programs, elected officials, landlords, parents, and other interested adults.

We do not see this AGENDA as a final thing. There were some issues not covered, and there are other people in East Harlem who might want to have input. So, we'd like to keep adding to this until it is really a full YOUTH AGENDA that East Harlem can unite behind.

However, we think it is a strong basic statement already, expressing the views of 500 people, so we hope you will read it carefully, let us know what is missing, and help implement the parts you agree with.

Following are the recommendations, by category. In some cases, the workshop recorders gave us summaries of the discussion; these have been included because they are interesting.

Employment

Forty people attended a dialogue between young people and employers and businessmen. The discussion turned mainly to how businesspeople could help youth, so the recommendations under employment are taken from 1980:

1. We want useful jobs which will build up our community: for example, renovating buildings, planting gardens, tutoring.

2. Full youth employment should be a national goal.

3. There should be less government spending on the military, and more attention to employment.

Business and the Community

There was great interest expressed by the young people in learning how to become businesspeople. The recommendations reflect this interest:

1. Successful adults should support young people. For example, each employer or businessperson could take one or two young workers "under their wing" in an apprentice-like relationship. Employers should make a special effort to help young people learn, get experience, make contacts, and move into better employment opportunities. We should form our own networks to help each other along.

2. Young people should focus first on getting an education and on getting work experience that will develop our knowledge and skills; getting into business can come later if we really want to.

3. We should explore bringing Junior Achievement into East Harlem, as a way for young people to learn more about the business world.

4. Young people should do careful self-evaluations and set goals; then we should work very hard to reach the goals.

5. The community should support local businesses and encourage them to stay in East Harlem. Businesses should work together.

Economics

A workshop on Reaganomics was held. The speaker, economist Bill Tabb, laid out the basic ideas of Keynesian economics and of supply-side economics.

- Keynesian (pronounced Cainsian) economics was a response to economic depression. Its solution was for the government to spend money employing people to rebuild the failing economy. It worked in the 1930s to end the Great Depression.

However, now we have a recession and an inflation at the same time. This has never happened before. Just spending government money might relieve the recession, but it usually makes inflation worse. As a result, the economists haven't known what to do.

Supply-side economists (who are the ones Reagan is following) say that business should be freed from regulation and taxation, and then they will re-invest their money and energy into the economy, making it strong again and providing lots of new jobs. They say government spending should be cut, and businesses should be supported.

But so far businesses are not re-investing: they are investing in other countries where profits can be higher due to lower costs; and they are buying up other companies. Also, the government is still spending just as much money, only now it is on the military instead of on people's programs, so government spending is even more inflationary than people-spending, because the military doesn't create anything for people to buy.

So, neither the problems of recession nor the problems of inflation are being solved, and meanwhile more people are out of work.

Our recommendations:

1. All solutions should focus on employment as a priority.

2. Military spending should be slowed down. Instead emphasize the government's role in seeing to it that its citizens have:

   A. Employment

   B. Housing

   C. Food

   D. Education

   E. Health Care

   F. Mass Transit

3. The government should create support for small businesses.

4. The government should create a safe environment for workers: health benefits and protection from job hazards.

5. Corporations should be taxed their fair share. Current efforts to relieve corporations of taxes are not helping.

6. There should be a national housing entitlement program.

7. We should encourage all forms of self-reliance among our people, not dependence on the government.

8. We should express our views through VOTING. And we should vote with our feet by attending demonstrations, conferences, and rallies.

Education

About forty people participated in a dialogue between teachers, School Board representatives, and students. The results of this dialogue were combined with the results of a 1980 position paper based on the ideas of 150 young people, to get the following summary recommendations:

1. General

    A. Make the curriculum relevant to the lives of students by including materials on ethnic heritage, jobs, and the issues of today.

    B. Establish programs with greater flexibility so that students can make choices that reflect their interests.

    C. Establish smaller schools, smaller classrooms, and a sense of community within each classroom.

    D. Make certain that the school relates to the community as a whole; provide access for community people and a forum for ideas and problems.

    E. Provide educational programs that help young people to respect themselves and others.

    F. Young people must get involved in influencing educational programs by going to School Board meetings, dealing with principals and other administrators, and participating in policy decisions.

2. Relations between teachers and students

    A. Establish clear expectations of behavior and work, possibly by using written contracts.

    B. Teachers and students must recognize that each are human beings with needs and problems and must try to treat each other with understanding.

    C. Teachers should establish contact with parents.

D. Teachers should keep personal problems out of the classroom.

E. Learning is the responsibility of both teacher and student.

F. Teachers and students should have opportunities to establish schools and other educational settings that fit their real interests.

G. Administration should provide training and support to teachers.

> *"It's sad that we as Spanish and Black children put ourselves down. But it's not our fault. It's a reflection of how society operates. It can be changed. We are already involved in changing it, because we understand it, and we care. That's why I want to join with everybody to build a community based on love!... Love is a strong force, the force that shall dominate the world if it is liberated.*

Johnny Rivera
Keynote Speaker

3. In order for students to participate more fully in school policy they must:

A. Establish effective communication with principals early, before problems arise.

B. Make alliances with adults who influence the principal.

C. Prepare carefully for meetings with administrators so that we can get our point across.

D. Upgrade student organizations: make them work.

4. Concerns specific to East Harlem schools:

A. Make sure that all students get what they need. Don't focus just on the most successful.

B. Question: What will happen to the students currently in Benjamin Franklin High School when it is closed? What schools will they go to?

Housing

Following are the recommendations from the dialogue between landlords and tenants:

1. We need government and private sector subsidies for housing in low-income communities.

2. We are against the replacement of the existing government subsidy programs with so-called housing vouchers.

3. We are opposed to the cutbacks and phasing out of the public housing programs across the nation.

4. We support the over-all and eventual goal of tenant ownership.

5. There is a need for more information in the community about the advantages of cooperative ownership of buildings.

6. There should be technical assistance for tenants wanting to buy or manage their own buildings.

7. Tenants should be encouraged to organize against gentrification and displacement.

8. The community should develop plans for renovating abandoned buildings and squatting in partially occupied buildings so as to use all the housing resources available.

9. There is a need to improve landlord—tenant relationships. There should be communication regarding the costs of running a building, what rent actually pays for, discussions of economic realities and tenants' rights. Landlords should be accessible for meetings, and should fulfill their responsibilities, such as cleaning sidewalks and back yards.

10. The issue of the homeless must be faced by public planners: according to news reports there are 36,000 homeless people in New York City.

11. The names of housing support groups should be widely publi-
    cized: East Harlem Triangle, East Harlem Council for Human
    Services, East 116th Street Block Association, Hope Community,
    Community Planning Board #11, Metro North, NERVE, Inter-
    cultural Resource Development, Renegades Housing Movement,
    Youth Action Restoration Crew, and others.

Crime Prevention and Law Enforcement

Summary of the discussion between young people and police:

- The young people felt that police behavior and attitudes
  toward young people in the community was disrespectful, uncaring, and at times abusive. The young people felt powerless
  to deal with these abuses.

- The police representatives said the police perceive the problem
  as one of extensive crime and lack of community support in
  helping the police do their jobs.

- Both sides felt there was a lack of communication between police and youth concerning what are the community problems,
  how police deal with them, how the community could help,
  and how the police could change.

RECOMMENDATIONS:

1. The City should strengthen community relations services in the
   police department.

2. The Police Department should give better training to its officers
   in community relations, especially relations with young people.

3. Groups in the community should hold meetings to let the police
   department know what the community needs and wants from
   police services; community and youth representatives should
   attend the Police Community Council meetings and give input.

4. The problems of crime cannot be solved alone. We must work together to solve all the problems of our community. All must be solved for any one of them to be truly solved. We need to keep organizing in a positive direction to oppose crime and the causes of crime, to get:

   A. jobs, better schools, parks, and recreational programs.

   B. more conferences like this one to continue steering young people in the right direction.

   C. more political power.

   D. more economic power through local businesses.

5. We need to develop a campaign against drugs.

   A. dry up the market for drugs through educating people against drug use. Strengthen peer groups to oppose drugs; strengthen ourselves to resist drugs.

   B. apply political pressure on law enforcement agencies to prevent the flow of drugs into our communities.

6. Prevent police abuses and hold police accountable for respecting the community.

   A. Police who do wrong should be required to suffer the consequences.

   B. People should help their friends or acquaintances who are arrested unjustly, or are the victims of police brutality, by testifying on their behalf. People need to follow through by going directly to the precinct when they see something wrong happen.

7. Form Youth Patrols to cut crime.

Youth and the Military

A far-reaching and intense dialogue between young people and representatives of the military led to the following recommendations:

1. In school and other settings young people need to be informed about various options that are available to them, not just the military.

2. Whenever the value of the military, especially in public schools, is presented, the opposite side should be presented as well.

3. Draft counseling should be used to present a total view of what military is and what it means.

4. Selective Service laws should be examined, and people should be educated about them.

Great disagreements existed among the group about the 'role of the military and about foreign policy and domestic spending policies.

It was agreed that individuals have the right to their own views, and to live their lives according to their views, no matter how difficult it may be for others to accept their views; but dialogue should not stop, because the process of reaching informed consensus about the role of the military is essential to the human race.

The Role of Women in the Community

Young women face special problems as we grow up in this community and this society. Some of these problems are as follows:

Education: Young women are not being encouraged to go into male dominated fields like law, science, and medicine. We are influenced by stereotyped male and female roles. Furthermore, the reality of family responsibilities, such as having children and caring for our parents, makes it difficult to go on with our education.

Sexism: There is widespread sexism (meaning the attitude that men are better than women and that women are meant to be sex objects or assistants for men) in the family, in the educational system, in the media. It affects everything.

Abuse of Women: The extreme form of sexism is rape and other physical abuse of women. There is a lack of preventative measures, and a lack of services, shelters, and counseling.

Family and Job/Career Problems: The men are not sharing enough with household work and child-rearing. Women are put in low-paying jobs and are paid less than men for jobs doing equal work. There are not enough family planning services and childcare services.

RECOMMENDATIONS:

1. We need more leadership training for young women.

2. We need more day care and support systems for young mothers.

3. There should be widespread human sexuality education.

4. We should have consciousness raising about sexism in the media, especially advertising.

5. We need a way to deal with rape, both preventing it and helping women who have been raped.

6. We should develop communication between young women and older women.

7. Approach working women in the community for assistance in career education.

8. Self-defense training for women should be a priority.

9. There is a need for dialogues between young women and young men about relationships, sex, and child-rearing, in mixed groups.

Sex, Pregnancy, and Relationships

A good part of this workshop was direct sex education. It was very well attended. Recommendations were as follows:

1. More sex education: dialogues between young men and women, discussion of attitudes towards sexuality everywhere — at school, at home, and in programs; more workshops, more communication between men and men, women and women, between partners, and in the family.

2. More outreach to inform people of clinics, sex education, and birth control.

3. Some kind of attention to helping people develop and sustain relationships based on mutual respect, serious relationships in which people are honest and not exploiting each other.

Youth Involvement in the Political Process

About 20 people, including 2 elected officials and many active youth, had a general discussion about youth involvement in the electoral process and the accountability of politicians. Their recommendations were as follows:

1. We should do a massive "Voter Education Campaign.

2. We should develop a structure for accountability of our public officials. The structure should include finding out exactly what our politicians are doing and how they are voting; and should include criteria for what we think is good political leadership.

3. A group of young people should meet with the politicians on a regular basis reporting back to the youth community on what the politicians are doing.

We young people need to be informed about specific issues and be clear about what we want.

The politicians should be accessible for meetings and should provide full reports on what they vote for and against. It should not be necessary to do complicated research to find out how our representatives are representing us.

4. There should be forums on politics for youth, including training in the actual electoral process and political history.

5. There should be internships for interested youth to work alongside elected officials (Councilman Robert Rodriguez and State Senator Olga Mendez offered to take initiative in raising funds for this.).

Leadership

Some qualities of good leadership are these: honesty, correctness of purpose, sincerity, being motivated, taking initiative, knowing oneself, listening to what other people want, sorting out emotional reactions from objective thinking, getting consensus from the group and delivering results to the whole group.

Some DO's and DONT's: Do be supportive and loving; DO care about yourself, see that you have a good support system, have a knowledge of what needs to be done and how, take criticism as feedback, treat all equally, consult with peers, be openminded, share information, take a stand, be organized, be visible; DON'T take on too many responsibilities, and don't engage in arm-twisting or threatening or bribing.

RECOMMENDATIONS:

1. We need more development and encouragement of women as leaders.

2. More training in organizing skills.

3. More ways of continuing to deepen our commitment to the community.

Youth Involvement in Programs and Institutions

We believe that all programs and institutions dealing with youth would be improved by involving the young people in decision-making and implementation. The programs would be more effective, more responsive to the real needs of the young people. Further, they would be helping the community through training our next generation of adult leadership, making the most of our human resources.

The main obstacles to increasing youth involvement are:

1. People with more experience tend to crowd out those with less experience by talking more. This includes both adults and experienced young people.

2. The process of involving young people in decision—making takes time, and adults are often rushed, or programs understaffed.

Nonetheless, we propose that:

1. People with more experience learn to be sensitive to those with less experience in order to get their input.

2. Administrators should allow the time to make decisions involving everybody's input. The benefits more than outweigh the difficulty.

Appreciations

We would like to thank the following people who did a wonderful job as resource people, moderators, cooks, recorders, and conveners at the Conference, because they showed that they really care about the young people in East Harlem. We're sorry we can't thank all the people who made wonderful speeches, because we don't have all the names. And really, we'd like to thank everyone who came!

Mark Alexander

Regina Ross

Freddy Acosta

Mary Kay Penn

Edgar Acevedo

Senator Olga Mendez

Ruben Acosta

Councilman Robert Rodriguez

Kenneth Askew

Irene Rivera

Emilio Bernard

Sargeant Nunez

Francisco Diaz

Jose Rivera

Tito Delgado

Naomi Rice

Shelley Inniss

Terry Scher

David Calvert

Hirazn Maristany

Linda Duke

Bill Tabb

Ena Fox

Victor Ortiz

Kathy Huber

Roberta Stallings

Peter Kleinbard

Gladys Padro

Chantay Jones

Daniel Rivera

Linda Gonzalez

Tony Minor

Linda Federici

Patrick Shields

Gloria Lattimore

Mario Morales

Cynthia Orchart

Steven Shapiro

Ismael Nunez

John Sainz

Mel Mungin

Milo Stanojevich

Ethel Velez

Kelly Vilar

Howard Harrington

Dorothy Stoneman

Frederick Williams

Kevin White

Winston Sweetie

Robert Anazagasti

Greg McCants

Questionnaire

Would you take the time to let us know what issues raised in the conference you think we should be most energetic about following up?

Please rate the following on a scale of 1 to 10, with 10 being what you'd most like to see us tackle.

- ☐ Sex education
- ☐ Youth employment
- ☐ Accountability of politicians
- ☐ Youth getting jobs in housing renovation
- ☐ Improvement of local schools
- ☐ Cooperation between businessmen and youth
- ☐ Police and youth relations
- ☐ Cutting the military budget and spending instead on human needs especially jobs
- ☐ Housing
- ☐ Leadership development for women
- ☐ Campaign against drugs
- ☐ Programs helping with rape, child abuse, child care, etc.
- ☐ Voter education campaign
- ☐ Mini-conferences on all issues
- ☐ Other?

East Harlem Youth Congress —
Background Information

The East Harlem Youth Congress was organized by the Youth Action Program of the East Harlem Block Schools to provide an organized voice for the ideas of young people.

The general purpose of the Youth Action Program is to assist young people in implementing their ideas for community improvement. Current projects of the Youth Action Program, all initiated and governed by young people, include the Youth Action Restoration Crew, the Youth Action Homes Away From Home, the Weekends Out of the City, the Youth Action Learning Center, a Job Referral Program, and the East Harlem Youth Congress.

The East Harlem Youth Congress gives young people an opportunity to think together about public issues, to learn about society, and to develop leadership skills as we reach for agreement and learn to take action in support of our ideas.

There are 500 members of the Youth Congress. It is open to anyone who is interested. It holds weekly educational forums on Friday evenings, has several operating committees, sponsors an annual Youth Conference, studies the political process, and will become as active as its membership desires in building for unity and action on issues.

This newsletter is a report of the East Harlem Youth Leadership Conference of 1982. The Conference was organized by the East Harlem Youth Congress, with the active assistance of staff and young people from the East Harlem College and Career Counseling Program, Mt. Sinai Adolescent Health Clinic, Casita Maria, the National Commission on Resources for Youth, LUCHÄ, Hotline Cares, Union Settlement, and all the projects of the Youth Action Program. The Conference was partially funded with a grant from the New York State Conference on Children and Youth. Additional funding came from the New York City Youth Board. Basic funding for the Youth Congress comes from the New York City Youth Board, the Field Foundation, and the New York Community Trust.

Members of the Steering Committee which organized this Conference are as follows:

Freddy Acosta	Victor Ortiz
Valerie Corsari	Rose Parrilla
Francisco Diaz	Eric Perdomo
Linda Gonzalez	Naomi Rice
Howard Harrington	Diana Rivera
Chantay Jones	Johnny Rivera
Shelley Inniss	Irene Rivera
Peter Kleinbard	Albert Quinones
Guillermo La Fosse	John Sainz
Hugh Lawrence	Patrick Shields
Richard Malavet	Dorothy Stoneman
Tony Minor	Winston Sweetie
Ismael Nunez	Frederick Williams
Cynthia Orchart	

Members of the Staff of the East Harlem Youth Congress are Otilio Colon, Dorette Grant, Richard Malavet, Mary Kay Penn, Ernesto Ramos, Johnny Rivera, and Dorothy Stoneman. Volunteers who helped with the Conference preparations, in addition to the Steering Committee, were Jackie Rivera, Sara Alavarez, and Gregory Rudd,

Reflections

Just approaching the registration area, one could feel the excitement and enthusiasm. Our theme for the day was "The Greatest Love".

After opening ceremonies by Irene Rivera and Morning Chairman Victor Ortiz, the conference was brought to its feet in response to the outstanding performance by the East Harlem Boys Choir. They seemed to rock with a spirit of life that can only be compared to that of church on Sunday Morning.

The keynote speech by John Rivera contained a message for all in attendance, that no matter what sex, race or color, we should never forget that in essence we are all one and should strive to work together and fight those things that constantly divide us.

For the third time, the conference was brought to its feet. There was lots of hugging and clenched fists as united we lifted our voices for the theme song "The Greatest Love of All," by George Benson.

Next on the agenda was the Open Speak-Out, which ran much smoother than expected. Most of the young people thought adults would do all the talking. However, this was not the case. Adults and young people emphasized the need for Blacks, Latinos, and other "Minorities" to wake up and begin taking pride in ourselves and our communities, by first respecting ourselves, avoiding those things that are negative, and by reaching out to help others get involved.

After the Speak-Out we were off to our dialogue sessions where young people had the opportunity to meet and exchange ideas with those in power concerning problems affecting youth. I shared moderating tasks in the dialogue on Landlords and Tenants, which ended earlier than expected. I used the time wisely and sat in on two dialogues: Elected Officials & Youth, and Businessmen and Youth. I found all three to be interesting discussions.

The lunch was deliciously prepared by members of the East Harlem Block Schools Board. The afternoon session was chaired innovatively by Dorette Grant. Resolutions from the dialogue ranged from How To Stay In School, Health & Self Care, and Drugs, to "HOT" issues like Reagonomics, Young Women in the Community, Sex, Pregnancy & Relationships.

By the end of the day, we all knew what Victor Ortiz meant in his remarks when he said, "**There is a lot of love in the Youth Action Program and WE'RE gonna spread it around the world.**" I am sure that those in attendance will agree that this was a day for all young people to come together, and indeed WE WERE. Young people came not only from East Harlem but from as far away as Brooklyn. We all realize now that in order to change today's world into that special place, we must begin first to look within ourselves, for there lies the key to a better tomorrow.

"There are many children out there with nobody to turn to. They turn to drugs. They drop out of school. It's our job to help them reach out. That's the purpose of this conference, to reach out.

"You 're not going to turn to Reagan, you 're not going to turn to the White House, or the people of Albany. You have to do it. We're going to show everybody here that a winner never quits, and a quitter never wins.

Ismael Nunez
Steering Committee Member

APPENDIX 4

A Different Point of View on Alzheimer's Disease
(Referenced in Chapter 18)

By Dorothy Stoneman, 1985

My mother was diagnosed with Alzheimer's disease four years ago. My husband and daughter and I have just moved into her house to take care of her, to ensure that she does not have to go to a nursing home, at least not in the immediate future. Whenever I tell anybody about it, they commiserate with great feeling. "Oh, how terrible!" "Oh, I know how terrible it must be for you. I am so sorry! Alzheimer's is such a terrible thing to have to live with!"

Because there has been so much publicity lately about the horrors of Alzheimer's, I'd like to tell about my mother from a completely different point of view. Once I had faced the tragedy and had wept in co-counseling sessions with my family and friends for at least twenty-five hours about the progressive loss of my mother right before my eyes, I began to look at the situation with a clearer sense of the current reality.

My mother is in no physical pain. She is still quite self-sufficient physically. She gets up in the morning, takes a shower, dresses herself, washes out her underpants and her panty hose, combs her hair and comes down to eat her breakfast. Her breakfast is something or other, with milk on it. It is usually something other than cereal. It might be peas, or lettuce, or turkey soup or mayonnaise. Whatever it is she chooses, she puts milk on top of it as if it were cereal. We let her choose what she wants to eat, as long as it will do her no harm.

After breakfast she struggles to make a list of foods we should buy. Since she doesn't remember the names of any of the foods, she systematically takes items out of the refrigerator or out of the cupboard, and copies down the names of them on a little slip of paper. After about forty minutes of painstaking and laborious research, she produces a list of about five items, usually including milk, cat food, and cookies. She gets one of us to drive her to the store where we help her to select the items, bring them home, and put them away.

After that, she often goes back to bed. When she wakes up, she starts over again. She comes down to breakfast again and eats something else with milk on it. During the rest of the day, she putters around. She wipes surfaces, she sweeps leaves off the front walk, she picks specks of dirt up off the floor, and she sits and reads Time Magazine. She can no longer decipher the words, nor can she understand the meaning of most of the words, but she sits and goes through the motions as best she can, turning the pages and looking at the pictures. She was always a diligent student. She puts the same effort into it now as she always did. She's been carrying the same Time Magazine around with her for the past six months.

If we go out, she's delighted to come with us. She enjoys movies, where she holds my husband's hand and pats it and sits with her eyes fixed on the movie screen. She likes concerts. She loves to go to the park and watch little children. She enjoys feeding her cats. In fact, she follows her cats around the house and the yard offering them full bowls of food all day. She actually tamed a squirrel, thinking it was a cat, by bringing it bowls of food several times a day. Now the squirrel eats in our kitchen. She is so generous that she leaves food out to feed the flies and the ants and any other living creature that she spies.

Even as my mother's intellectual faculty has faded and unraveled to a point where she is really quite incapable of communicating in even simple sentences, her character has become ever more clearly revealed. She is an angel. She is a benign and loving presence. At every moment she is busy trying to improve the environment by cleaning it or fixing it up in one way or another. When she is not cleaning, she is trying to feed a person or an animal. Otherwise, she is still trying to learn and trying to read. She is an example of a person who is functioning at the peak of her ability, even as her abilities diminish. Being with her fills me with admiration and awe for my mother, as I watch her doing her best at every moment with what little she has left.

For my mother, Alzheimer's is not the worst way to die. She is quite happy. At least, she's always in good humor, smiling lovingly at the people around her, saying, "Oh, I'm so glad to see you." "Very good!" "Oh, really!" "Oh, I'm so glad you came to my place!" Perhaps most important, she is surrounded by her family, who love her dearly. Without Alzheimer's she would not have been surrounded by her family, because she has always been completely self-contained and self-sufficient. She never asked anything from her three children. She never resented anything we didn't give her. She never seemed to expect any attention.

Had she died like her mother did, with a quick heart attack, when nobody expected it, none of us would have had the chance to express how deeply and dearly we love her. This long, slow, painful dying process of Alzheimer's has allowed my brother and me, in turn, to move in with her to care for her, to give her back what she gave us as children. It is already a year since she recognized any of us or called anyone by name. Nonetheless, we know that she is she. We see her behaving in a way completely consistent with her entire life. We are able to give her pleasure by caring for her attentively. We love her very much, the way I imagine a parent would love a child with disabilities. We hang on her every sentence, and we enjoy her every humorous comment.

She does many very funny things. Last night, when we went to visit a family with a dog, she tried to feed the dog. She pulled a ten-dollar bill out of her pocketbook, tore it in half, and offered the dog half of her ten-dollar bill. For the last three years she has mixed up the words for food and money, but this is the first time she mixed up the objects.

At the stage where she was just mixing up nouns it was particularly funny. She would look out the window at the car and say, "Oh, there's my nice little potato." Or she would pat my daughter on the head, and say, "You're such a nice kitty." Family members often gather in the kitchen at the end of the day and share humorous stories of the things Mommy has said or done that day.

As my mother has lost her intellect, she has also lost some of her inhibitions. Three years ago, I first noticed this when she was unexpectedly willing to climb up to the top of a very tall slide in the playground, a double height slide, and slide down it with my daughter. Two years ago, she went with my husband and me to watch people play tennis. I had decided that the energetic activity of the game would appeal to her. I wanted to give her a chance to observe the action. As the players stepped onto the court, she said, "Oh, are we going to do this?" Realizing that she would be willing to try, I went home quickly to fetch her sneakers. Sure enough, she donned the sneakers, took the tennis racket firmly in hand, stepped out onto the court and prepared to play tennis. She had on a dress, stockings, and it was high noon on a hot summer day. She is seventy-three years old and had not played tennis in thirty years. With heart in mouth, I lobbed the ball over the net to her and sure enough, "Whack", she slapped it back across the net. Back and forth, and she never missed the ball.

My husband and I were agog. Every time she hit the ball, we caught each other's eye with sheer delight and amazement. We were also a little scared. If she dropped dead of a heart attack it would be hard to explain why we had her playing tennis! But she was neither scared nor amazed. She seemed to think it was quite an ordinary occurrence. She only commented when she hit the ball into the net, at which time she would say, with great disappointment, "Oh, I can't do it!" After forty minutes, she said she'd had enough. Climbing into the car, she said, "We should have started that sooner. That was fun." But who would have thought that my mother would have been eager and able to play tennis?

This event gave us a clue to many subsequent days of pleasure. We took her canoeing. We took her to play ping pong. We took her out to play baseball with a plastic bat and a whiffle ball. She was completely successful at each of these activities. To find that my mother, who could no longer speak in simple sentences, could actually play croquet, tennis, and ping pong better than my nine-year-old daughter was quite amazing.

We find we do her a disservice whenever we assume we know her limitations. Two years ago, she unexpectedly sat down at the piano, which she hadn't touched in twenty years, took out a Christmas carol and began to sight-read Christmas Carols. She was most critical of herself, expressing disappointment at each note that she missed. But we were amazed. She could no longer read English, yet she could sight-read music after not having done it for twenty years. She can still do this.

A year or so ago she lost interest in going to movies because she couldn't understand them. She simultaneously stopped watching television. Now, however, we find that she has a renewed interest. She no longer realizes that she doesn't understand them, so she enjoys the colors and movement and the action. She sits in the audience at the movie theatre exclaiming loudly, "Oh, my gosh!" whenever anything dramatic occurs.

She can still figure out new things that are consistent with her age-old principles. For instance, recently we had a foster dog staying with us. The dog was large and vicious toward my mother's cats, so we had him locked in a kennel in the back yard. My mother, however, doesn't like to see creatures locked up. Again and again, she would go out to the back yard and let the dog loose, without understanding that he might hurt her beloved cats. Each day we tied the door with a more complicated knot to prevent her from opening it. Each day she figured out how to open the door to let the dog free. She would get up in the middle of the night, since she doesn't know the difference between night and day, come downstairs and let the dog out.

Oftentimes, it's clear that her logical process is in advance of her linguistic capacity. She does have ideas. She is thinking. But she can't communicate in sentences, and she can't name objects or use appropriate verbs. Now, three months after I wrote the first part of this article, she is down to four or five verbs. Almost all her sentences go like this: "But then, is it going in there?" It doesn't matter what she intends to say, it usually comes out in the same sentence. Her other favorite sentence, said when she looks at any of us directly, is, "Oh, you're a good one!" She no longer knows any of our names.

We have followed certain principles in caring for my mother. We have tried to surround her with what she enjoys, let her do everything she's capable of, and avoid conflict with her over minor things. If she wants to sleep in her clothes, and get up at 3:00 A.M., we don't insist that she sleep in pajamas, and we don't give her sleeping pills to ensure that she's on our schedule. Instead, we leave a plate full of food out for her in the breakfast nook, and we leave four or five dirty dishes in the sink, so she'll have something useful to do in the wee hours of the morning. She likes to clean things up. We have to leave the plate full of food, to make sure she gets a balanced diet. Left to herself at this stage she would just eat Pepperidge Farm cookies. Or, worse, we recently caught her digging into three raw onions and a garlic flower doused with water in a cookie tin. But if she wants to eat in the middle of the night, it's O.K. If she wants to get dressed by putting her pajamas over her suit, we don't mind. Who cares, after all? The people in the grocery know her, and we find the rest of the world to be warmly welcoming to her as well.

We think letting her do things her way, as long as it's not dangerous, is important. It preserves her dignity and her place in the world. She can also be quite stubborn if we don't respect her wishes. She will say, "No!" She'll stamp her foot, and thump someone on the arm with her fist. "No! I'm not going in there!" Forcing her to do trivial things our way could mean conflict that would demean and dehumanize her. It might even end up with our thinking she needed to be drugged or restrained somehow.

In fact, when she had a little heart palpitation and had to go to the hospital, within an hour the hospital staff had decided she needed to be restrained, because she didn't want to do what she didn't understand. We can see the potential, even at home, for routine dehumanization stemming from a need to force her into routines and structures that no longer matter to her. So, we avoid coercion, and try to maintain our own sense of humor and flexibility. If she wants to put food on the floor to feed the ants, so what? If she wants to keep the back door open in the winter to let the cats in and out, we might as well put on our sweaters, or cut a swinging panel in the door.

Of course, at certain points we have had to take important things away from her. Two years ago, she was still driving her car to the store every day. She was driving it very well. But when the license came up for renewal, we had to respond to a question on the application that asked if she had been diagnosed with any new disease. We had to write that she did indeed have a new disease involving memory loss. At the Registry of Motor Vehicles, they asked us to go and speak with the supervisor. My mother tried to persuade him. "I can do it," she said. "I can do it." He asked how old she was, presumably to check her memory. "I'm seven and three, "she said. "I'm not too old. I'm seven and three. I can do it." He responded, "No, you're not too old – seven and three. Ten is not so old. But I need a letter from your doctor saying you can do it." The doctor did not agree to write that letter.

For a year, my mother kept looking at the car, saying "I'm not too old. I can do it." But we couldn't let her. This was sad, because the car was always part of her self-sufficiency. Now, two years later, she still enjoys riding in the car as a passenger. She delights in every other passing car, warns us to wait at every intersection, calls attention to every change of light, points with wonder at the amount of traffic, and giggles delightedly at every large truck.

Recently we have had to take away her matches, because she started trying to light the ends of pencils and pens to smoke them, and then she started eating her cigarettes when she couldn't figure out how to light them. She often tries to light her cigarettes by putting the end under the water faucet. She would labor for half an hour, trying to figure out how to get a cigarette lit, trying all sorts of methods, a few of them risky. So now we carry the matches and light one for her whenever she seems to be searching for a smoke.

Knowing that everything is always going to get worse, that she will lose more of her skills and her concepts and her words and her memory as time goes on, is painful. But we try to keep our attention on the amazing amount that she still does know. We focus on the fact that she is apparently quite happy, as long as we keep responding to what she is trying to tell us, hugging her and smiling at her and looking affectionately and deeply into her eyes, and surrounding her with friendly people and joyful music.

I find it endlessly fascinating to talk about my mother, but I do not need to tell everything in this brief article. I merely want to make the point that Alzheimer's is not always a scourge. Alzheimer's is just one of many ways of dying. It happens to be one that allows a family to say good-bye, over and over, and over, and over, and over again. In some cases, it allows an older person to enjoy life in a simple way, without physical pain and without the awareness that she is dying.

One day my mother will cross the line between physical self-sufficiency and total dependency. At that time, this long dying process may become very much more difficult in every respect. But for these past four years since she was diagnosed, and probably for at least one year more, taking care of my mother has been an odd sort of a blessing. It has allowed us to look in wonder at the true goodness of her character, to be awed by her kindness, and to witness every day how precious and delightful life is in all its forms, especially the form of my mother.

(Later note, from 2021: My mother died in my arms, in her bed, at home, on March 27, 1987. Her last words, that she spoke directly to me, were, "Going in there." I was blessed to be able to stay close to her until the very last minute of her wonderful life.)

Research Studies on YouthBuild

Research studies conducted on YouthBuild between 1996 and 2018 are listed below in reverse chronological order. This is not a complete list, but it is representative of the large amount of research done. It doesn't include all local studies, research done for PhD studies, nor studies since 2018. If you are interested in the full study, most can be found through Google.

- **Laying a Foundation: Four Year Results from the YouthBuild Evaluation**, MDRC, May, 2018, Cynthia Miller, Megan Millenky, Daniel Cummings, Andrew Wiegand (SPRA).

- **Life After Lockup: A Special Report on Successful Recidivism Reduction**, YouthBuild USA, 2016. (Study of outcomes from nine SMART YouthBuild sites funded by DOL's High Poverty/High Crime Youth Offender grant)

- **Building a Future, Interim Impact Findings from the YouthBuild Evaluation,** MDRC, Cynthia Miller, Megan Millenky, Lisa Schwartz, Lisbeth Goble, Jillian Stein. November, 2016 (Funded by the US Department of Labor)

- **Developing Positive Young Adults: Lessons from Two Decades of YouthBuild Programs, MDRC, May 2015.** (Funded by YouthBuild USA)

- **Creating New Pathways to Postsecondary: Evaluation of the Bill & Melinda Gates Foundation's Postsecondary Success (PSS) Initiative,** Brandeis University, Heller School for Social Policy and Management, December 2013. (Pilot YouthBuild sites were evaluated. Funded by the Gates Foundation)

- **Youth Development Through Service: A Quality Assessment of the YouthBuild AmeriCorps Program,** Kathleen A. Tomberg, Research and Evaluation Center, John Jay College of Criminal Justice, City University of New York, 2013. (Funded by AmeriCorps)

- **Pathways into Leadership; A Study of YouthBuild Graduates,** Peter Levine, PhD, CIRCLE, Tufts University. 2012. (Funded by Knight Foundation)

- **An Analysis of GED Attainment at YouthBuild AmeriCorps Programs,** SPR — Social Policy Research Associates, Michael J. Midling, Jillianne Leufgen, 2010. (Funded by AmeriCorps)

- **Costs and Benefits of a Targeted Intervention Program for Youthful Offenders: The YouthBuild USA Offender Project,** Mark Cohen, PhD., Alex Piquero, PhD, 2008. (Funded by YouthBuild USA)

- **The YouthBuild Program for Ex-Offenders, A comprehensive Qualitative Review,** Social Policy Research Associates, 2008. (Contracted by the US Department of Labor)

- **Youthbuild Program: Analysis of Outcomes Needed to Evaluate Long-Term Benefits,** US Government Accountability Office (GAO), Report to Congressional Committees, William B. Shear, Feb. 2007. (The government spells Youthbuild with a small b, as it is seen in the authorizing legislation.)

- **YouthBuild USA Youthful Offender Project, Year 1,** Anne Leslie, 2007, YouthBuild USA.

- **Fast Growth High Impact Nonprofits Research** Leslie Crutchfield and Heather McLeod Grant, Duke University's Center for the Advancement of Social Entrepreneurship. 2007.

- **The Efficacy of Education Awards in YouthBuild AmeriCorps Programs** Andy Hahn, Heller School, and Tom Leavitt of Analytic Resources. 2007 (Funded by AmeriCorps)

- **YouthBuild USA: Achieving Significant Scale While Guiding a National Movement.** The Bridgespan Group, Inc., 2004.

- **The Growth of YouthBuild: A Case Study** Center for the Advancement of Social Entrepreneurship. Greg Dees, Fuqua School of Business, Duke University, 2004.

- **Life After YouthBuild: 900 YouthBuild Graduates Reflect on Their Lives, Dreams, and Experiences,** Hahn, Andrew, Leavitt, Thomas D., Horvat, Erin M., Davis, James E. Brandeis University, Temple University, 2004.

- **YouthBuild Program: A Measurement of Costs and Benefits to the State of Minnesota,** Minnesota Department of Employment and Economic Development: Minnesota 2003.

- **The Evolution of YouthBuild USA: A Case Study of Organizational Innovation and Growth in a Changing Social Policy Environment.** Perkins, Jr., Jeffrey, University of Pittsburgh, 2002.

- **The YouthBuild Welfare-to-Work Program: Its Outcomes and Policy Implications.** Anne Wright, YouthBuild USA 2001.

- **YouthBuild in Developmental Perspective: A Formative Evaluation of the YouthBuild Demonstration Project,** Ferguson, Ronald F., Clay, Philip L., Snipes, Jason C., and Roaf, Phoebe. Harvard University, Massachusetts Institute of Technology, and Public/Private Ventures, 1996. (Funded by the Ford Foundation).

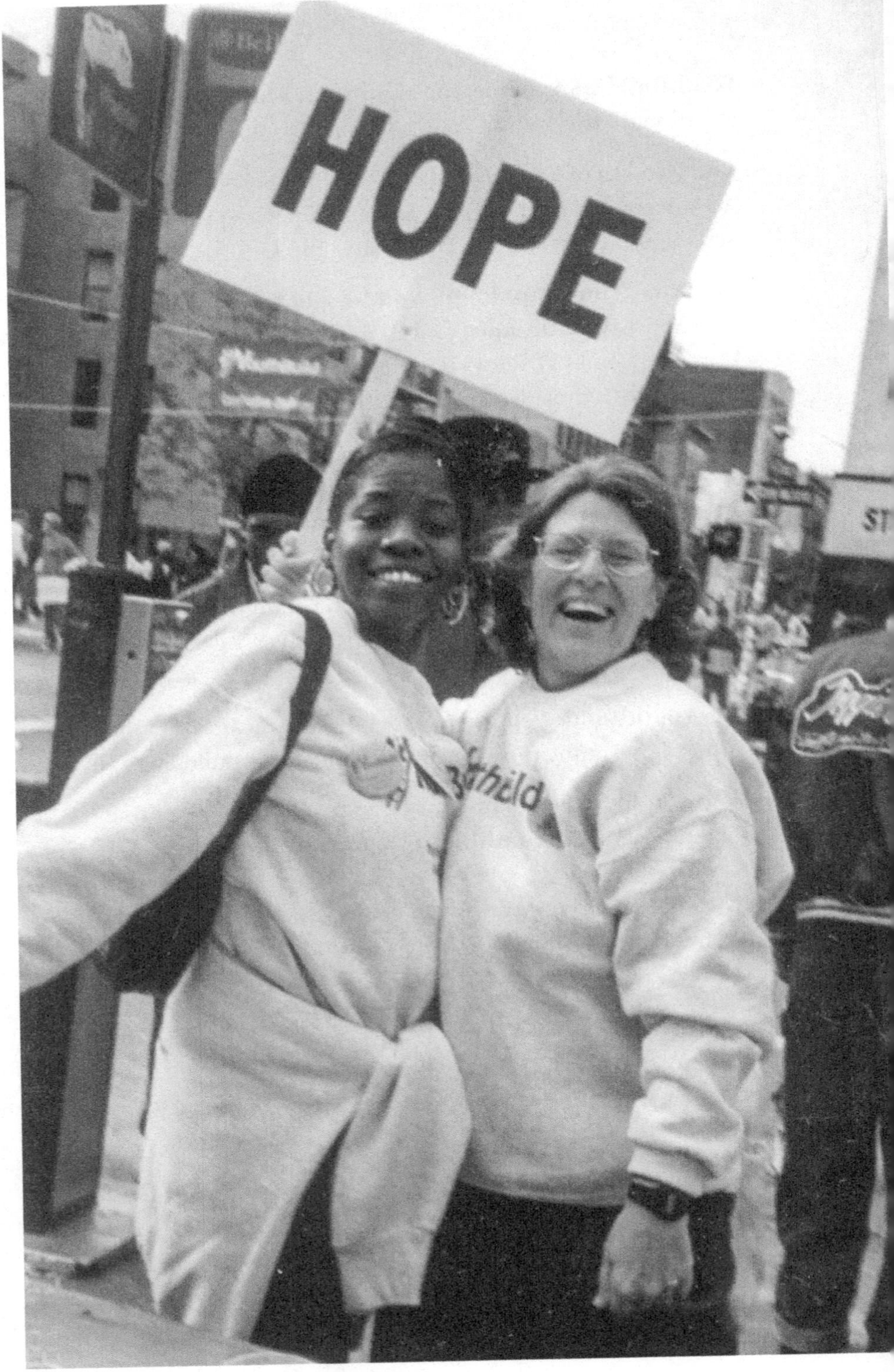
HOPE

Made in United States
North Haven, CT
25 January 2025

64941316R00202